Hooray for

SIMON AND SCHUSTER   NEW YORK

LEO ROSTEN

YĪDDĪSH !

A Book About English

A cheerful lexicon of Yiddish words
which have become part of the English language,
plus English words and phrases
which have been transformed into Yinglish;
the whole garnished with stories, jokes, parables,
reverent quotations from the Talmud and
a glittering gallery of writers, rabbis, sages, wits,
with impulsive side trips into the faith, folklore,
genius and history of the Jews—
from their servitude in Babylon
to their magnitude in Beverly Hills.

Library of Congress Cataloging in Publication Data

Rosten, Leo Calvin.
Hooray for Yiddish!

1. Jewish wit and humor.   2. Yiddish language—
Glossaries, vocabularies, etc.   3. English
language—Foreign elements—Yiddish.   I. Title.
PN6231.J5R66   437'.947   82-646
ISBN 0-671-43025-4   AACR2

To the memory
evergreen,
of
my Mother and Father:
Aleyhem ha-sholem

INTRODUCTION:

About This Book

The Joys of Yiddish was an unabashedly personal lexicon of words from Yiddish that are often heard or read in English. Their number has grown—enormously—since we last met.

In the book you now hold in your hands, I cast my net considerably further. This work contains:

1. Yiddish words that have won acceptance in English dictionaries: the brazen *chutzpa,* the intrepid *kibitzer,* the skulking *gonef* (and so on).*

2. Hybrids, formed out of English, that have been taken to the bosom of Americans: alrightnik, fancy-shmancy, crazy-doctor.

3. Phrasings and syntax, indigenous to Yiddish, which are racing through spoken English: Enjoy. Big deal. Get lost! Smart, he isn't. Could be.

4. *Mama-loshn* clamoring at Webster's gates: the endearing *bubeleh,* the picturesque *shlep,* the all-purpose *shtik.*

5. Entirely new words, not minted of English elements, for which there simply are no Anglo-Saxon competitors: *shmegegge, doppess, ipsy-pipsy,* etc.

6. Yinglish expressions, *sui generis,* that I recommend for admission into the ranks of colloquial (at *least*) English: the sardonic *Go know,* the raffish *gefutzevit,* the delicious *tsatske,* the unspeakable *paskudnyak.*

---

* The foothold established on the hospitable shore of English may be glimpsed if you scan the entries beginning with *ch, k, sch, sh, y* in any good English dictionary or the invaluable *Thesaurus of American Slang* compiled by Lester Berrey and Melvin van den Bark, and the *Dictionary of American Slang* compiled by Harold Wentworth and Stuart Berg Flexner.

About Yiddish

No Jew speaks "Jewish," any more than any Canadian speaks Canadian. A journal printed in English may be a Jewish journal, if it deals with Jewish concerns; a book about Idi Amin is a Yiddish book if it is printed in Yiddish.

Yiddish uses the letters of the Hebrew, not the Roman, alphabet, and is written or printed from right to left:

ybab   eht   em   dnaH

Hebrew and Yiddish are entirely independent languages. You may be a wizard in Hebrew and not understand a line of Yiddish; the same is true vice versa.

The vocabulary of Yiddish is drawn from

German	72 percent
Hebrew	18 percent
Slavic tongues	16 percent
Romance languages (Latin/French/Italian)	5.60 percent
English	3.55 percent

The fact that these numbers add up to more than 100 demonstrates the limitations of statistics. I *know* the figures are to be trusted: I made them up myself (but only after an exhausting analysis of the clashing estimates of debonair philologists).

Whatever the percentages, do not sniff with superior nostrils over a tongue once said to be "jargon." English draws 53.6 percent of its vocabulary from Latin-French-Italian-Spanish; 31.1 percent from German-Dutch-Scandinavian-Old English; and 10.8 percent from Greek. *These* figures come from the editors of the *Concise Oxford Dictionary* (preface). To illustrate the astonishing number of foreign words you and I use in everyday English, I once concocted a children's tale of 172 words; it contained thirty-two different languages.*

Yiddish is not a "new" language. It is, strictly speaking, older than English. It is a "fusion" language that has drawn upon Hebrew, Loez (Jewish correlates of Latin, Old French, Old Italian), German and Slavic. Over two hundred manuscripts, plus several

---

* "In the kitchen there were coffee, tea, goulash, chowder, taffy and a bottle of shampoo" harbors aliens from, respectively, Old Saxon, Turkish, Chinese, Hungarian, Creole, Tagalog, Medieval Latin, Hindustani.

hundred printed pages, in Old Yiddish (1200–1500) have so far been discovered. A Hebrew-Yiddish dictionary of the Bible was published in Cracow as long ago as 1534.* You may estimate the significance of this by recalling that Modern Latin lexicography began with a thesaurus in 1531, and that Nathan Bailey fathered English dictionaries in 1721.

It will be no news to you that I find Yiddish a beguiling tongue. Indeed, I was once driven to exclaim that it is a tongue that never takes its tongue out of its cheek. To me, Yiddish is the Robin Hood of languages.

> Yiddish lends itself to an extraordinary range of observational nuances and psychological subtleties. Steeped in sentiment, it is sluiced with sarcasm. It loves the ruminative, because it rests on a rueful past; favors paradox, because it knows that only paradox can do justice to the injustices of life; adores irony, because the only way the Jews could retain their sanity was to view a dreadful world with sardonic, astringent eyes. In its innermost heart, Yiddish swings between *shmaltz* and derision.
>
> I have always marveled at how fertile this *lingua franca* is in what may be called the vocabulary of insight. Jews *had* to become psychologists, and their preoccupation with human, no less than divine, behavior made Yiddish remarkably rich in names for the delineation of character types. Little miracles of precision are contained in the distinctions between such simpletons as a *nebech*, a *shlemiel*, a *shmendrick*, a *shnook;* or between such dolts as a *klutz*, a *yold*, a *Kuni Lemel*, a *shlep*, a *Chaim Yankel*. All of them inhabit the kingdom of the ineffectual, but each is assigned a separate place in the roll call. And Yiddish coins new names with ease: a *nudnik* is a pest; a *phudnik* is a *nudnik* with a Ph.D.
>
> Were I asked to characterize Yiddish—its style, its life story, its ambience—in one word, I would not hesitate: irrepressible.
>
> —*The Joys of Yiddish*, PREFACE

My earliest awareness of the marvelous resilience and will to live of my mother-tongue came when I was quite young. An old woman, bowed under the weight of shopping bags, stopped me:

---

* The most decisive work on Yiddish is the monumental *History of the Yiddish Language* by the late Max Weinreich (University of Chicago Press, 1980). That master's lifelong work, a stupendous achievement, was translated into English by Shlomo Noble and Joshua Fishman, who deserve a tribute all their own. That Weinreich is crotchety at times only puts him in the sublime company of Samuel Johnson. Weinreich deals with the origins of many "Jewish languages," *i.e.*, languages prior to, and feeding into, the Yiddish we know: four Loez tongues, Dzhudesmo (or Judesmo), a correlate of Spanish, Catalonian and Portuguese, Chuadit, etc. If you are often dazed by Weinreich's erudition, polylinguisticism, and sheer, dogged minutiae, do not feel guilty: you are in good company.

"Yinger mon, ir farshteyt Yiddish?" ("Young man, do you understand Yiddish?")

　　"Yaw," I answered.

　　"Vat time is it?"

On Humor and Pedagogy

Humor is the affectionate communication of insight. I feel no shame in using jokes, anecdotes or stories to illustrate the meaning of a word or to convey the bouquet of a phrasing. This is, of course, unorthodox lexicography, but it seems to me unexcelled for pedagogical power. A joke is an art form, a very swift, very short short story. It is a structured narrative, designed to make a point with force. That force is intensified by the comic ingredient of surprise.

The Jewish joke has revolutionized the humor, wit and repartee in the mass media (many examples garnish the pages of my text). Jewish humor has its own special characteristics; it is shot through with mockery and paradox. Since the culture of the Jews exalts reason, no less than faith, it is not surprising that so much Jewish wit hinges on logic to celebrate illogic. A liberating kind of lunacy dances through Jewish jokes.

When I was five years old, my father (*alav ha-sholem*) led me into a wholly new palace of laughter with this japery:

> Three cross-eyed witnesses stood before the bench of a cross-eyed judge.
>
> "What's your name?" the judge asked the first man.
>
> "Eli Krantz," replied the second.
>
> "I wasn't talking to you!" snapped the judge.
>
> "I didn't *say* anything!" cried the third.

It was at that moment that I realized that shining continents of wit stretched, unexplored, before me.

Another mind-boggling example of the inversion of reason came to me in a letter from a logician named Marx:

> *Dear Junior:*
>
> Excuse me for not answering sooner. I have been so busy not answering letters that I have not been able to get around to not answering yours in time.
>
> —GROUCHO

You will find hundreds of jokes in my text. The vast majority will be as new to you as they were to me. You may recognize some as old friends. And before you growl "I read that one before!" let me say "So what?" Do you stop a pianist who is playing Chopin because you heard that piece before?

Besides, I have completely rewritten, relocated or freshly embroidered every "old" *mayse* in this book. There simply is no substitute for certain classic jokes. They have an independent life, and immortal viability. (Who would want to forget the one that ends with the grandmother exclaiming "Delicious!" or the *moyl* scowling, "And what would *you* put in the window?!")

Jewish culture is a joke-making culture. (Is Portuguese? Is Turkish?) I am always astonished when I contemplate the sheer quantity, range and bubbling variety of Jewish humor. I do hope you are not foolish enough to think humor a category of trivia. The humor of a people is as illuminating as its patterns of pride, guilt and ambivalence. Humor is an isotope that locates the insights of a people. It was gloomy Hobbes who cried, "Laughter is sudden glory."

On Language

The human community has invented some 3,000 different languages, of which Yiddish is one. And each language is honeycombed with singularity. What human tongues have in common is only purpose: the use of sounds to communicate sensations; the deployment of words to capture the swarming multitude of impressions on the self; the fashioning of symbols to express the infinite fantasies of the imagination; the devising of methods to teach what has been learned to those who do not yet know it; the creation of words, words, words that may just possibly convey the divine and the godawful parameters of the human condition.

> Of all man's marvelous inventions, language is surely the most amazing. It distinguishes him from the animals; it makes abstract thought—generalization, discrimination, analysis, hypothesis—possible. Without language, there could be no science or technology, no poetry or physics, no transistor or computer, no laser, maser, zipper or Hollandaise sauce. The Bible says, "In the beginning was the word." If that means anything, it means that language existed *before* man. The great Rabbi

> Akiba's disciples took it for granted that an alphabet existed before God created the world. I have no way of proving this; but there is no way of disproving it either.*

No language is born of logic, nor ruled by reason. Were English logical, the opposite of "in-law" would be "outlaw," a female ghost would be a "ghostess," and the past tense of "squeeze" would surely be "squoze." An unknown prankster earned my thanks with this doggerel:

> One fowl is a goose but two are called geese.
> Yet the plural of mouse should never be meese.
> If I speak of a foot and you show me your feet,
> And I give you a boot, would a pair be called beet?
> If one is a tooth and the whole set are teeth,
> Why should not the plural of booth be called beeth?

Translation

"Japanese is in some respects untranslatable," says Herbert Passin, in his *Language and Cultural Patterns*, "but so is every other language.... The more deeply you go into a language the more unique it becomes."

To translate is to re-create portions of a culture to someone not raised in that culture. To translate Yiddish is to translate an entire style of life, a construct of apperceptions, a complex system of values, subtleties of thinking and feeling which are imbedded in the history of European Jews and the life of their descendants. Maurice Samuel, a remarkably sensitive and elegant translator, put it this way:

> The Yiddish masses were strangers to earthy joys that lightened the lives of their neighbors. Their consolations were to a large extent [those] of the imagination. Therefore their language, besides serving a normal need, had an esoteric function unimaginable to their neighbors. All languages have their peculiarities and impenetrable privacies . . . The spirit of Yiddish sets it apart from contiguous languages. The difficulty of translating Yiddish . . . lies less in the absence of corresponding vocabularies than in the Jewish-Yiddish conception of the meaning of life and the destiny of the people.
>
> —*In Praise of Yiddish* (COWLES)

---

* My *Treasury of Jewish Quotations*, PREFACE.

That prince of Jewish writers, I. L. Peretz, once said:

> Yiddish bears the marks of our expulsions from land to land, the language which absorbed the laments of generations, the poison and the bitterness of history, the language whose precious jewels are undried, uncongealed Jewish tears.

On the English Spelling of Yiddish Words

"Standard Yiddish," as prescribed and propagated by the Yivo Institute for Jewish Research, has been accepted by leading linguists, the Library of Congress, the *Encyclopedia Judaica,* and the continuing journal, *The Field of Yiddish.**

1. I shall respect the rules of standard Yiddish, *except* where a different spelling, in Roman characters, has already been well established. The contrast between the two is often startling:

Standard Yiddish	*Established in English*
b'yali	bialy
khale	challa
matse	matzo
meyvin	maven

To spell *shamus* as *shames,* which standard Yiddish urges upon me, is to suggest that iniquity attends even the most respectable detective.

2. I also depart from standard Yiddish where its spelling discombobulates the innocent reader. To give the name of the Sabbath as *Shabes,* instead of the almost universal *Shabbes,* is to cue a reader into making the holy day rhyme with "slaves" instead of "novice."

3. Wherever there are several ways of spelling a word, I list those ways in columnar form; the first spelling is the one that has

---

* The standard orthography follows the Northern (Lithuanian or "Litvak") spelling and pronunciation—a somewhat surprising state of affairs, given the fact that the overwhelming majority of Jews who spoke or speak Yiddish (surely over 70 percent) did not follow the Litvak articulation but used the Polish, Galician, Czech, Ukrainian, Russian vocalizations. You will understand the dilemma Yivo presented to many Jews, including the writer of these words. The scholars of Vilna, that Jerusalem of Jewish learning, were commanding figures, to be sure. Unfortunately, they would not pronounce (I mean this literally) the *yi* that characterizes the speech of Polish Jews. They said "Idish" and "ingele" for "Yiddish" and "yingele." They have prevailed—at least in the spelling.

so widely taken root in English periodicals and books that it must be given preference. Example:

Chanuka

Khaneke (standard)

Channuka

I may add that I have also seen Chanuka Englished as Chanukah, Chanuke, Channukah, Khanuka, Khanuke, Hanuka, Hanuke, Hannuka, Hannuke, etc.

4. To make sure that my readers, of whatever persuasion or complexion, do not pronounce a three-syllable word in two syllables (because of the English spelling) I employ blunt orthographic cues: *meshugge,* for instance, is clearly better for American vocal cords than the standard *meshuge.* This was driven home to me by a friend who displays his fondness for Yiddish by pronouncing the priceless adjective *m'shug.* (He knows from nothing about *mama-loshn.*)

5. I double consonants in certain words to squelch the possibility that the word will be pronounced with a long, rather than a short, vowel. Standard Yiddish orthography uses *rebe.* I would hate to have a rabbi addressed as "Reeb," a syllable obviously from Jabberwocky.

6. I use *sh* at the beginning of a word instead of the oft-encountered *sch.* The *sch* is German; in English it usually calls for the cluster *sk.* It is foolhardy to encourage the unwary into calling a shlepper a "sklepper."

7. I prefer to use *h* for the uvular fricative instead of *kh,* although I follow standard Yiddish by using *kh* where it seems feasible. But I cannot bring myself to inflict *khutzpe* (or even *hutspa*) upon *chutzpa.*

8. Where a terminal *e* dictates the lengthening of the preceding vowel (*mat, mate*) I often checkmate the rule by adding a minatory *h:* thus, *opstairsekeh* escapes the fate of rhyming with "Mozambique."

On all of the above, I should warn you, I could not achieve complete consistency. I was, after all, raised in Southern (Polish) Yiddish. That was the language we spoke all through my childhood. It was the language used in the school where I learned to read and write the lovely tongue. It was the accent and cadence I heard in the marvelous Yiddish theater. There is no point in pedants lamenting my occasional lapses. For my part, I hold no grudge against the Humboldt Current.

Of one thing I am sure: Sholom Aleichem would understand, if for no other reason than that I refuse to change his pseudonym to Shol'm Aleykhem.

Standard Yiddish uses the following letters for the following pronunciations:

a	as in "father"
ay	as in "bite"
dzh	as in "Joe"
e	(never silent, even when it is the last letter in a word) as in "red"
ey	as in "they"
i	(when final or only letter) as in "machine," otherwise as in "lid"
o	as in "mother" or "cloth"
oy	as in "toil"
u	as in "rule"
kh	as in (German) *Ach!*
ts	as in "hats"
zh	as in "measure"

Acknowledgments

Since *The Joys of Yiddish* was published (1968), studies of and in and about Yiddish have exploded all over the provinces of linguistics, literature, psychology, ethnology, sociology, philology, psycholinguistics, history.* To keep my heart from sinking, and my will from paralyzing, I sought the help of an informal panel of experts: Dr. Shlomo Noble of Yivo, Professor *emeritus* Nathan Susskind of City College, Professor Joshua A. Fishman of Yeshiva University, Professors Joseph Landis and Samuel Heilman of Queens College. For questions about Hebrew and theology I consulted Professor Seymour Siegel of the Jewish Theological Seminary. These good men were endlessly instructive in coping with my ignorance, and endlessly diplomatic in coping with my innocence. I thank them heartfully; and you should, too.

---

* See, for example, Professor Marvin I. Herzog's massive *The Yiddish Language in Northern Poland: its Geography and History* (Indiana University); Samuel Heilman's germinal study of the *shnorer:* "The Gift of Alms," *Urban Life and Culture,* January 1975, pp. 371–395; Gerald Cohen's extensive forays, in *Comments on Etymology,* at the University of Missouri, into *shmuck, shlemiel* and other Yinglish words; *The International Journal of American Linguistics: The Field of Yiddish* (now in its 26th year of publication); the remarkable *Journal of Psycholinguistic Research.* I must separately cite the many admirable investigations of the sociologist-linguist-Yiddishist Joshua A. Fishman of Yeshiva University, whose "Yiddish in America" (*International Journal of American Linguistics,* Vol. 31, No. 2) is something of a bench mark in the field. Professor Fishman also edited a huge anthology: *Never Say Die: A Thousand Years of Yiddish in Jewish Life and Letters* (Mouton, The Hague).

My greatest debt is entered in the golden book of *mitzves* next to the name of Dr. Nathan Susskind. That unretiring scholar—classicist, philologist, master of Hebrew and German and Yiddish and English, *maven* on the history, religion and ethos of the Jews down the ages—inched his way through my manuscript with admirable and painful (to me) exactitude. I am profoundly grateful to him.

It is customary to crown prefatory plaudits with the shopworn "but none of the above is responsible for any errors." I go further than that. My errors are mine. They are mine alone. I absolutely refuse to share credit for them with anyone.

—LEO ROSTEN

Reader: Please Note!

1.

When an entry is preceded by this symbol ✡, it means that more information may be found in *The Joys of Yiddish*.

2.

If you do not find an entry under *ch* look for it under *kh* or *h*.

3.

To pronounce the guttural *kh,* pretend you have a fishbone stuck in the roof of your mouth.

4.

In spelling certain words, I sternly drop the *c* from the *sch* of the German from which the Yiddish was cloned. This orthographic surgery protects the innocent, who might otherwise say, "Don't be a *sklemiel.*"

5.

Where a Yiddish word has been Englished in different ways, I list the different spellings; the first is either the one I prefer or the one most often encountered in English.

6.

Three major (six minor) geographical variations are involved in the pronunciation of Yiddish. I have accepted, not without sighs, the Lithuanian (Litvak) phonetic regime installed by authorities (see Introduction). This in no way reflects upon the accents of Galitzianer, Poylish, Ukrainian, Romanian, Grik, Toikish or Japanese Jews. They are all free to act aggrieved.

—L.R.

A

Accusing someone of asininity by echoing a question

The true *maven* of Yiddish knows the sweet uses of scorn:

> Q. Don't you want to meet a wonderful boy and get married and have a fine family?
>
> A. No, I don't want to meet a wonderful boy and get married and have a fine family. (Meaning: "How stupid can you be to ask such an idiotic question?")

Accusing someone of idiocy by denying the obvious

This deadpan ploy is typical of Jewish sarcasm:

> Q. How would you like an all-expenses-paid trip to Hawaii?
>
> A. I prefer to spend the winter in a foxhole in the Bronx. (Meaning: "How can you even *ask* such a stupid question?")

Adjectives fronted for purposes of irony or emphasis

This is a distinctive characteristic of Yiddish usage, and a glittering feature of advanced Yinglish. (Yes, I know it is occasionally found in Dickens.)

> Smart, he isn't.
> Beautiful, she's not.
> Lucky, they are.

Note how much more effective "Funny, he isn't" is than "He isn't funny."

The transposition of predicate adjectives (or nouns) is particularly loved by speakers of Yiddish. If you say, "Harry isn't a hero," that's hardly interesting: but "A *hero*, Harry isn't" suggests that Harry may be intelligent, kind, good-looking, even honest, but of one thing you can be sure: Harry is no *shtarker (q.v.).*

△ △ △

What I call "fronting" is dubbed "topicalization" by more earnest students of linguistics. One pioneer, Dr. Mark H. Feinstein, has published a study of one hundred college students which demonstrates that Jews are more likely than non-Jews to accept the fronting of certain "indefinites." See Feinstein's "Ethnicity and Topicalization in New York City English," *International Journal of the Sociology of Language,* No. 26 (Mouton), page 15ff.

△ △ △

The three condemned men faced the firing squad in the courtyard of the prison in Leningrad.

"What is your last request, Nikolai Karpovich?" barked the officer.

"I want my ashes spread on the Russian-Chinese border . . . in honor of Mao Tse-tung!"

"All right. Squad: ready . . . aim . . . fire!"

Down dropped Nikolai Karpovich.

To the second man, the executioner said, "And what is your last request, Andrey Basilovich?"

"Bury me in Tiflis, where glorious Stalin was born."

"Fine. Squad: ready . . . aim . . . fire!"

Down sank Andrey Basilovich.

To the third condemned man, the executioner said, "And your dying request, Yitzchok Sheinberg?"

"Please . . ." wheezed old Sheinberg, ". . . spread my ashes over the grave . . . of Leonid Brezhnev."

"Brezhnev? But Comrade Brezhnev isn't dead!"

Said Sheinberg, "I don't mind waiting."

(Dumb, he wasn't.)

Adjectives used as nouns

> Yinglish, as in "She's a crazy!"

Please don't rise in wrath to cry, "But that *is* English!" Don't rush to cite the delirious sixties, during which we were subjected to a succession of outrages by hirsute fanatics who were dubbed "the crazies."

Long before that gaudy time, American Jews were converting adjectives to nouns with equanimity. Early in the 1920s (and perhaps earlier), on the Lower East Side, in Brooklyn, in the Bronx, in the Jewish enclaves of Chicago, Detroit, Los Angeles, our parents and grandparents were coining nouns such as "a skinny . . . a silly . . . a crazy." My generation extended the practice: "a nasty . . . a goofy."

Please note: I am *not* talking about nouns such as "smarty . . . toughie . . . softie . . . sharpie." These are adjectives made into nouns by adding *y* or *ie.* I refer to adjectives which, entirely unchanged, are used as nouns.* Jewish children and professional comedians bandy "a funny" about instead of "a joke."

△ △ △

PSYCHIATRIST: Sit down, Mr. Lichtman. Now what brings you here?

MR. LICHTMAN: People. Stupid people. Doc, I despair about the whole human race!

PSYCHIATRIST: Mmh. What is it that people *do* that—

MR. LICHTMAN: They call me—a crazy. No matter what I say, right away they holler I am a crazy! What do you *do,* Doctor, about such stupid, stubborn people? They won't listen to a word of truth!

PSYCHIATRIST: Mr. Lichtman, perhaps you ought to start at the beginning.

MR. LICHTMAN: Good! In the beginning, I created the heavens and the earth. And the earth was without form and void . . .

Adonai

Hebrew: My Lords. (Note the plural.)

The sacred title of God, usually translated into English as "Lord."

Adonai is pronounced by a pious Jew only after his hands have been washed, with head covered, during prayer. In all other circumstances, the devout say *Adoshem.* In Hebrew, the singular name is *Adoni,* the plural is *Adonim,* and the plural plus the possessive *i* is *Adonai*—i.e., "My Lords" or "My Masters."

Why is the Hebrew word for God a plural? You must now bear with conjecture. Before the second millennium B.C.E., the Hebrews were polytheists; they spoke not of their God but of their gods. The Hebrew language simply did not change to accommodate the epochal shift from a multiplicity of deities to One Omnipotent Being.

---

* And before you rush to the *Oxford Dictionary of the English Language:* I looked it up. "Skinny," for instance, is described only as an adjective, never as a noun. And authorities such as William and Mary Morris (*Dictionary of Contemporary Usage,* Harper & Row), and Harold Wentworth and Stuart Berg Flexner (*Dictionary of American Slang,* Crowell) cite no usage that would contradict my claims.

As hyperthyroid MC's say: "Let's hear it for the Jews!"

Such supreme sanctity became attached to the Name (see YHVH) that it was rarely used outside of the synagogue.*

Clever readers will of course pounce upon the possible connection between *Adonai* and "Adonis." Their pounce is not foolish: "Adonis" happens to be the Greek form of the Semitic *adon*. Adonis was one of the Syrian gods, presiding over the crucial realm of agriculture. And there was a magical cult of Adonis worship in ancient Greece.

See ADOSHEM, JEHOVAH, YAHVEH, YHVH.

△ △ △

Jewish folk sayings about God are endless, befitting His scope. Here are a few of my favorites:

> What the Lord does is certainly best—probably.

> God may love the poor, but He helps the rich.

> Oh, Lord: help me. If you don't, I'll ask my uncle in New York.

> Dear God: You help total *strangers*—so why not me?

> God is closest to those whose hearts are broken.

> Dear God: I know that You will provide: but why don't you provide *until* You provide?

> Oh, Lord: do not inflict upon us all that you know we can endure.

> If God lived on earth, men would knock out all His windows.

△ △ △

Have you never wondered why the Lord waited until the last day of His initial labors before creating our common forebear? If so (and even if not so) the reason is staggering:

> Why was man created on the last day? So that he can be told, when pride takes hold of him: God created the gnat before thee.
>
> —TALMUD: *Sanhedrin,* 37a

△ △ △

A question bothered theologians for centuries: Why did the Almighty create Adam alone? I have always been grateful for the answers in three different passages in the Talmud:

---

* In English, Orthodox Jews still write or type "G–d." To very pious Ashkenazim, every Hebrew word is too sacred to be uttered until you have washed your hands, hence the saying *Danken dem di hent nit gevashn* ("Thanks to the One whose Name I may not utter because my hands have not yet been washed"). All these taboos ended in the anomaly that the word for "pray," in Yiddish or other Jewish vernaculars, is taken from another (not Hebrew) tongue. See DAVEN.

Why did God create only one man? So that no one could say virtue and vice are hereditary.

—Sanhedrin, 4a

Why did God create Adam alone? In order to teach us that whoever destroys a single life is as guilty as though he had destroyed the entire world; and that whoever saves one life, earns as much merit as though he had saved the entire world.

—Sanhedrin, 4:5

Why did God create but one man? So that no one of his descendants should be able to say, "My father is better than your father." (Or, "My race is superior to yours.")

—Sanhedrin, 37a

△ △ △

Chaim Mintz went off alone one day to scale the sheerest face of Mount Carmel. As he dug his boot onto a ledge it gave way, and Chaim fell 150 feet—managing, by a miracle, to grab a branch from a gnarled tree. "Help! Help!" he yelled.

A great voice far above intoned, "My son, do you have full faith in Me?"

"Yes! Yes!"

"Do you trust Me without reservation?"

"Oh, yes, Lord!"

"Then let go of that branch."

"What?"

"I said, 'Let go of that branch!' "

A pause; then Mintz said, "Excuse me, but—is there anyone else up there?"

Adoshem

From Hebrew: formed from the first syllable of *Adonai* and the last syllable of *Ha-Shem:* the Name.

The spoken name used instead of the sacrosanct *Adonai.*

Adoshem is used for "the Lord" by believing Jews in ordinary conversation or outside formal religious observances.

Many names are used by pious Jews for God, depending upon which aspect of Him is intended. When God's justice is involved, the Lord is *Elohim;* the Creator of the World is *Bore Olam;* when God's mercy is involved, the Lord is called *Ha-Shem;* when the Ruler of the World needs a designation, it is *Ribon,* more commonly *Ribono shel Olam* (in Yiddish: *Riboyne shel Oylem*).

The use of synonyms suggests no ambivalence about monotheism: I believe humankind has a psychological need to prolong and adorn its venerating. (Hindus use 108 different names for the Ganges, the holy river.)

If you thirst for more, imbibe "Names of God" in the *Encyclopedia of the Jewish Religion,* edited by R. J. Werblowsky and G. Wigoder (Holt, Rinehart and Winston).

See JEHOVAH, YHVH.

△ △ △

A rabbi in Persia found a great ruby that belonged in the crown of the Emperor. An official crier went about the capital crying, "Whoever returns the Emperor's ruby within thirty days will be rewarded. But if it be found on him after thirty days, his head will be cut off!"

On the thirty-first day, the rabbi returned the ruby.

Asked the Emperor: "Did you not hear my proclamation?"

"Yes, your majesty. On the first day."

"Then why did you not return the jewel until now?"

Said the rabbi, "I did not return it within the thirty days so that you could not say I returned it because I feared you. I returned it because I believe in Adoshem."

Whereupon the Emperor exclaimed, "Blessed be the God of these Jews!"

Affirming indignation by repeating a question in the form in which it was asked, with varying intonational emphasis

This is a favored ploy in Yiddish, and a major contribution to the scornful persiflage of Yinglish. Note the dramatic effect achieved by the shift of stress, *seriatim:*

1.

Q. Did you send your mother flowers on her birthday?

A. *Did* I send my mother flowers on her birthday? (Meaning: "Are you implying that I could forget an important occasion like that?")

2.

Q. Did you send your mother flowers on her birthday?

A. Did *I* send my mother flowers on her birthday? (Meaning: "What kind of monster do you think I am—not to send my mother flowers on her birthday?")

3.

Q. Did you send your mother flowers on her birthday?

A. Did I *send* my mother flowers on her birthday? (Meaning: "And suppose I didn't send them? Suppose I brought them in person? Is that a crime?")

4.

Q. Did you send your mother flowers on her birthday?

A. Did I send *my* mother flowers on her birthday? (Meaning: "Have you forgotten that I sent *your* mother flowers on her birthday? If I sent flowers to your mother would I forget to send flowers to mine?")

5.

Q. Did you send your mother flowers on her birthday?

A. Did I send my *mother* flowers on her birthday? (Meaning: "You know that I always send flowers on their birthdays to my wife, my sister, my aunt, my cousins in New Jersey, so are you implying that I am the kind of *paskudnyak* who would send flowers to them and not to my own *mother?*")

6.

Q. Did you send your mother flowers on her birthday?

A. Did I send my mother *flowers* on her birthday? (Meaning: "Flowers were just the *beginning* of what I gave my mother on her birthday!" which suggests anything from a round-trip ticket to Israel to a condominium in West Palm Beach.)

7.

Q. Did you send your mother flowers on her birthday?

A. Did I send my mother flowers on *her* birthday? (Meaning: "If I always send my mother flowers on *my* birthday, what kind of *grubyan* would I be not to send her flowers on hers?")

8.

Q. Did you send your mother flowers on her birthday?

A. Did I send my mother flowers on her *birthday?* (Meaning: "Flowers you don't have to send your mother on New Year's or the Fourth of July—but on her *birthday?!*")

Again . . . ?

English used as Yinglish. From Yiddish: *Vider . . . ? Shoyn vider?*

Yiddish is rich in what the Germans call *Flickwörter*, expletives or particles tacked on to words to endow them with color: the stab of sarcasm, the nuance of scorn, the *shmeer* of *shmaltz*.

1. What?!
2. Already? So soon?
3. For God's sake!
4. Don't *tell* me.
5. You mean to say . . . ?
6. Over and over.
7. Can you beat that?
8. You must be crazy!
9. Once more.

In Yinglish, the jejune English adverb "again" undergoes a delectable transformation, for it does not mean simply "once more" but is an irritated, impatient, ejaculatory gloss. It reeks innuendo. Thus:

1. *Again* he's here? ("But he was just here yesterday!")
2. Again she needs money? ("She needs money so *soon?*")
3. Again he left her? ("Oh, for God's sake! This is becoming absurd.")
4. I know, I know: Weinstein again. ("Don't tell me; it's an old story; he *always* blames Weinstein.")
5. *Again* he married a teen-ager? ("You mean to say that that *shlemiel* has gone and married a teen-ager after all the misery he went through with his first wife, also a teen-ager?")
6. Again I had to write him how to get here! ("You can't begin to know how many times, over and over, I have written that dummy instructions on how to get here.")
7. Again she forgot my birthday! ("Can you beat that?")
8. *Again* I should apologize to that *chainik-hocker?* ("You must be crazy even to suggest a thing like that!")
9. Oh, my. I'll tell her again.

△ △ △

My favorite story about the scathing Yinglish use of "again" is this:

Timid Pinchas Herzog stammered to his boss, "Mr. Elchin, I absolutely can't live on the s—salary you're paying me! For a year already my wife has been nagging me I should ask for a raise, a r—raise of ten dollars a week!"

Mr. Elchin stroked his chin, muttered *"Mnyeh,"* and sighed. "So okay. You got it."

It was an overjoyed Pinchas Herzog who hurried home.

The next week, when Pinchas opened his pay envelope, his face fell. He hurried into the boss's office. "Mr. Elchin, what h—happened to my raise?!"

"Your raise?" echoed Elchin. *"Again* you want ten dollars more?"

Again with . . . ?

From Yiddish: *Shoyn vider mit?*

This interrogation adds the Yinglish use of the preposition to the already complaint-laden "again."

△ △ △

WIFE: So how many drinks *did* you have?
HUSBAND: *Again* with the drinking?

△ △ △

HUSBAND: What was that guy's name?
WIFE: *Again* with your jealousy about who I dance with?

△ △ △

GREENBLATT: In January, my wife asked me—in addition to the household expenses—for eighty dollars. In February, she asked for ninety dollars. In March, *again* with ninety!
HOFFMAN: Migod, Nathan! What does she do with all that money?
GREENBLATT: Who knows? I never give her a penny.

Agreement as a vehicle for scorn

Experts in Yinglish employ the device of nominal agreement to carry the freight of blistering disagreement. Example:

Q. But won't you feel bad if you have to have surgery?
A. Yes, I'll feel bad if I have to have surgery.

The repeated understatement magnifies the scorn.

A variant of this *tu quoquery* lies in altering the adjective: "Yes, I'll feel miffed if I have to have surgery."

Or dramatizing the event: "Yes, I'll feel bad if I have to have my arm cut off."

△ △ △

MRS. BIRNBAUM: Is it true that you're going to have a baby?
MRS. KLINEMAN: It's true, it's true.
MRS. BIRNBAUM: *Mazel tov!* Do you want a boy or a girl?
MRS. KLINEMAN: Certainly.

Agreement enlarged for purposes of mockery

1.

MINNIE: Are you going to his funeral?
HENRY: Abso*lute*ly. ("I can hardly wait.")

2.

SAM: I hear his new wife is beautiful.
JOE: Beautiful? She's gorgeous—all 280 pounds of her.

3.

NETTIE: Do you think she's a virgin?
SARAH: Oh, absolutely. Her daughter calls her "Lucy"—never "Mother."

△ △ △

"Plotnickoff, you owe me forty dollars!"

"I know, and first thing tomorrow—"

"Tomorrow, tomorrow, I'm sick of your tomorrows! Last week you said you couldn't pay. Last month you said you couldn't pay. Last *year* you said—"

"Enough! *Didn't I each time keep my word?*"

Aha!

Expletive (of surprise, comprehension, triumph, etc.).

Do not confuse this vigorous, versatile exclamation with the English "Ahhh . . ." Do not even confuse *Aha!* with its Yiddish clone *Hoo-ha!* (*q.v.*)

Aha!, which can be pronounced with resonance of pleasure or astonishment, sudden illumination or invidious triumph, covers an altogether unique gamut of meanings:

1. Delight: "*Aha!* Then *I* win the bet!"
2. Astonishment: "Past the *moon* we sent a rocket? *Ah-ha-a-a.*"
3. Illumination: "*Aha!* So *that's* why they called off the party!"
4. Triumph: "*Aha!* So *now* do you admit you're wrong?"
5. Resignation: "You want *me* to go with you? . . . *Aha!*"
6. Defeat: "So it's no use? We lost . . . Well (sigh) . . . *A—ha.*"

Certain Yiddish words are so distinctly and emphatically Jewish in their emotional aura that they may be called quintessential to the character of the language—and the people who fashioned it. Among such words *Oy* probably ranks first. Then comes *Nu,* no doubt. But not far behind, surely, is *Aha!*

△ △ △

The classic use of *Aha!*, combining cunning manipulation with climactic triumph, is illustrated in the tale of old Mr. Fishbein, a widower, who for years and years had been eating every Friday night at Moskowitz and Lupowitz (of blessed memory).

On this night, as usual, Mr. Fishbein sat down at his usual table, and Shlomo, the waiter, as usual, put before him the usual chopped liver.

Mr. Fishbein ate the chopped liver; the waiter removed the plate, as usual, replaced it with a bowl of chicken soup, and started off.

Fishbein called, "Eh–eh! Shlomo!"

"What?"

"Taste this soup."

"Hanh?" frowned the waiter. "It's the soup you *always*—"

"Taste it."

"Listen, Mr. Fishbein! In all these years did you ever *once* have here a bad bowl chicken soup?"

"I said: Taste—the—soup!"

"Okay," scowled the waiter. "I'll—where's the spoon?"

"A*ha!*" cried Fishbein.

△ △ △

Mr. Weinberger was returning from New York by bus to his home town, Ellenville. Across the aisle sat a young man. Mr. Weinberger sang out, "My name is Weinberger and I live in Ellenville."

"My name," said the young man, "is Glickman. And I'm going to Ellenville."

"On business?"

"No."

"To visit family?"

"It's not family."

"Are you—married?"

"No."

"Aha." Mr. Weinberger leaned back in his seat, closed his eyes, and reasoned thusly: "Not on business; no family in Ellenville; not married. So he must be going to meet a girl. And if he's going this far, it must be serious. So—which girl? Hinda Rozinski? No: she's engaged to that dentist from Brooklyn. . . . Is he going to the Baskins? N–no, the Baskins' daughter was married two years ago. . . . To the Arkins? N–naw, Shirley Arkin is only fourteen. . . . Maybe to the Pizarcheks? But Lily Pizarchek is away, at college. . . . To the Gorelicks? Never! Gorelick would never let his Sandra marry a boy who has to travel on a bus because he hasn't enough money to own a car. . . . The Shlaum girl? Ah. The Shlaums have three daughters: Annie, Eva and Grace. Annie is big and fat, and this young man is good-looking enough to pick and choose. Eva? Eva is a widow with young children. . . . Grace? Grace! There is a live number! And last weekend she went to New York. *Aha!*" Mr. Weinberger beamed. "Mr. Glickman, congratulations."

"Eh? What—?"

"On your forthcoming engagement to Miss Grace Shlaum."

The young man blushed furiously. "But—we haven't told a soul. Not even her mother and father. How did you ever find out?"

"How I found out?" echoed Mr. Weinberger. "My boy, it's obvious."

ai-ai-ai

See AY-YAY-YAY.

A.K.

Initials for the taboo *alter kocker:* old defecator.

(Vulgarism)
1. An old man.
2. A constipated man.
3. A slow-moving, slow-thinking man.
4. (Affectionately) Old codger.

△ △ △

I am told that an *alrightnik* named his cocker spaniel "Alter."

△ △ △

OLD MR. BARNOFF (answering phone): Hello.

WOMAN'S VOICE: Hello. Is this 922-4861?

MR. BARNOFF: No, lady. You got the wrong number.

WOMAN: Are you sure?

MR. BARNOFF: Listen, lady, did I ever lie to you before?

△ △ △

The board of the synagogue was astounded when their rabbi, age seventy-eight, announced that he was going to marry—a twenty-nine-year-old girl. "How can you *consider* such a scandalous thing?" exclaimed the Chairman of the Board.

"It will be a disgrace to the congregation!" cried a trustee.

"It could be dangerous for you!" cried a doctor. "Do you realize, *Rebbe,* that sometimes there's a heart attack . . . sometimes death. . . ."

The old man nodded. "That is in the hands of God, blessed be His Name. If He, in His infinite wisdom, decides on death—I certainly will miss her."

△ △ △

SCENE: *Telephone Exchange, Los Angeles*

OPERATOR: Long Distance. May I help you?

MR. SHOSHKIN: You soitinly can. Give me, in Pokipsee, New York, 744-8032.

OPERATOR: Would you mind repeating the name of that city, please?

MR. SHOSHKIN: Po–kip–see. In New York. Po–kip–see.

OPERATOR: Sir, would you mind *spelling* that?

MR. SHOSHKIN: Listen, lady: if I could spell it, I would send a postcard.

alav ha-sholem (m.)

olav a shol'm (standard)

aleha ha-sholem (f.)

aleyhem ha-sholem (pl.)

alavasholem

> Hebrew, often heard in Yinglish. Rhymes with "olive-a roll 'em." The two words for the masculine are pronounced as if one, usually, dropping the *h* sound. Pronounce the feminine form ah-LEY-a ha-SHO-lem (Yiddish) or sha-LOAM (Hebrew).
>
> 1. Literally: Unto him (her), peace.
> 2. May he (she) rest in peace.

This invocation is obligatory whenever you mention someone who is no longer breathing. The English equivalent, of course, is "May he [she] rest in peace."

Whenever you hear, say, "My Tante Bessie, *aleha ha-sholem* . . ." it would be scandalous to ask, "And how *is* your Aunt Bessie?"

When I was growing up, I was puzzled by the negative embroidery which blithely surrounded *alavasholem: e.g.,* "Charley? That no-good! That liar! That *plosher, alavasholem.* . . ."

In time I learned the emotional acrobatics. Those named are dead, and one *must* wish the dead well. The pro forma invocation of kindness is a ritual, and rituals offer sanctioned outlets for the discharge of warring emotions. The obligatory reduces anxiety by eliminating choices. In this way one can rage, "That s.o.b. should only fry in hell," adding the immediate, petitionary *alav ha-sholem* to assuage conscience. Invoking the deity's mercy takes the edge off malediction—*after* hostility has been healthily vented.

△ △ △

A bearded sage once patted my head when I was ten and said, smiling, "You're a nice boy. You should live to be a hundred and twenty-one!"

I told this to my father, *alav ha-sholem,* who explained: "Moses is supposed to have lived until a hundred and twenty."

"Oh—but why did the old man say 'a hundred and twenty-*one*'?"

My father chuckled, "Maybe he didn't want you to die suddenly."

△ △ △

Even *alav ha-sholem* is used by Jews for comic effect. Thus:

"I have a doctor, a regular genius. Such important patients! For instance: Samson Rothschild, *alav ha-sholem;* Lena Buchholz, *aleha ha-sholem;* Professor and Mrs. Mintzhoff, *aleyhem ha-sholem.* . . ."

△ △ △

My dear mother, *aleha ha-sholem,* adored this little story.

"So, Jennie," said Sadie, "Goldie tells me you have had a very hard time."

"What do you mean, 'had'? You think everything now is hotsy-totsy?"

"So—what happened?"

"Last June, my dog was run over. In July, my daughter got a divorce. In August, my darling husband, *alav ha-sholem,* dropped dead. And next week—" Jennie sighed—"the painters are coming."

Aleichem sholem

Aleykhem shol'm (standard)

> Pronounced in Yiddish: a-LAY-khem (gargle the *kh*) SHO-lem. From Hebrew. In Hebrew, the accent is otherwise: sha-LOAM.

> 1. (As a greeting) Unto you, peace.

When two Jews meet, one says, *"Sholem aleichem,"* and the other replies, *"Aleichem sholem."*

> 2. (As an expletive) Can you beat that?

"He was kissing her passionately when—*sholem aleichem*—someone busted into the room!"

"That someone—*aleichem sholem*—was me!"

> 3. (As an ejaculation) Oh, for God's sake!
>
> △ △ △
>
> SCENE: *Obstetrics Ward, Beth Israel Hospital*
>
> WOMAN: How come all you obstetricians are so busy—*sholem aleichem!*—these days?
>
> DOCTOR: Because so many men—*aleichem sholem!*—are working for us.

See SHOLEM ALEICHEM.

alevay

halevay (standard)

> Often used in conversations between Jews. Pronounced "olive eye." Aramaic: May it be so.

1. If only . . .
2. May it come to pass.
3. I hope (wish) . . .
4. (Ironically) That'll be the day!

Halevai, usually pronounced without the voiced aspirate *h,* is found in abundance, like a Greek chorus fortifying hope, in the pages of the Talmud. The petitionary utterance is often heard in spoken Yiddish, especially by women.

Alevay is a signal that what follows it, or preceded it, is "devoutly to be wished." Thus:

"He should come home safely, *alevay.*"

"*Alevay* we should have good weather."

"If only, *alevay,* the war would end!"

When used ironically, *alevay* means "Forget it," or "I'd like to see the day *that* happens!"

△ △ △

JOE: You want to see *Star Wars* tomorrow?

MINNIE: Yeh! If, *alevay* we're still alive.

JOE: So if we're not, we'll go Wednesday.

MINNIE: *Alevay.*

△ △ △

"That crook!" exclaimed Mr. Popoff. "May he drop dead and leave enough insurance to pay his debts!"

Sighed Mrs. Popoff, "*Alevay,* God forbid."

aliyah

aliot (pl.)

> Hebrew: going up; ascent. Often found in English.
>
> 1. The honor of being called to the stage, during a synagogue service, to read a portion of the Torah or to recite the blessings before and after. (More properly called *aliyah la-torah.*)
> 2. Migration to the State of Israel.
> 3. A visit or pilgrimage, usually to Jerusalem.

To read aloud from the Hebrew text takes considerable skill, because no vowel sounds are indicated, no punctuation(!), no signs for oral accent. Today the one "called up" often does not read at all (rabbis do not want to embarrass the many who don't know Hebrew); instead, the text is chanted by an appointed reader or elder. *Autre temps, autres moeurs.*

Don't say "I went on an *aliyah*," but "I made *aliyah*."

The many problems that attend immigration to Israel are set forth by Kevin Avruch's excellent examination of the lives and the personal accounts of certain families. See his *American Immigrants in Israel: Social Identities and Change* (University of Chicago).

△ △ △

Arnold Kalbfleish made *aliyah* to Israel. Soon after his arrival, he went to an optician. "I'm having a lot of trouble reading, Doctor. Maybe I need stronger lenses."

The optician placed a large chart before Kalbfleish. "Read off the letters on the bottom line."

Mr. Kalbfleish squinted and squirmed. "I can't."

"What about the next line up? The letters are larger."

Kalbfleish stared and shook his head.

"Then try the top line."

"I can't."

The optician cleared his throat. "Excuse me, mister. Are you blind?"

"Oh, *no*, Doc. I just never learned Hebrew."

alkay

> Rhymes with "fall day."
>
> 1. Okay.
> 2. Everything's in order.

This is one of the most common malformations of colloquial English by colloquial Jews. I never could get my father, who became quite fluent in English, to say "Okay." I often tried: "It's '*o*kay,' not '*al*kay,' " I would say.

"They don't mean the same thing?"

"They do mean the same thing, Pa; but *alkay* is wrong."

He gave me one of his all-purpose smiles. "*Zuneleh* (dear son of mine), the people to who I say *alkay* don't know it's wrong."

On another occasion my father said, "*I* don't use okay when I mean *alkay*. Take our automobile. If you ask, 'How is the engine?' I say 'Okay.' If you ask 'How is the battery?' I'll say 'Okay.' But when I want to say that everything—motor, lights, brakes—is hotsy-totsy, I say, '*Alkay!*' "

Little did I dream that my Papa was performing a feat of what is now called "psycholinguistics."

Space engineers and cosmonauts have coined the expressive "A.O.K." to mean "All systems working."

Had my father been alive to hear this, he would, I think, have smiled. "Ufcawss! *Alkay*."

△ △ △

LEVKISH: Did you hear the story about the two Jews who—

YABLON: Stop! Why is it always two Jews? Wouldn't the story be just as funny if it was about two Irishmen? Or two Mexicans? Or two Zulus?

LEVKISH: *Alkay.* Two Zulus met at the U.J.A., and the first Zulu said, "Ikey, when is your son going to be Bar Mitzve?" So the second Zulu said—

YABLON: Forget it.

already

From Yiddish: *shoyn* and *nokh.*

1. By now ("He's not convinced already?").
2. It's about time ("So come on, already.").
3. Premature ("Already he's arguing?").
4. With no further ado ("Enough already!").
5. I *mean* it ("Stop already!" "I'm mad already!")

When used at the end of a sentence, as in "Come on already!," English shows the direct infiltration of Yiddish, where *shoyn* (already) does a lively trade: ordinarily, English usage would be "now."

Jews of the Bronx, the Lower East Side, the West Side of Chicago adapted English words to Yiddish patterns to create new idioms. The amusing, or simply expressive, ring of the neologisms swiftly led writers, actors, comedians, then talk-show regulars to adopt the Yinglish modes. (This may be called idiomatic feedback, though food is not involved.)

See also AGAIN, ALRIGHT ALREADY, ENOUGH ALREADY, YET.

△ △ △

PATIENT: Doctor, I'm going crazy already! I just can't remember a damn thing. If you asked me what time I got up this morning, or what I ate for breakfast, or where I had lunch—I couldn't tell you one thing!

PSYCHIATRIST: How long has this been going on?

PATIENT: How long has what been going on?

△ △ △

Hymie Shoenfeld, an old waiter at a restaurant famous for the independence (not to say insolence) of its waiters, died. Some of his friends decided to hold a seance in the quarters of

ROSA PENELOPE LEVITSKI

SEER—ORACLE—MEDIUM

SPIRITUAL INTERMEDIARY

Now, ten of Hymie Shoenfeld's friends sat around the table, under a shaded lamp, as Rosa Penelope Levitski went into a trance, intoning, "Hymie . . . Hymie . . . are you happy? . . . I will rap three times, then you should answer. . . ." Mme. Levitski rapped—slowly, solemnly— three times.

The friends sat, hushed.

"Hymie, Hymie," crooned the oracle, "*please* pay attention. Are you in Heaven? In bliss? I will now knock *four* times." And four times— loudly—did Mme. Levitski rap on the board. But the room stayed silent as the grave. . . .

"Hymie! Hymie Shoenfeld! What's the *matter*? We want to hear you already!" And now the seeress firmly knocked five times—in vain. "Hymie!" cried Mme. Levitski. "Stop pretending! I know you're there! *Why don't you answer?*"

Came the disembodied voice of Hymie the waiter, "Because . . . that's . . . not . . . my . . . table."

△ △ △

"Doc," said Elmer Byfeld, "you know I'm seventy-nine. You know how with me making love maybe once a month is already good. Well, I have a friend who is eighty-one. And last week he told me, man to man, that he makes love three times a week! Doc, what should I *do?*"

Said the doctor, "Tell him the same thing."

Alright already

> Yinglish to the core. From the Yiddish *Shoyn genug,* or *Genug shoyn,* which means "Enough already."

1. Enough!
2. Say no more, for God's sake!
3. Will you please shut up?
4. I can't *stand* any more!

"Alright already," a thriving export from the Bronx, is, to be exact, a version of "Enough already!" (*q.v.*) And in that context "Alright already!" signifies exasperated agreement:

5. Okay, okay, just stop nagging me!
6. You win: save your voice.
7. I give up: you shut up.

"Alright already" is not always rooted in disgust. It may be used simply to betoken agreement—and cut off further discussion:

8. Okay, okay: let's get on with it.

This last usage is beautifully illustrated in the playlet I now give you.

ACT 1

TEACHER: Who blew down the walls of Jericho?

BENJAMIN: Don't look at me, ma'am; *I* didn't.

ACT 2

TEACHER: Mr. Fardroos, I must talk to you about your boy, Benjamin. When I asked him, during Bible study, who blew down the walls of Jericho, he answered, "Don't look at me; I didn't!"

MR. FARDROOS: Miss, I assure you: if my boy said he didn't do it, he didn't do it!

ACT 3

PRINCIPAL: Miss Skorskie, I hear that little Ben Fardroos, when asked who blew down the walls of Jericho, answered, "*I* didn't." Is that true?

TEACHER: Absolutely. And his father vouches for the boy's honesty!

ACT 4

PRINCIPAL: Mr. Binter, as chairman of the board of trustees of our synagogue you will be interested in something that involves Mr. Fardroos. When his boy's teacher asked who blew down the walls of Jericho, little Ben replied: "Not me." Mr. Fardroos assured the teacher that his son could be trusted. I asked the teacher what she thought, and she—

CHAIRMAN: Alright, alright already! I'm a busy man. Get the wall fixed and send the bill to me.

alrightnik

alrightnikeh (f.)

alrightnitseh (derisive)

> Yinglish, *sans doute*, from English: all right.
>
> 1. A man or woman who has done "all right" monetarily and shows it in tasteless display, vulgar manners, gaudy dress or tactless boasts.
> 2. *Nouveau riche* but neither well-read nor respectful of learning.

The use of the pungent Slavic particle -*nik* tells you that the mood is barbed. When -*nik* is tacked onto an otherwise sober English word, the intention is to draft scorn into the service of derogation.

Alrightniks may be envied for their wealth, but they are despised for their ostentation. Within traditional Jewish values, *alrightniks* are offensive because they are not sensitive, not *eydel.* Above all they are neither learned nor devoted to the pursuit (or support) of learning. The wealthy who *are* learned are not called *alrightniks.*

Alrightnik was introduced into Yiddish (therefore into Yinglish) by Abraham Cahan, the legendary editor of the *Jewish Daily Forward.* He did not have to explain *olraytnik.*

△ △ △

Joe E. Lewis, a night-club wit in a class by himself, once philosophized: "Show me a Jew who comes home in the evening, is greeted with a big smile, has his shoes taken off, has his pillows arranged for him, is served a delicious meal—and I'll show you an *alrightnik* who lives in a Japanese restaurant."

△ △ △

As the lifeguard pulled Mr. Sossheim, a well-known *alrightnik,* out of the water, an excited throng cried, "Give him air!" and "Call a doctor!" and "Get his wife!"

"Stand back!" boomed the lifeguard. "I'll give him artificial respiration!"

"Never!" cried Mrs. Sossheim. "Real respiration or nothing!"

△ △ △

A rabbi came to a rich man asking for a contribution to the Jewish community fund to provide food to the town's poor people.

"Nonsense," scoffed the *alrightnik.* "They're not poor, they're loafers! They don't *want* to work."

Said the rabbi, "Come to the window. Look out. What do you see?"

"Why, I see—people."

"Now, please, look into this mirror. What do you see?"

"Why, myself."

Sighed the rabbi, "Amazing. When clear glass is coated with silver, all you can see is yourself."

△ △ △

The essential creed of *alrightniks* is best stated in folk sayings such as these:

> It's no disgrace to be poor—and that's the only good thing to be said for it.

> If the rich would only hire the poor to die for them, the poor would earn a very good living.

And the poor (and the envious) have this to say of *alrightniks:*

> If you rub elbows with the rich, you get a hole in your sleeve.

> If you're rich, people will say you're intelligent, handsome—and sing like an angel.

> You can live like a king and still die a fool.

And the sages of Israel have taught us:

> The rich have heirs—not children.

> Whenever there is too much, something is lacking.

> Pity the man who has nothing but money.

And the Talmud:

> No one is as poor as he who is ignorant.
>
> —*Nedarim,* 41a

> Some people are slaves—to silver.
>
> —*Shabbath,* 54a

A.M.

> Yinglish acronym for *able momzer*—not the abbreviation A.M., for *ante meridiem* (before noon).
>
> 1. Verbal shorthand for *able momzer* (able bastard)—meaning someone very clever, competent and tough.
> 2. Code name for a smart, resourceful but not likable person.

△ △ △

Boris Acklitz was deep in sleep when his phone awakened him. "Hollo," he grunted.

"Mr. Acklitz, in apartment Four-C?"

"Yeh."

"This is Mrs. Brodsky in Three-B. It's half-past three in the night and your dog's barking is driving me absolutely *crazy!*" The phone slammed down.

The next night, at 3:45 A.M., Mrs. Brodsky's phone rang. "Hello," she mumbled.

"Mrs. Brodsky?"

"Yeah."

"Mrs. Brodsky in apartment Three-B?"

"Yeah!"

"This is Boris Acklitz. I want to tell you something."

"At a quarter to *four* in the morning?"

"Yeh. I don't own a dog."

(I think you will agree that Boris was an *A.M.*)

△ △ △

Dr. Hitzel examined the cardiogram and, smiling at the patient, said, "You're in perfect health, Mr. Iskorov, heart, lungs, blood pressure—everything."

"Mazel tov," sighed Mr. Iskorov.

"I'll see you next year."

Doctor and patient shook hands. Mr. Iskorov stepped out.

In a moment, Dr. Hitzel heard a loud crash. He leaped into the reception office. There, flat on his back, lay Iskorov. Dr. Hitzel's nurse cried, "He fell down like a rock!"

The doctor knelt, listened to Iskorov's heart. "He's dead." Dr. Hitzel put his hands under the corpse's arms. "Quick, nurse; take his feet!"

"What?" she gulped.

"For God's sake, let's turn him around—make it look like he was coming *in!*"

(Dr. Hitzel was an *A.M.*, too.)

Amen

See OMEYN.

America gonef! (standard)

America ganev! (standard)

From Hebrew: *ganov:* thief.

1. (Literally) America, the thief.
2. Miraculous America!
3. Wonderful America!
4. Where, except in America, could such a thing happen?

The ejaculation is also used to hail:

5. Anything exceptionally clever, ingenious, resourceful.

And so manifold is its potential, *America gonef!* may be used as the equivalent of

6. Can you beat that? Isn't that astonishing?
7. Wow!

All the admiration, gratitude, awe and wonder of immigrant Jews was poured into the apodictic cry of *America gonef!* The expression celebrated the land where everything good, fortunate and marvelous is possible.

In my family and in our circles in Chicago, "Only in America" was a little-used and pallid encomium beside *America gonef!* My father, an incurable enthusiast and passionate extoller of America's virtues, would cry *America gonef!* at least five times a week.

△ △ △

A greenhorn wandering around New York, fascinated, came to the famous Fulton Fish Market, where he saw two huge barrels, side by side. On the first barrel was painted a sign:

FRESH CRABS: $5 a dozen

The next barrel had a sign:

CRABS: $3 a dozen

As the newcomer watched, he saw a crab crawl slowly over the rim of the $3 barrel and drop into the $5 barrel.

Clucked the *greener,* "*America gonef!*"

△ △ △

On Moishe Caplan's first day home from school, his proud mother ran out to meet him. "So, Moisheleh, what did you learn?"

"I learned how to write."

"Already? The first day? *America gonef!* So what did you write?"

"Who knows? I can't read."

△ △ △

In the cardroom of a Catskills hotel, four strangers arranged a bridge game. As they sat down, the first man said, "Let's introduce ourselves. I'm Henry Garfield."

"My name," said the second player, "is William Garfett."

"I," said the third man, "am Arnold Garford."

The fourth man: "I'm Jack."

"Jack what?"

"Also Garfinckel."

America gonef!

Anger via sardonic exoneration, deploying "only," "merely," or "just" to convert the factual into the embarrassing

"Don't apologize, dear: you're merely twenty-eight minutes late; our plane is only over Cincinnati by now."

"He was very generous about the deal: he gave us 4 percent of the profits, which just left him 96."

"How could you know that Denver was west of Detroit? After all, that made us drive only 240 miles in the wrong direction."

△ △ △

Ezra Brenner extolled the vacuum cleaner he was peddling to Mrs. Thornycroft. "A better machine you won't find anyplace!"

Sighed Mrs. Thornycroft, "I can't ever make up my mind. Come back tomorrow. But I warn you: don't be disappointed if you find me —in a dilemma."

"Disappointed? Me? Lady, only yesterday I found my prospect in a kimono!"

Annihilating a statement with an outlandish observation

Yinglish is a category of psychological posture no less than wording or syntax.

The culture of the Jews is so steeped in orality, so responsive to wit, so studded with repartee, so impatient with the obvious, so merciless to banality, that it is not surprising that Jews prize swift deflation.

△ △ △

"Do you realize, Grampa, that it cost the United States about ten billion dollars to put a man on the moon?"

"*Tchk, tchk*—including meals?"

a nothing

100 percent Yinglish. From Yiddish: *a gornit (gornisht):* a nothing.

1. A person of no consequence.
2. A zero in the mathematics of respect.

The use of the article *a* is entirely Yiddish: no American or Englishman would say "a nothing." And *gornisht* is often extended, for effect or vehemence, to *gornisht mit gornisht:* "(It amounts to) nothing plus nothing."

"That Ungerman is a live wire. But his partner? A nothing."

"He went to three schools and how did he turn out? A nothing? Worse: a nothing with nothing."

3. Chic, because understated.

In advertising copy, one often runs into "a nothing" in the argot of women's fashion, "a little nothing" meaning very chic and expensive, but simple.

The most conspicuous example, of course, is "the little black dress" of Chanel, which swept through the salons of Europe and America and remains, to this day, the epitome of "understated elegance." (The French have adopted the pastiche *Un petit rien.*)

In the Talmud, "I am a nothing" appears as the paraphrase of the end of the solemn Amida prayer of Yom Kippur (*Berakot,* 17a).

△ △ △

On Yom Kippur, that most awesome of days, Jeremiah Hershenhorn, that most successful of merchants, beat his breast and swayed back and forth as he intoned the Confession, that catalogue of fifty-six categories of sin, and as was his wont, Jeremiah Hershenhorn would periodically moan, "Forgive me, O Lord: for I am a nothing, a nothing . . ."

Next to Mr. Hershenhorn, the well-known *shnorer* (beggar) of the neighborhood, Itzik Krivitz, boomed out *his* Confession and, beating his breast, cried, "Forgive me, O Lord, your humble servant, for I—am a nothing, a nothing!"

Hershenhorn shot his face toward heaven and, jabbing a finger toward Krivitz, cried, "Look, look who's calling himself a nothing!!"

A-1

A-Number One

> The second is more emphatic than the first.

1. Best.
2. Matchless.
3. Most admirable.

I am not unaware that some readers will demur: "But this is straight English!" And so it is—the *words,* I mean; the usage is another barrel of *tsimmes (q.v.).*

I call "A-Number One" Yinglish because I have heard it used thousands of times in noncommercial discourse by Jews, but rarely, outside of business matters, by Gentiles.

I do not claim that Jews invented "A-Number One." My claim is that Jews used and spread the verbal tag with avidity, funneling it back into English with the nuances of Yinglish. The Yinglishization of "A-1" parallels the Yinglishization of "customer" (*q.v.*).

△ △ △

Young Mischa Minkoff, the new reporter on the staff, was called to the office of Mr. Slansky, the managing editor.

"Mischa, I want to tell you, your work is excellent—A-One!"

"Thank you, Mr. Slansky."

"How much are we paying you?"

Sighed Mischa, "Thirty dollars a week."

Slansky beamed. "I'm glad."

Same story, different ending:

". . . How much are we paying you?"

"Thirty dollars a week."

Slansky nodded. "That's good."

Same story, different ending:

". . . How much are we paying you?"

"Thirty dollars a week."

Slansky pondered. "That's enough."

△ △ △

The woman stormed into Weizelbaum's Laundry. "You call yourselves experts? You say your work is A-Number One? Well, just look! Look what you did!"

Mr. Weizelbaum studied the object. "Lady, I don't see a thing wrong with this lace."

"Lace?" echoed the customer. "What I brought in was a sheet!"

appeal

Yinglish usage of English word.

1. A campaign to raise money for a worthy cause.
2. A program or lecture containing a solicitation of funds.

The Jewish conception of charity as a solemn and sacred duty, not philanthropy, has resulted in a plenitude of "appeals."

Anyone raised in a Jewish immigrant home became accustomed to "appeals": for orphans, the blind, abandoned girls, planting trees in the Holy Land, hot lunches for schoolchildren in Bessarabia, relief for the victims of pogroms around the world, HIAS, ORT, et cetera. No month went by, in my early life, without "appeal" raffles, bazaars, recitals (piano, violin, vocal), plays, dances, lectures, debates. My mother (*aleha ha-sholem*), a woman of indomitable will and astounding energy, organized many a committee for many a crying cause.

△ △ △

Sonia: Mama, you must come to the Community Chest appeal. The speaker is a famous professor.

Mother: What is he talking about?

SONIA: The role of sex in marriage.
MOTHER: I already gave.

△ △ △

Lena Kronin, after a month in Golden Ways Retirement Colony, sought out Mrs. Haas at the weekly Ladies Arts and Crafts class. "Sophie, you're probably the best friend I have here, so I have to get your help." Lena paused and began to blush. "It's—uh—a very personal matter. Sophie . . ." she blurted, "how do you go about starting an affair?"

"You came to the right party," beamed Sophie Haas. "*I* always start with 'God Bless America'!"

appetizing

In Yinglish: a noun.

The part of a delicatessen or supermarket devoted to appetizers.

American cities are witnessing the spread of "appetizing" as a noun—to designate that part of a delicatessen or supermarket devoted to such delicacies, much loved by Jews, as chopped liver, *gefilte* fish, smoked whitefish, lox, herring in sour cream, shmaltz herring, *et alia*.

Only the supremely confident would dream of so outlandish a designation: not "appetizers," but "appetizing." The first time I saw the word on a delicatessen window, I stood as if struck by thunder. (One cannot, of course, be struck by thunder; how, then, explain "thunderstruck"?)

I did not see "appetizing" used as a noun in Chicago, Washington or Los Angeles. I encountered the tantalizing adjective-as-noun in New York very occasionally in the 1950s, and frequently in the 1970s. But Stuart Berg Flexner (*I Hear America Talking*, page 165) says that Russian Jews have been talking about "an appetizing store" since the 1890s. *Nu?*

△ △ △

A fancy-shmancy (*q.v.*) delicatessen in New York has this proud slogan emblazoned on its shopping bags:

THE ULTIMATE
IN
GOURMET APPETIZING

I would not call this the ultimate in gourmet English.

Ashkenazi

Ashkenazim (pl.)

> From *Ashkenaz:* Hebrew for Germany; the Biblical name of a kingdom in ancient Armenia.

> A Jew (or Jewish tradition) in or from Central and Eastern Europe; contrasted with *Sephardi* or *Sephardim* (*q.v.*)—Spanish or South European Jewry.

The name *Ashkenazim* has been applied, since the sixteenth century, to the Jews of Central and Eastern Europe—ancestors of the vast majority of Jews in the United States. (The first Jewish immigrants were Sephardim.)

The Sephardic Jews mostly came from Babylon, the Greek islands, Africa, Portugal, Spain, southern France, the Orient. The Ashkenazim moved from Rome to northern France, then to Germanic cities down the Rhine, around the eleventh century, then to Central and Eastern Europe—where they found settlements of Jews who had emigrated, long before, from Palestine and Rome.

The Ashkenazim followed the religious practices and traditions of the rabbi-scholars of Palestine; the Sephardim continued and elaborated the practices and traditions of the Jews in Babylonia and the Greek diaspora.

Ashkenazic Jews are distinguished from Sephardic Jews in their style of thought, their pronunciation of Hebrew, aspects of their liturgy, many customs, food habits, ceremonials. Yiddish is the Ashkenazic language—and universe; the vernacular of Sephardic Jews is Ladino (or Judesmo, or Dzhudesmo), a dialect of Spanish and Portuguese.

You may hear it said that the Sephardim were the aristocrats of Judaism, the deepest philosophers, the first Jewish mathematicians and astronomers, the vanguard of rationalism and enlightenment. The Sephardim were certainly more worldly than the Ashkenazim. But the Ashkenazim created a distinctive civilization—in a Yiddish literature that Sephardic Jews could not understand, about a kind of person the Sephardim had never seen, celebrating passions and visions Sephardim could scarcely comprehend. It was in the Ashkenazic world that *Yiddishkayt* (Jewishness) reached its golden age. (See SHTETL.)

Were I asked to cite the works that best portray the culture of the Ashkenazim, I would name the following: *The Brothers Ashkenazi*, by I. J. Singer, a stupendous novel, fit to rank with Dickens and Balzac (be sure to read the translation by Maurice Samuel); *Yoshe Kalb*, also by I. J. Singer; *The Dybbuk*, by S. Anski; *Three Cities*, by Sholom Asch; the matchless stories of "Mendele" (Mendele Mokher Seforim); and, of course, the rollicking tales of Sholom Aleichem. Recently discovered memoirs with memorable (if episodic) material are *The Samurai of Vishgorod* (Jewish Publication Society) and *The Journeys of David Toback* (Schocken).

For sociological-ethnological studies, I recommend *Life Is with People*, by Zborowski and Herzog; *Studies in Judaism*, by Solomon Schechter; *The Jews: Their History, Culture and Religion*, edited by Louis Finkelstein; *The Jews of Poland: A Social and Economic History*, by Bernhard D. Weinryb; *On the Edge of Destruction*, by Celia Heller; the essays in *The Golden Tradition*, edited by Lucy Dawidowicz.

Aspersion (ridicule, irony) through apparently innocent interrogation

Nothing is more characteristic of Yiddish humor (or Yinglish sarcasm) than the deployment of a simple question to:

1. Demolish whatever validity the substance of a question may have seemed to possess: "Now he wants to take a vacation?"
2. Castigate the gall of anyone who did what is questioned: "To my wife he complained about my *mother?*"

△ △ △

A variation of this ploy appears in the guise of the apparently innocent afterthought:

Mickey Yarloff's success as a life-insurance agent was the talk of all his colleagues. One day a friend asked, "Mickey, what's your secret?"

Yarloff shrugged. "Whenever a prospect can't make up his mind, I say, 'Think it over. Sleep on it. Let me know tomorrow —if you get up.' "

—atsh

Slavic suffix and emphasizer.

A suffix for a class of person who possess the attributes of an adjective or noun. The suffix endows the new word with a certain affection—*or* no uncertain scorn.

Examples:

Yingatsh: a young man *(ying)* of special and appealing youngness—*i.e.,* strength, courage, bravado; or, an uncouth fellow.

Piskatsh: a big talker, a loudmouth (*pisk*).

Smarkatsh: a brash slob, an immature punk.

See YINGATSH.

△ △ △

They sat on a bench, watching the cars go by. Then out of the blue, Kastner exclaimed, "You know something, Julius? My wife just doesn't understand me. Does yours?"

"I don't think so. I never heard her mention your name." (Julius was a *smarkatsh*.)

Automatic apposition

Note the absence of commas:

My son the doctor . . .

My son the professor . . .

My son the astronaut . . .

This construction, spoken boldly, as if "son-the-doctor" were one word, an adjectival noun, in a usage that does not require a pause (or, in writing, a comma) is perhaps the most commonly used, and surely the most often lampooned, locution of this nature in Yinglish. The particular pleasure-*cum*-pride of Jewish mothers that is represented by the Yiddish word *naches* (with a guttural *kh*) is transferred, kit and kaboodle, into English vernacular.

To be more exact, this entry transcends automatic apposition; it is presumptive compounding.

△ △ △

NACHMAN: So how's your daughter?

ABELSON: What a girl! My daughter the pianist plays all over America.

NACHMAN: And your son Al?

ABELSON: My son the attorney is too busy to take new clients.

NACHMAN: Wow! And your son Elmer?

ABELSON: Ah, Elmer, Elmer. Still sells pickles. . . . And if not for him, we'd all be starving.

△ △ △

"Did you know my son the doctor opened his new office? You positively should go get a checkup!"

"Who needs a checkup? I'm in perfect health."

"Don't be so sure. My son, I guarantee, will find *some*thing!"

ay-li-lu-lyu

Onomatopoeia. Pronounce it "I-li-lu . . ."

1. The sounds of a lullaby often sung by Jewish mothers.
2. A refrain often contained in Jewish (Yiddish/Hebrew) folk
   songs.
3. The ruminative noises old Jews hum to themselves.

△ △ △

Early one morning, Room Service in a Tel Aviv hotel answered a call.
An old man was on the line. His voice was quaky and he was humming,
"*Ay-li-lu-lyu.*"

"Room service," called the manager of the dining room.

"Room soivice?" asked the old man. "Good. *Ay-li-lu-lyu.*"

"Sir, will you please tell me what you want?"

"What I want—is breakfast. *Ay-li-lyu* . . . A glass orange juice, it
should be *bit*ter. . . . Toast, it should be burned black. . . . Coffee, it
should be cold and sour and—"

"What?" gasped the manager. "I can't fill an order like that!"

"Why not? You did yesterday. *Ai-li-lu-lyu.* . . ."

ay-yay-yay (standard)

ai-ai-ai

Rhymes with "my, my, my!" Can be accented on different levels
or attuned to different keys, depending on the emotion to be
conveyed—just as long as you do not confuse it with *oy-oy-oy*.

Ay-yay-yay is an eloquent and hardy star in the repertoire of Yiddish
vocalization. Sounds and facial expression are used to reinforce intentions; hence, the singing out of the liquefied *y* accompanied by a laugh
or a beam of bliss designates delight; sheep-eyes and low moans coun-
terpointing *ay-yay-yay* unmistakably telegraph dismay; a sneer or snicker
will emphasize the derisive *ay-yay-yay*.

I always admire the range and pitch that maestros of the *ay-yay-yay*
can bring to the utterance of the triple vowel:

1. Pleasure: "What a supper—*ay-yay-yay!*"
2. Regret: "She left her husband? Ay-yay-*yay!*"
3. Congratulations: "You were first in the whole class? *Ay-yay-
   yay!*"
4. Astonishment: "He refused the offer? Ay-*yay*-yay!"
5. Scorn: "Mrs. Kotch will choose the menu? *Ay-yay-yay!*"

6. Anguish: *"Ay-yay-yay,* such a tragedy . . ."
7. Warning: "Drive slow, be careful, don't rush . . . *ay-yay-yay.*"
8. Apprehension: "She *must* have the operation . . . *ay-yay-yay.*"
9. In reprimand: "Enough already! Don't make such an *ay-yay-yay.*"

You may wonder wherein *ay-yay-yay* differs from the ultra-Jewish *oy-oy-oy!* The zones of communicative affect are not easy to demarcate, but the following folk saying makes a shrewd beginning: "To have lots of money may not be so *ay-yay-yay,* but to have no money at all is surely *oy-oy-oy!"*

△ △ △

When her little son swallowed a fistful of aspirin tablets, Mrs. Stolper frantically telephoned her pediatrician, old Dr. Itzman. "Doctor, Doctor! My Yusseleh just swallowed half a bottle aspirin!"

"Ay-yay-yay! Is he crying?"

"No."

"Is his color funny?"

"No."

"Did he throw up?"

"No, Doctor! I'm scared *sick!* All that aspirin—shouldn't I *do* something?"

"Sure," said Dr. Itzman. "Try to give Yusseleh a headache."

△ △ △

MRS. SORKIN: Is it true you had triplets?

MRS. CASNER: Yes.

MRS. SORKIN: *Ay-yay-yay!* A miracle!

MRS. CASNER: The doctor told me it happens only once in two million times!

MRS. SORKIN: My God, Tilly! When did you have time to do the housework?

△ △ △

When Herman Balin, a *k'nyaker* who owned three haberdashery stores, returned from an American Express tour of Europe, he held forth to his friends about his experiences. "And the *climax* was—we had an audience with the Pope!"

"The Pope?!"

"Ay-yay-yay!"

"What kind of man is he?"

"In manners," said Herman, "a prince! In looks, strong but spiritual. In size, a 44 portly."

See also AHA!, FEH!, MNYEH, HOO-HA, OY, PSSSH.

B

✡ Baal Shem

> Hebrew: master of the (good) Name.

> The name given saintly men, men believed to possess mystical powers because they were chosen by God for the performance of divine intentions.

The most famous *Baal Shem* was *Baal Shem Tov* (good), the legendary Israel ben Eliezer, born in 1700, also known by the acronym "Besht." He was a visionary, a miracle worker, an apostle of religious ecstasy. He founded the Hasidic movement.

> The Besht said to the poor and the ignorant: God is in everything, including man. Every man, therefore, is good, and even a sinner can approach God with devotion. It does not matter that a simple Jew is unlearned—honest prayer is as important as erudition. . . . Man must enjoy human passions, not repress them or run from them. . . . An entire culture within the culture of the *shtetl* grew up around the liberating visions of the *Baal Shem Tov*—and ended, as movements begun by simple men often do, in a cult.
>
> —*The Joys of Yiddish*, page 24

Elie Wiesel's moving *Souls on Fire* (Random House) opens with a chapter on the Besht.

bagel

bayg'l (standard)

> Rhymes with "Nagel." From German: *Beugel:* a curved or round loaf of bread.

> A roll, hard and glazed on the outside, soft (one hopes) in the center, shaped like a life preserver.

Bagels are called "doughnuts with a college education." They were prized among poor Jews, to whom white flour was a great luxury. (See CHALLA.)

Bagels and hard-boiled eggs were the traditional offering to mourners after a funeral, in the home of the deceased. Why? Because bagels, being round, symbolized the unlimited continuation of the process of life and death. For the same reason, bagels were thought to be lucky. Do not snicker: the sophisticated Greeks thought so, too: a circle, having neither beginning nor end, was celebrated as the "perfect" form. This also accounted for the certainty that all the celestial orbits were round —a concept that stymied astronomers from Thales to Kepler.

Bagels smeared with cream cheese and laden with lox (*q.v.*) are among the triumphant inventions of the Jews.

On St. Patrick's Day some stores in New York sell green bagels. This is the best example of cultural cross-fertilization on record.

△ △ △

"He lies in the earth and bakes bagels" is a Yiddish expression that does not mean that someone lies in the earth and bakes bagels. It means "He's not doing so well."

But to say, "*May* he lie in the earth and bake bagels" indubitably means "May (I hope) he drop(s) dead!"

△ △ △

The proverbial man from Mars entered a Jewish bakery. "Hey, what are these small wheels?"

"They're not wheels," said the *balebos*. "They're bagels. Here, try one."

The Martian did. A beatific smile crossed his lips. "Wow! These would go *great* with cream cheese—and lox!"

△ △ △

On January 15, 1981, Teddy Kolleck, mayor of Jerusalem, shared the pulpit, wearing the red robe of an Episcopalian cleric, at the Cathedral of St. John the Divine in New York.

After the service, the Right Reverend James P. Morton, dean of the cathedral, invited the audience of seven hundred "to an informal reception with loaves and fishes—otherwise known as bagels and lox." (*New York Times*, January 16, 1981). America *gonef!*

balebos (m.)

baleboste (f.)

> From Hebrew *baal:* master, and *bayis:* house. Pronounced bol-e-BOSS and bol-e-BUS-ta.

1. The head of the house.
2. The owner of a store or shop.

Great prestige was accorded the Jewish immigrant who escaped working for a boss by saving enough money to become his own *balebos*.

Many Jewish women "worked in the store" (grocery, stationery, cigar, notions) alongside their husbands. In time, the women moved from the store to a flat above the store. And with greater *mazel* and success, the wives made homes in neighborhoods farther from "the store."

3. A conscientious, immaculate housewife-cook-laundress-cleaner.

The highest compliment paid a *baleboste* is "She keeps a home so absolutely clean, *you could eat off the floor!*" My mother-in-law (*aleha hasholem*) polished the brass drainpipe under her sink so often and so vigorously that a glow bounced off it to light up the kitchen.

△ △ △

A Texan oil magnate was touring Israel. Driving across a long stretch of desert, he beheld an old Jew leaning on a fence in front of a bungalow. The Texan pulled to a stop. "Hiya, neighbor."

"*Shalom.*"

"What in the world do you do, way out here in the middle of nowhere?"

"I raise chickens."

The Texan surveyed the barren environs. "How much land do you own?"

"My lot is sixty by a hundred."

"Miles?"

"Oh, no. Feet."

"Well, well." The Texan grinned. "You know what, mister? Back home, I've got me a spread where I get in my car at nine A.M. and drive and drive—and I don't even get to see the fence at the back of my property until four-thirty that afternoon!"

"My, my," sighed the *balebos*. "You know what, mister?"

"What?"

"I used to have a car like that."

△ △ △

On Houston Street, the window of Shimmel Brindel's Hardware Store contained this sign:

EVERYTING

FOR THE KITHCEN

A passer-by read the sign and promptly went in. "Where's the *balebos?*"

"You are looking at him," said Brindel.

"Listen, do you realize there are two mistakes in English spelling in your window sign?"

"I know."

"So why don't you correct it?"

"Why should I correct it?" echoed Brindel. "At least ten people a week come in to tell me about the mistakes—and at least six, once they're in, buy something."

Bar Mitzve (standard)

Bar Mitzvah

> Pronounced bar MITS-veh. Hebrew: literally, son of the commandment; more accurately, man with duties.
>
> The ceremony in which a thirteen-year-old Jewish boy reaches the status of a man, with attendant obligations and duties, *i.e.*, becomes committed to the lifelong religious and ethical obligations of an adult—and becomes countable for *minyens* as one of ten men, the quorum required for public prayer.

The ceremony is held in a synagogue or temple on the *Shabbes* closest to the lad's thirteenth birthday. The ritual was unknown until the fourteenth century, albeit ancient rabbis decreed that after his thirteenth birthday a Hebrew lad was responsible for observing all the *mitzves.* Since there are no less than 613 of these, many Jewish parents think the recording angel does not keep strict account.

Many Jews resent the ostentation of modern Bar Mitzve parties. What I find more striking is the unalloyed joy of parents and grandparents, whether poor or rich. Consider what it meant to a community of Jews, in other times and places, to add a young male to the tribe: the very existence of Jewry depended on that.

Note: Do not say "Eddie was *Bar Mitzved,*" converting *Mitzve* into a verb; Eddie *became* (Yiddish: *iz gevorn*) *Bar Mitzve,* a son of the commandment.

△ △ △

Bar Mitzves are an excellent trading mart for Jewish jokes. Here is one I recently heard amidst the festivities:

Two natives of Plitz, a small, distant planet, unknown to each other, landed in St. Louis. The first, walking through the shopping district, suddenly heard the ultra-high-frequency signal, not unlike the plucking of the shortest string on a harp, that only Plitzians make. He looked around. His radar homed in on a *landsman.* "Hey, there!" called the first Plitzian. "Been on earth long?"

"Since dawn. And you?"
"Since last night. *Crazy* place. What's your name?"
"5-J-968. What's yours?"
"I'm 73-Q-76."
"That's funny. You don't *look* Jewish."

baruch ha-Shem

barukh ha-Shem (standard)

> Hebrew. Pronounced bah-RUKH ha-shem.

> Blessed be the Name (of the Lord).

If you talk to an orthodox Jew, a pious Jew, a rabbi of whatever denomination, you will hear *Baruch ha-Shem* uttered often, just as you hear "God willing," or "If it please the Lord," from a devout Christian.

A recent telephone call with one of my panelists ran:

"Shalom."

"Shalom, Leo."

"How have you been?"

"Very well, *baruch ha-Shem.* You know my wife had an operation, but—*baruch ha-Shem*—she's fine. Then I flew to Israel, *baruch ha-Shem.* Our conference was a great success—"

"Baruch ha-Shem," said I.

"Thank you," said he.

bath

> Yinglish, as in "I have him (you) in the bath." Here "bath" does not mean a tub, or any form of ablution. Nor does "I have her in the bath" mean what you think. (See TOOK A BATH.)

> A malediction: "I have him (you, her) in the bath" (from the Yiddish *Khob'm in bod*).

This curse is less drastic than, say, "To hell with him!" and more refined than "I have him in the earth!" (*Khob'm in drerd!*)

"A bath" is symbolic, of course; it is used in expressions that dismiss someone's objections, arguments or demurrer:

> "Henry says you owe him an apology."
> *"Khob'm in bod."*

> "Bess wants to make up with you."
> "I have her in *bod."*

△ △ △

The classic use of the execration is in the following story:

"Sasha, I couldn't believe my two eyes! I walked into the bedroom and there was Fishbein—in bed with my wife!"

"Oh migod! What did you do?"

"Without a word, I turned on my heel, went into the kitchen and made myself a big glass tea!"

"B–but, what about Fishbein?"

"Khob'm in bod! Let him make his own tea."

△ △ △

Mr. Kipnis was riding home on the train from New York to Hartford. A pleasant young man sat down opposite him, and in a moment said, "Excuse me, sir. What time is it?"

Mr. Kipnis studied him. "You Jewish?"

"Yes, I am."

"Understand Yiddish?"

"Yes."

"So, *kh'hob dir in bod!"*

The young man reddened. "What a nasty thing to say! I ask a polite question—"

Kipnis raised a hand. "Don't jump to conclusions. Your question *was* polite; but if I give you a polite answer, you go on with 'Nice day' and 'What time do we arrive?' and 'Do you take this train often?' and soon it's what business I'm in and then what do *you* do, and soon I invite you to my house. And there you meet my wife and my daughter, Sylvia. A *beau*tiful girl, believe me, also very smart, a wonderful cook, a big reader—and you make a date, naturally. And you are positively sure to fall in love with her! So you come to me, popeye, saying, 'Please, Mr. Kipnis, I want your blessing. I want to marry your Sylvia!' So, young man, how can I break your heart? Could I let my Sylvia marry a young man *who don't even own a watch?!* That's why I stopped the whole business before it can even start: *'Khob dir in bod!'* "

B.C.E.

Initials for "Before the Common Era."

Hebrew scholars and historians, no less than Yiddishists, faced an uncomfortable problem in the use of B.C. and A.D. Given their beliefs about the Messiah, they could hardly accept Jesus as *Our* Lord. Maimonides said that the Messiah will restore the State of Israel, gather in the Exiles, rebuild the Temple; after that will come the Resurrection and then the Day of Judgment.

Since the Nazarene did not restore the State of Israel, gather in the Exiles or rebuild the Temple, the folk and rabbis of Palestine could not think him their Messiah. Ever since, Jewish historians were not at ease with B.C. and A.D.

Fortunately, "common" begins with the same initial as "Christian" —hence: "Before the Common Era." A.D. is rendered in Jewish encyclopedias and scholarly works as C.E.—"Common Era."

Begin already!

From Yiddish: *Fang* (or *fong*) *shoyn on* (or *oon*).

Impatient entreaty ("Will you please begin, for God's sake?").

There was nothing quite like "Begin already!" available in conversational English until the phrase, a translation from Yiddish, appeared in all its naked exasperation.

"Stop already!" is, obviously, a tocsin of desperation.

△ △ △

Mrs. Briskin, leader of the Hadassah tour of Europe, had long complained about the dilatory habits of the local guides. As her group now stood at Runnymede, Mrs. Briskin hissed to the Cook's agent, "Be*gin* already!"

"Ladies," proclaimed the guide, "on this very spot was signed the historic, the immortal Magna Carta!"

"When?" asked Mrs. Briskin.

"1215."

She glanced at her watch. "We missed it by twenty minutes!"

△ △ △

Fong oon (without the *shoyn*) is the point of departure for many a Yiddish play on words: my favorite involves a merchant on Mott Street named Fong Oon, who had a father named Oon Fong ("beginning"); and Oon Fong, an impatient Chinese, often rasped: *"Fang oon fun oonfang, Fong Oon!"*

benefit

A sponsored theater performance, in which the proceeds go for the benefit of the subsidizing organization.

The "benefit" was a play, musical comedy, concert or lecture underwritten by a Jewish fraternal society guild, *verein*, trade union, or organization composed of immigrants from the same city in the Old Country (Warsaw, Vilna, Odessa, Bialystock)—hundreds of which flourished in New York and other cities with growing Jewish populations.

The organization would put up the money for the production, paying the theater/producers in advance, then selling tickets to its membership (and, on weekends, to the public at large). The price of the tickets provided a profit to the sponsoring group.

See "SECOND AVENUE."

Better you (he, she) should . . .

From Yiddish: *Beser zolst du . . .*

The English equivalent is, of course, "It would be better if you . . ." The Yinglish formulation is crisper, but much less stylish; indeed, it offends my ear. I hope it bothers yours.

Today the phrase appears more often in novels, plays and short stories (by Jewish writers) than it does in life.

△ △ △

Old Sol Lenkowitz, on his deathbed, was dictating his last will. "To my son, Pinchas, I leave $50,000. To my darling daughter, Rosie, I leave $100,000. To my son Solomon I leave $50,000 . . ."

"Just a minute," said the lawyer. "Your whole estate comes to $4,000. How do you expect your loved ones to get $50,000, $100,000?"

"Get it?" croaked the old man. "Better they should work their heads off for it, the way I did!"

△ △ △

Milly Benjamin was plain, shy, thirty-two—and unmarried. Her parents grieved sorely over her plight.

One day, Mrs. Benjamin said, "Don't get mad, Milly—but I have a good idea. To end this sitting around, night after night, hoping maybe some nice man—from where? from the clouds? from a star?—will ask you—"

"Mama!"

"Better you should put an ad in *The New York Times.*"

"Mama!" gasped Milly. "You have to be joking!"

"I'm not joking."

"But the *shame*—"

"What shame? You don't give your *name*. Like this." She handed her daughter a paper, on which she had printed:

JEWISH GIRL FROM FINE FAMILY, EDUCATED, GOOD COOK,
BIG READER, AGE 28, WOULD LIKE TO MEET
INTELLIGENT, REFINED JEWISH GENTLEMAN.
OBJECT: MATRIMONY. BOX 703.

Milly stammered and gulped protestations, but her mother insisted. "What's to *lose*, Milly? And just think of what could happen!"

The advertisement appeared. And each morning the girl known as "Box 703" hastened down three flights of stairs to meet the postman. On the fifth day, she came running up and burst into the apartment: "Mama! An answer! Forwarded from the paper!" With flushed cheeks, Milly ripped open the envelope, devoured the contents—and burst into tears.

"Milly!" cried Mrs. Benjamin. "What's wrong?"

In a strangling voice, Milly gasped, "It's from Papa."

Be well

Stay well

> From Yiddish: *Zay gezunt.*

"Be well" and "Stay well" seem to be perfectly proper English—but the usual English salutation of farewell is "Take care of yourself," or, in England, "Mind your health."

Was it the energetic use of "Be well" and "Stay well" by Jewish speakers and writers that fortified the beachhead of those phrases on the shores of English usage?

△ △ △

Mr. Opshutz approached a young man on Collins Avenue. "Excuse me, my boy. Are you Jewish?"

"No, I'm not."

"Are you sure?"

"Of course I'm sure!"

"You're not just teasing me?"

"No. Why should I tease you?"

Mr. Opshutz sighed. "I don't know. Stay well . . ."

"Wait." The young man glanced around and, lowering his voice, said, "I'll tell you the truth. Not a soul in Miami knows it. I am a Jew."

"That's funny," clucked Mr. Opshutz. "You don't *look* Jewish."

bialy

b'yali (standard)

> A slightly underbaked roll shaped like a rubber wading pool, with baked onion sprinkled in the declivity.

The name *bialy* is the affectionate diminutive for Bialystok, the city in Poland where Jewish bakers perfected this extraordinary confection. If you ask me, the bakers made Bialystok immortal.

△ △ △

The Rudolf Ohrensteins bought a large home in Oyster Bay, staffed it with four English servants, and invited three couples out for their first Sunday brunch of the season: the Steins, the Frolichs and the Pysers.

On Sunday morning, Mrs. Ohrenstein noticed that the table was set for twelve. "Henshaw!" she called.

"Yes, madam," said the butler.

"You have set the table for twelve."

"Yes, madam."

"But I told you *three* couples were coming. Plus me and my husband, that makes eight."

"Yes, madam."

"Then *why* did you set plates for twelve?"

"Well, madam, Mrs. Pyser phoned just an hour ago. She is bringing the Bagels and the Bialys."

Big deal!

> This withering dismissal comes right from Yiddish: *A groyser kunst!* ("Some big art!") or the sarcastic *Khokhma!* with the accent on the *ma* ("Stroke of genius!").

I can hear the auditorium ring with objections: " 'Big deal' is English!" and "What is Jewish about 'Big deal'?" So I'll tell you what's Jewish about "Big deal." The phrase is sarcastic. The mood is derisive. The phrase is not descriptive, but deflative. It is uttered with emphasis on the "big," in a dry, disenchanted tone. In such usage (as against, say, "He signed a big deal today"), the exclamation was launched in the 1940s (see Wentworth and Flexner, *The Dictionary of American Slang*). It swiftly gained popularity as a blasé retort among the young, especially on our high school and college campuses:

"He made the Ping-Pong team!"

"Big deal."

△ △ △

Query: Who slipped the phrase into English, and for English-speaking audiences? Three Jews. The comedian Arnold Stang, who played Sad Sacks and *shlemazls*, used "Big deal!" as his distinctive put-down. The Henry Morgan show, on a radio network, regularly featured Stang. It was the enormously influential Milton Berle television show on which Stang often appeared. And "Big deal!" enlivened the Jack Benny program. In due course, "Big deal!" became a familiar—indeed, a commonplace—wisecrack in television talk shows, comedy skits and movies.

△ △ △

Huffing and puffing, a Jew frantically runs to catch a train. A second before he gets there, the train zooms away. The Jew stops, mops his brow, and shouts after the train, "Big deal!"

Same situation, different ending:

Albert Nussman, passing by, asks, "Mister, why are you so angry?"

"I," puffed the Jew, "missed that train by two *seconds!*"

"Hm. The way you're carrying on, I thought you missed it by two hours!"

bim-bom

bim-bum

A charming, meaningless hum (in song, tale or monologue).

Old folk songs use *bim-bom* for euphony or meter. Some used nothing but the repeated sound.

Hasidim use *bim-bom* a good deal—but so did my father, and he was no Hasid.

Bim-bom appears to great effect in the conversations created by Sholom Aleichem.

The English equivalents of *bim-bom* are many: "hey-nonny-non," "ta-ra-ra," "tra-la-la," etc. Many of these recur in Shakespeare's songs.

△ △ △

Mr. Alkin went to see a famous *tsadik*, a man known far and wide as a seer who, it was said, communed with angels and could actually see into the future. "O dear *Tsadik*," sighed Alkin, "if only I knew what awaits me after death! I have been a good man, a pious Jew in every way—"

"What is it you want to know?"

"I want to know if, after I die, I will go to heaven and remain forever among the angels—and bask in the Divine Presence for all eternity."

The *tsadik* sighed, nodded, closed his eyes and began to hum, *"Bim-bom, ta-ra-ra-re-rom, bim-bim-bom . . ."* and slipped into a trance.

Alkin held his breath and waited.

Finally the old man's eyelids fluttered and opened. "So, I spoke to a fine angel, and I have the answer for you."

"Really? Wonderful. Tell me—"

"It's in two parts, good news and—eh—bad news. First, the good news. Yes—count on it! When you have left this world of travail, because you have been such a good man, a kind man, a pious Jew, the angels will waft you to heaven—where you will forever remain, near the Golden Throne, blessed by the divine *Shekhine* (radiance). . . ."

"Oh, *Tsadik!*" cried Mr. Alkin. "How glorious! How wonderful! After that, how can any news be *bad?*"

"Tonight," sighed the *tsadik.*

Bite your tongue!

> From Yiddish: *Bays di tsung* or *Bays dir di tsung.*
>
> Stop talking! Say no more! Be quiet!

Why is this Yinglish? Because in English one says "Hold your tongue!" or "Bite your lip!"

The imperative is particularly pictorial: Biting your tongue is an absolutely foolproof way to stop acting the fool, by imprisoning or paralyzing your chief vocal messenger.

△ △ △

SCENE: *Bench on New Jersey boardwalk*

MRS. RABIN: O–o–y.

MRS. LUTSKI: Oy–oy.

MRS. BICKEL: Oy–oy–oy.

MRS. FARBER: Bite your tongues! Didn't we agree not to discuss our children?!

blintz (sing.)

blints (standard)

blintzes (pl.)

> From Ukraïnian: pancake.
>
> A pancake folded around cottage cheese (or strawberries, cherries, blackberries, potatoes, apples, peaches) and fried to a crisp golden brown.

Usually, *blintzes* are covered with cold sour cream. But latter-day converts to this confection have taken to capping *blintzes* with brown sugar, honey or jam. (The only justification I can see for not using sour cream is that you don't have any.)

△ △ △

The astonishing and historic victory of Israel in the Six Day War was hailed by the wits in Tel Aviv as a *Blintzkrieg.*

There is no shortage of wits in Tel Aviv. When I was there, I sometimes felt I was caught behind the lines in a *Vitskrieg.*

△ △ △

WAITER: Try the *blintzes*. The best in years!
DINER: No, thanks. I'll wait for some fresh.

bluffer

blofer (standard)

> Yinglish extension of the English: bluff.
>
> 1. A pretender, boaster, hot-air artist.
> 2. A cheat, faker, crook. ("He bluffed me out of ten dollars.")

This use of *bluff* or *bluffer* is not like the English words, which describe a strategy or strategist in, say, the game of poker.

A female practitioner of deception is, of course, a *blufferkeh*.

△ △ △

The most effective salesgirl I ever heard of was the one who sold perfumes and confided to female customers, "Don't use this brand if you're bluffing!"

bobkes

> Show-business cant. Rhyme with "took this" or "tuck this." From Russian: beans, and Yiddish: goat droppings.
>
> 1. Something so small or cheap that it is outrageously disproportionate to expectations—or fair value.
> 2. An absurd idea.
> 3. An insulting sum, price or proposition.

Bobkes may mean beans, but Jews use it for a more emotional expression: scorn. (They use *beblach* for beans.) *Bobkes* comes from the Yiddish for goat dung, and is the overheated expletive that transcends "Nuts!" "Baloney!" or "Peanuts!" Thus, numbered as above:

> 1. "I worked five weeks on that sketch, and what did they offer? *Bobkes!*"
> 2. "What do I think of their suggestion? *Bobkes!*"
> 3. "Fifty dollars to fix the faucet? You must think I don't know *blintzes* from *bobkes!*"

As was said by a writer who shall remain unnamed: ". . . those who yell '*Bobkes!*' understand the place of pride in the protocol of humiliation. . . . Only the proud cry '*Bobkes!*' "

△ △ △

I have heard *Bobkes!* howled in the old Lindy's on Broadway and in the new Polo Lounge in Beverly Hills. In fact, I heard it so often that I began to forgo the expletive, sneering *Shmontses! Shmontses!* (*q.v.*) owes nothing to vegetables and gains admirable evocativeness from the wedding of the insidious sibilant *sh* to the seductive nasal *m*, climaxed by that earthy phoneme of disgust, the post-dental fricative *ts*.*

△ △ △

Bernie Brendel was a door-to-door salesman with an astonishing sales record.

One day his friend, George Umglick, sighed, "Bernie, I can't tell you how much I envy you. We both go out for a day's work, and I come back with *bobkes*. I can't even get inside a house. But you come back with twenty–thirty good sales. How do you do it?"

"It's simple, George. Every time a housewife answers the bell, I say, 'Lady, what *I* just saw in your neighbor's house!' They let me in."

bonditt

Pronounced in Yinglish as bon-DIT.

1. Bandit (literally).
2. A likable rascal.
3. A clever, mischievous person.
4. A son-of-a-gun.

This loan-word takes on an entirely fresh bouquet as Yinglish, where it is deployed with a smile or a chuckle of affection: "That son of mine, what a *bonditt!*" My parents called Charlie Chaplin or Douglas Fairbanks "some *bonditt!*" Today Burt Reynolds plays the role perfectly.

I was astonished to learn that Jews used *bonditt* in Eastern Europe long before they ever saw a movie or heard a syllable of English. The appellation was popular in Italy (Italian, *bandito*) and in other European countries to characterize a clever romantic hero: Robin Hood or D'Artagnan.

△ △ △

The waiter brought the Today's Special fish to a customer, who stared at it, then leaned over and began to whisper, then placed his ear close to the plate.

"Mister!" cried the startled waiter. "What are you doing?"

"I'm talking."

---

* If you pine for a translation of the jargon of the new linguistics, try to find it in *A Dictionary of Linguistics*, by Mario Pei and Frank Gaynor (Littlefield, Adams) or, even less illuminating, the formidable *Dictionary of Language and Linguistics*, by R. R. K. Hartmann and F. C. Stork (Applied Science Publishers, London).

"Talking to a *fish??*"

"Certainly. I happen to know nine fish languages: Carp, Salmon, Pike—"

"But what did you *tell* the fish?" asked the goggle-eyed waiter.

Sighed the *bonditt,* "I asked him where he was from. He answered, 'From Peconic Bay.' So I asked, 'How are things in Peconic Bay?' And he answered. 'How should I know? It's *years* since I was there.' "

△ △ △

A *bonditt* said to his wife: "The new doctor in the neighborhood charges twenty-five dollars for the first visit—but only ten dollars after that. Well, I'm going to outsmart him. I'll go in and say, 'Hi, Doc, here I am again!' "

Off he went to the doctor.

When he returned, his wife asked, "So what happened?"

"I said 'Hi, Doc, here I am again!' So he examined me and said, 'Continue the treatment I recommended before.' "

(The doctor was a bigger *bonditt!*)

boo-boo

> Yinglish origin, now accepted English slang. Possibly from *bulba:* potato. (See BULBENIK.)

> 1. A verbal mistake; a *faux pas.*
> 2. An embarrassing error.
> 3. A blunder.
> 4. (Originally) Accidental loss of bowel contents by a baby or child.

This euphemism rocketed to public attention around 1949–1950 as a trademark of the comedian Jerry Lewis in night-club and television skits with his then-partner, Dean Martin.

Boo-boo began as a parent's/nurse's code word (like B.M.) for a child's "accident," in diapers or panties. It was, because expressive and amusing, inevitably taken up by children.

Boo-boo became popular among radio and television performers for it was a funny-sounding, indispensable label for any *faux pas:*

"In front of the whole class? What a *boo-boo!*"

"If I don't get to a men's room fast, will I make a *boo-boo!*"

Among Gentiles in the Bronx and other boroughs, the tympanic *boom-boom* served as the genteelism for "bowel movement." The character Edith, in television's *All in the Family,* missed no chance to greet her grandson's full diaper with a blinding smile and congratulations to the *boom-boom*er.

△ △ △

Jesse Jurow, Hollywood producer, met a fetching, if dim-witted, chorus girl in New York, married her, brought her back to Bel Air, and invited his friends to meet her at dinner in his palatial home.

"Jesse," sighed the new bride, "I hafta tell you, I'm nervous. Writers, directors, highbrows—what can I *talk* to them about?"

"Darling, there's not a thing to worry about. They'll talk your ears off! All you have to do is smile and nod and say 'How interesting!' They'll adore you."

Jesse was right. The new Mrs. Jurow charmed one and all, listening, wide-eyed, smiling. Only after the dessert did she make a *boo-boo*. Jesse stood up at the table, saying to the guests, "Shall we have coffee in the library?" and his doll trilled, "Honey, I don't think it's open this late at night."

✡ borsht (standard)

> Beet soup.

On restaurant menus, *borsht* or *borscht* is sometimes spelled *bortsch* or even (what looks like a misprint) *borshch,* which I encountered in a Russian café.

However it's spelled, plop sour cream onto the surface.

boychik

boychikel (diminutive)

boytshik (standard)

> Rhymes with "coy tick."

> 1. Little boy.
> 2. Affectionate/admiring term for a male.
> 3. Scalawag.
> 4. A shrewd corner-cutter.

This neologism, which tacks the Slavic *-chik* particle onto the otherwise neutral *boy,* is deployed with various shades of meaning:

> *Proudly:* You know my brother? Some *boychik!*
> *Fondly:* Take my word, *boychik;* she's not your type.
> *Ironically:* Pushing seventy, he's chasing after girls. Some *boychik!*

In warning: When you deal with that *boychik*, leave your wallet at
home.

Boychikel diminutizes the diminutive for enhanced fondness—or sar-
casm:
"Listen, *boychikel*, I can give you lessons in brains."
"You know, you're not a *boychikel* anymore, Moe. Go slow."

△ △ △

Freud's favorite story, the one he used to crown his analysis of the
manipulation of reason in Jewish jokes, concerns the two traveling sales-
men, competitors, who meet in a railway station. They exchange *Sholem
Aleichem*'s, then eye each other.
"So—eh—where are you going?"
"I'm going—to Pinsk."
"Pinsk? Mmh . . . Listen, *boychik:* when you tell me you're going to
Pinsk, you expect me to figure you're going to Minsk. But I happen to
know you *are* going to Pinsk—so why are you lying?"

△ △ △

"And another thing, Harry. The reason you are not popular is that you
are such a smarty pants—always know the answer, always ready with
criticism. *Boychik*, you are just too pretentious!"
"Pre*ten*tious?" echoed Harry. *"Moi?"*

bread

From Yiddish: *broyt.*

(In slang, jive, rock-and-roll cant and drug culture)
1. Money.
2. The wherewithal.

Yiddish makes widespread use of *broyt* as a substitute for "money": *a
shver shtickl broyt* ("a hard little piece of bread"); *"Er hargert zikh zu makhen
a shtickl broyt"* ("He kills himself to earn a piece of bread"). Jazz musicians, of whom many were Jewish, began to use "bread" to mean money
or a living.
I distinguish the slang and Yinglish use of "bread" from the
straightforward English, as in Conan Doyle, say: A blackmailer tells
Sherlock Holmes, "Here's how I make my humble bread."

bris

brith

Bris is Yiddish; *brit* or *brith* is Hebrew. (There was no *th* ending in Hebrew until Gentile scholars of the Bible introduced it several hundred years ago.) Hebrew: *Brith Milah:* covenant.

The ceremony attending circumcision.

The *bris* occurs on the eighth day of a boy's life. Genesis 17:10 tells us that the Lord decreed: "This is my covenant . . . every man child among you shall be circumcised." (Abraham, a great and *very* brave man, circumcised himself.) *

Many were the punishments Jews suffered down the ages for circumcising their boys: Hadrian forbade the rite (which in part led to Bar Kochba's rebellion); Antiochus Epiphanes, a friend of Caligula (but not quite as crazy), instituted the death penalty for circumcision; a monarch of the Visigoths named Sisebut, about whom I know no more than his startling name, demanded that Jews replace circumcision with baptism. None of these mighty monarchs could force the Jews to stop their fulfillment of what they considered God's commandment.

Not all Jews: those who longed to "pass," notably the Hellenized Hebrews, were driven to undergo an operation which removed the visible evidence of circumcision. Outraged rabbis responded by decreeing that the penal glans be laid bare by pushing back the little boy's skin before the solemn slitting.**

When the medical and hygienic value of circumcision became known (a fact denied by many modern pediatricians), hordes of non-Jews had their baby boys circumcised; it is no longer possible to tell Jews from *goyim* in the showers of gymnasia. (My research in this area has not been systematic.)

△ △ △

Mr. Morgenstern appraised the swaddled baby: "Krevetz, you have a *beau*tiful boy!"

Frowned Mr. Krevetz, "First, it's not a boy, it's a girl. Second, let go of my finger."

---

* The Jews did not invent circumcision. The custom is described by Herodotus. Phoenicians, Syrians, and Ethiopians performed the cutting of the foreskin. Among Muslims circumcision (called "purification") is mandatory, pun or no pun. Eskimos and American Indian tribes practice circumcision. In some cultures, women refuse sexual union with an uncircumcised *bravo.* Circumcision rites have been noted by anthropologists in Africa, Indonesia, Australia. (The rites are usually held at puberty and *en masse.*)

** For a fascinating survey of Greek influences upon the Jews, both before and after the conventional "beginning" of the Diaspora (70 C.E.), see Victor Tcherikover's erudite *Hellenistic Civilization and the Jews* (Atheneum).

bubbe

bobe (standard)

bube (standard)

> From Slavic: *baba:* grandmother; midwife. (There is a Hebrew *buba*, but it means "little doll" and is not the Yiddish word for grandmother.) *Baba* is grandmother in Japanese, too—but do not jump to conclusions.

> Grandmother.

△ △ △

I pass on to you a piece of pointed doggerel:

> A pharmacist named Abe Leisen,
> So loved his *bubbe* from Meissen,
>   That to honor her name
>   And propel her to fame,
> He invented the drug Bubbemycin.

I hope this will replace the overlong, overworked "Chicken soup is Jewish penicillin."

△ △ △

Arlene Balaban brought several classmates home for the weekend. With considerable intensity they discussed Darwin and the revisionists' criticism of the theory of evolution.

Arlene's *bubbe* said, "Heredity . . . environment . . . Young girls, just ready to start life—already you worry about such things?"

"It's a complicated subject, Gramma."

"Complicated-shmomplicated. In my time, we knew the answer. If the baby looks like his father, that's heredity. If he looks like a neighbor, that's environment."

△ △ △

"*Bubbe*, thank you so much for your present!"

"I'm glad you liked."

"What bride wouldn't, Gramma? A whole sewing basket, with thimble, scissors, . . . but *Bubbe*, where are the instructions?"

△ △ △

Jerry wanted to give his eighty-two-year-old *bubbe* a birthday present. And when he heard about a pet shop that had a mynah bird who talked Yiddish, Jerry hurried over. It was true: Herman's Pet Shop had a mynah bird that talked excellent Yiddish. "Why not?" shrugged the bird in Yiddish. "My father was Jewish, my mother was Jewish. I went to a *heder*."

Herman wanted $300 for the mynah bird. "Think of the hours and hours your old lonely *bubbe* will spend talking to this pet, unburdening herself of sorrows, recalling old times—"

"I'll take it!" cried Jerry. "Deliver it tomorrow, her birthday. To Mrs. Abe Silberberg, 275 West 108th Street."

The next afternoon Jerry called his grandmother. "Happy birthday. And you should have a hundred more!"

"*Alevay* I should have *one* more," sighed Grandma.

"*Bubbe!* Did you get my present?"

"Certainly I got your present."

"And how did you like it?"

"De-*li*-cious!" cried *Bubbe*.

P.S. I always thought this an unimprovable joke. Then I heard this topper:

The grandson sputtered, "D–delicious? *Bubbe*, that bird—spoke—Yiddish!"

Bubbe chuckled. "You're such a joker."

"I'm not joking, *Bubbe!* That bird spoke perfect Yiddish!"

"Don't be silly! If he could talk, why didn't he *say* something?"

bubbe-mayse

bobe-mayse

baba-myseh

> Pronounce it BUB-eh MY-seh or BAW-beh MY-seh.

1. (Literally) Grandma's story.
2. An absurd account or explanation.
3. An old wives' tale.

This compound noun is used with zest to pulverize an account, excuse or explanation:

"Imagine that man trying to get away with such a *bubbe-mayse*."

It is interesting to examine the origin of *bubbe-mayse*. Historian-linguists trace it to the Italian *Story of Bovo* (or *Buovo*), a romantic tale of the fifteenth century chronicling the adventures of a hero yclept Bovo. The fantastic adventure became immensely popular among Jewish women after a leading Jewish scholar and poet, Elijah Bochur, adapted it into Yiddish. The story has been published in over a hundred editions. One can learn the history of Yiddish by noting the succession of changes in these editions.

△ △ △

"Well, my boy," beamed Mr. Lowber to his twelve-year-old, "what did you study in your Bible class today?"

"We learned how the Pharaohs chased the Hebrews to the Red Sea, and our people were goners, so the Lord tossed an A-bomb. And that parted the waters so the Jews—"

"Wait a *minute!*" cried Mr. Lowber. "Rabbi Garfein told you that?"

"Naw, Pop. But if I told you the *bubbe-mayse* he tried to put over on us you wouldn't believe it either."

bubeleh

babele (Galician/Slovakian Yiddish)

bubee (Yinglish, diminutive, affectionate)

> Be sure to pronounce the *u* as in "put," not as in "but."

1. The affectionate form of *bubbe, baba, bobe, bawbe*.
2. Little grandma.
3. Grandchild.
4. Term of endearment used between a husband and wife, parent and child, relatives, friends.
5. Synonym for "dear," "darling," "honey."
6. A delicious, fluffy pancake; a Passover treat.

In theatrical circles, where hugs and kisses and terms of endearment luxuriate in all seasons, *bubeleh* and *bubee* (pronounced to rhyme with "goody") have become familiar Yinglish words:

"Well, *bubee,* long time no see!"

"*Bubeleh,* where have you *been?*"

"*Bubeleh,* couldn't you tell me, your own husband, about it?"

Do not quail before the many-splendored uses of this neologism, which conveys the no doubt shmaltzy love Jews bear their grandmothers. (It is no greater than the mooning, moist miasma in which Italians swathe *their* grandmothers.)

When a Jewish mother or father addresses the *baba* in the cradle as *bubeleh,* it is not only an expression of love; it carries the hope that the child will one day be a parent (and grandparent), too, and will address *its* offspring the same way.

Hollywood and television talk shows have become veritable hothouses of *bubeleh.* Even the Waspiest of actors and the blackest of singers cleave the air with threnodies of Yinglished affection. I suspect that natives of Alabama, Utah and even Fresno think the glamorous folk are calling each other "little boobs."

△ △ △

The classic (to me, immortal) story about *bubeleh* concerns the proud mother who was sending her six-year-old boy off to school for the very first time. "So, *bubeleh*, you'll get off the school bus carefully and hang up your clothes on a hook, don't throw them on the floor. And to the teacher you'll always say 'Yes, ma'am' or 'No, ma'am.' And you'll be a good boy and do everything she says. And when it's time to come home, I know you'll button up good, *bubeleh*, so you won't catch cold . . ." (on and on).

When the lad returned that day, his mother smothered him with kisses. "You liked school, *bubeleh*? You learned something?"

"Yep," said the lad. "I learned that my name is Nathan."

△ △ △

"*Bubeleh*, it's good to see how clean your face is. But how did you get your hands so dirty?"

"Washing my face," said *Bubeleh*.

bulbanik

Rhymes with "pull a trick." Polish: *bulba:* potato.
Yiddish slang used by actors/connoisseurs of the theater.

1. A stammerer; one who "talks as if there's a potato in the mouth."
2. Anyone prone to committing outlandish malapropisms.

I recommend this gorgeous word to all who love effervescent nomenclature. My first encounter with this theatrical term came at the old, never-to-be-forgotten Café Royale, the Sardi's of Second Avenue. You will find my adventure embalmed in *The 3:10 to Anywhere*, my memoirs about travel.

The reason for "hot potato" is that poor Jews were often so hungry that they would not wait for a potato (a treat) to cool before jamming it into their mouths.

bummer (m.)

bummerkeh (f.)

Yinglish, derived from English, not Yiddish.

1. Bum; a low-life.
2. A promiscuous man or woman.
3. One of shady reputation.

4. An unhappy or unsuccessful deal.
5. (Drugs) A bad trip.

This neologism offers a pungent example of the capacity of Yinglish to embellish and embroider an ordinary English word. We saw the same linguistic process of adaptation in *bluffer*.

△ △ △

"Hello, Sid Klopstein?"

"Speaking."

"This is Julie Metzner. Listen, can you join our poker game Thursday night?"

"I'll look at my calendar, Julie. . . . No, I can't. Moishe Belinski is playing at Carnegie Hall."

"So how's about Tuesday?"

"Hold on. . . . Nope. Belinski is playing at Town Hall."

"What about a week from today?"

"Uh—no. Belinski's at Lincoln Center."

"Migod, Sid, you are a real fan of Moishe Belinski!"

"I never laid eyes on him."

"B–but—"

"Whenever Belinski gives a recital, I visit Sonya."

"Who's Sonya?"

"His wife."

(Mr. Klopstein was a *bummer;* and in my opinion there is little reason to doubt that Mrs. Belinski was a *bummerkeh.*)

by (for "at")

Yinglish, regrettably.

In Yiddish one says "She's by Nelly" more often than "She's at Nelly's (house)." I see no reason for using such diction in English. The phrase was a favorite of immigrant Jews.

△ △ △

SCENE: *Hurvitz's Restaurant*

"Hello, friend!" Mr. Blumberg sang out.

"I don't think I know you," said the stranger.

"We both ate here last night!"

"So?"

"I wouldn't of recognized you—except for the umbrella by your side."

"Ha!" snorted the stranger. "Last night I wasn't carrying this umbrella."

"I know," said Blumberg. "I was."

by me (you, him, her, them) for "to me (you, him, her, them)"

From Yiddish: *bei mir.*

1. To me.
2. With me.
3. In my opinion.
4. In my (our) house.
5. In my (our) circle.

I must record my disapproval of this phrase. I must also confess that when deliberately used for purposes of deflation ("By him, he's a master of English!") it is deadly.

The use of "by" for "with" (or "in my opinion") probably began through casual slang linkage with "okay" ("That's okay by me," or "You can't prove it by me"). The substitute won great popularity in literary and theatrical circles through a story told about Samson Raphaelson, playwright and screenwriter:

Having struck it rich early in his career, Mr. Raphaelson bought a yacht. Dressed in blazer, white flannels and cruising cap, he proudly came to his mother. "Look, Mama!" He pointed to the braided "Captain" above his visor. "How do you like your son the Captain?"

Mrs. Raphaelson surveyed her son's splendor, read the gold braiding and replied, "Sammy, by me you're a captain. By you you're a captain. But tell me, by a *captain* are you a captain?"

Mr. Raphaelson assured me that this anecdote, too good to be true, is.

Some years ago, a song called *"Bei mir bist du schön (sheyn)"* ("To me you are so beautiful") soared into popularity. And soon wits from Boston Common to Muir Woods were mocking staid English with startling improvisations:

By me, you're practically a genius.
By her, I'm a snake in the glass.
By us, it's open house every Sunday after five.

△ △ △

CUSTOMER: How much do you charge to press a suit?
TAILOR: Three dollars.
CUSTOMER: Three dollars?! Why in Miami I can get a suit pressed for a dollar and a half!
TAILOR: Okay by me. But how much is the plane?

C

canary

A Bronx version of the Yiddish/Hebrew incantation against the evil eye: *kayn ayn hore,* or—as gasped, flung or spit—*kineahora.*

1. From the hocus-pocus phrase (above) used in the hope of warding off an evil eye.
2. A hex one can receive—or bestow.

"Canary" was used by Bronx and Lower East Side children of Jewish immigrants in various ways, from the placating to the admonishing to the threatening. Thus: "Don't gimme a canary!" ("Don't lay the evil eye on me!"), or "I'll give her a canary!" ("I'll put such a curse on her she won't be able to avoid the evil eye!"), or "Did I get a canary!" ("Did he jinx me good!").

None of these was uttered in an aviary.

△ △ △

Mrs. Balin sent her ten-year-old son Marvin to the store for bread, eggs and three pounds of grapes. After he returned, Mrs. Balin phoned the grocer. "Listen, Mr. Ponish, I just weighed your grapes. There are only two pounds four ounces. Your scales are a disgrace!"

"*My* scales?" cried Mr. Ponish. "Don't give me a canary! And don't weigh the grapes, lady; weigh the boy."

Castle Garden

Pronounced by Jewish immigrants "Kessel Goddin."

The port of entry in New York City for millions of immigrants.

"Castle Garden" was often used as a synonym for Ellis Island, but there was a difference.

Castle Garden was a huge music-hall/cabaret on a little island just off the tip of the Battery in Manhattan (the water has long since been filled in), made famous by such performers as Lola Montez and Jenny Lind, "The Swedish Nightingale." Castle Garden was converted to an immigration port of entry by the State of New York around 1855. Thousands of newcomers poured into the island each week. The processing was beset by dreadful "cattle car" congestion, sanitary nightmares; corruption, bribery and blackmail were visited upon bewildered aliens who could not speak a word of English.

> These immigrants packed their few household belongings, pots and pans, samovar, pillows, and bedding, much of which would be lost or pilfered on the way, and forsook their native towns and villages to embark on the greatest journey of their lives. They parted with loved ones, seemingly forever, and made their way by foot, coach, and train to the bewildering port cities of Western Europe. At a cost of thirty-four dollars . . . crammed into steerage for as long as three weeks, Jewish immigrants were confined to herring, black bread, and tea by their loyalty to dietary laws. It was "a kind of hell that cleanses a man of his sins before coming to Columbus' land," insisted a popular immigrant guidebook that attempted to minimize the torments of the ocean voyage. Whatever the spiritually therapeutic values of that epic crossing, few immigrants would ever forget its terrors.*

In 1892 the huge tide of immigration and the abominable conditions led the Federal Government to take over, and Ellis Island, in the bay, superseded Castle Garden.

Among some Jews, the "Golden Portal" became known as *Trer'n Indz'l,* "Isle of Tears." I give you one harrowing incident from Stanley Feldstein's book.

> Among the last to pass through the gates are a Russian Jew and his son. "Why did you come?" the inspector asks abruptly. "We had to" is the reply. "Are you willing to be separated; your father to go back and you to remain here?" The two look at each other with no visible emotion, for the question came too suddenly. Then . . . something in the background of their feelings moves, and the father, used to self-denial through[out] his life, says quietly, without pathos and yet tragically, *"Of course."* After casting his eyes to the floor, ashamed to look his father in the face, the son repeats, "Of course." Thus the healthy youngster is permitted to enter America, and the physically depleted father is detained, "for this was their judgment day."

Some 3,000 immigrants (of all nationalities) committed suicide there after they were denied admission to the United States—because they

---

* Moses Rischin, *The Promised Land: 1870–1914* (Corinth Books). Also see Oscar Handlin's *The Uprooted* (Atlantic Monthly Press) and Stanley Feldstein's *The Land That I Show You* (Doubleday).

had an eye disease, a limp, tuberculosis, an infection, seemed "subnormal," had inadequate "papers."

About 16,000,000 immigrants passed through Ellis Island: the ancestors of some 100,000,000 living Americans (!) came through the fabled Great Hall. The voluminous "Reports of the U.S. Immigration Commission" (Government Printing Office) form an extraordinary chunk of Americana.

△ △ △

Mr. Orlitsky glowed with pride, although shaking with apprehension, as he stood before Judge Cranborn to become a citizen, back in 1919.

"How many states are there in the Union?" asked Judge Cranborn.

"Forty-eight!"

"Good. And into how many branches is our Government divided?"

"President, Judges and—Congress."

"Fine. Now, Mr. Orlitsky, will you solemnly swear to support the Constitution?"

A moan escaped Orlitsky. "I would like to, believe me, Judge. But I have a wife and four children in Romania."

C.E.

Initials for "Common Era."

Jewish encyclopedias and reference works usually avoid A.D. and B.C. 1492 C.E. is when Columbus discovered America, for which Jews have been grateful ever after.

Columbus, by the way, took several Jews along on his historic voyages—as interpreters. He assumed that any Indians or Orientals he would encounter would probably be primitive, and would therefore speak God's language: Hebrew.

See COLUMBUS' MEDINA.

Chaim Yankel

Hayim Yank'l (standard)

> *Please* don't rhyme *Chaim* with "fame." Rhyme it with "Priam." The *Ch* needs to be *yecched* as if you have a fishbone stuck in the roof of your mouth. Pronounced KHA-yim YON-k'l.

> 1. The generic name for a *shlemiel, shnook,* Sad Sack or poor Joe.

Yankel, alone, is:

2. A condescending way of addressing someone ("Listen, Yankel: put up or shut up!").

3. The equivalent of "Mac" ("Hey, Yankel, watch where you're going!").

Chaim is a common Jewish name for a male: in Hebrew the word means "life." During an illness, parents would call a boy *Chaim* even if his name was Zachariah—because *Chaim* was thought to put a magical whammy on death. How? By confusing the *Molech ha-Moves* (Angel of Death), who sought his victims by name—and would never dream that the lad in bed, whom everyone loudly addressed as *Chaim*, was, in truth, Zachariah Ginsberg.

△ △ △

Jake Chadish, a *Chaim Yankel*, came into the office of his boss.

"Mr. Brankoff," quavered Chadish, "can I maybe take tomorrow off?"

"What's tomorrow, a national holiday?"

"No, no, Mr. Brankoff. It's—for me and my wife—our golden anniversary!"

"Your golden anni— Listen, Chadish, am I going to have to put up with this nonsense every fifty years?"

△ △ △

Feinstock and Sholmeier could bear the Nazi regime no longer. They decided to assassinate Adolf Hitler. They bought rifles with precision sights and concealed themselves inside a building Hitler was scheduled to ride past.

They waited, hour after hour.

Finally Sholmeier whispered, "I hope nothing's happened to him!"

chairlady

Yinglish, 100 percent pure.

A female presiding officer.

The women in my mother's circle were pioneer feminists. None was more ardent, articulate and confident than my mother.

In our living room, meetings of "the ladies" were often held in answer to her summons: to form a committee to send clothes to Poland; to raise funds for free milk for schoolchildren; to petition the city to offer certain courses in night schools. It was in our living room that I first heard the clarion "Mrs. Chairlady!"

Now this was a linguistic invention of some consequence. These feminists rejected "Mrs. Chairman" out of hand; they gave short shrift to the oxymoron "Madam Chairman"; easily, effortlessly, they said, "Chairlady."

Were they not wiser than those who promulgated the grotesque appellation "Chairperson"? It is not enough to defend the word by saying that it removes gender from the title. Many of us would like to know the sex of the presiding officer. Female cops are called policewomen without damage to civil liberties.

Mr. Hyman Kaplan once argued, "If the feminine of 'host' is 'hostess,' why shouldn't the feminine of 'ghost' be 'ghostess'?" I am on Mr. Kaplan's side.

△ △ △

After a candidate for mayor finished a long, boring speech, the chairlady stepped to the lectern. "Are there any questions?"

"Yes!" A dowager in the second row stood up. "Who else is running?"

△ △ △

Now that a Hollywood studio has appointed a woman as head of production, we may expect an old Hollywood tradition of the yes-man to be perpetuated in this manner: "Let's put it to a vote: All in favor of my proposal say 'Ay.' All opposed say 'I resign.' "

△ △ △

At a PTA meeting the chairlady said "—and now let's discuss the petition about raising teachers' salaries on a strictly merit basis."

Up rose a hand.

"Yes?"

"It shouldn't matter if they're merit or single. They should be treated the same."

✡ challa

khale (standard)

> Pronounce it KHOL-leh, with a German or Scottish *kh*.
>
> The braided white bread, glazed with egg white, which is a Sabbath delicacy.

△ △ △

A beggar came to Mrs. Isaacson's back door. "Lady, I'm absolutely starving!"

"You poor man. Come in. On the table is bread. *Challa* and dark bread. Start while I get you some food."

The beggar fell upon the soft, sweet *challa*.

"Eh, mister," murmured Mrs. Isaacson. "There's *black* bread, too."

"I know." More slices of *challa* were wolfed down.

"Mister . . . the *challa* is much more expensive!"

"Lady," observed the beggar, "it's *worth* it!"

✡ Chanuka

Khaneke (standard)

Channuka

Hanuka

> The Feast of Lights, an eight-day holiday in December. In Hebrew, *Hanukkah* means "dedication."

Chanuka is called "the festival of freedom," for it memorializes the victorious rebellion of the Jews, under the leadership of the Maccabees, against Greco-Syrian despots. The story is recounted in the Apocrypha: Maccabees I and II.

The Maccabean revolt began in 168 B.C.E. In 165, with victory, the Jews celebrated the recapture and rededication of the Temple and the high altar. *De facto* independence was not achieved until 161.

Judas Maccabee, or Judah the Maccabee, son of Mattathias, was the military hero who led the revolt. (Do not confuse this Maccabee with the Hasmonean dynasty, nor with the name given to seven martyred Christian children of Salome who refused to practice idolatry.) Judas and his brothers assigned eight days of Chanuka celebration and thanksgiving to the Lord, after the recapture of the Temple.

△ △ △

One of my favorite jokes, a telling commentary on Jewish mothers' capacity to lay on guilt, involves the mother who gave her son two neckties on Chanuka.

The boy hurried into his bedroom, ripped off the tie he was wearing, put on one of the ties his mother had brought him, and hurried back. "Look, Mama! Isn't it gorgeous?"

Mama asked, "What's the matter? You don't like the other one?"

charley

> Bronxese for *shayle:* Hebrew: question. Pronounced SHY-leh.

> 1. A difficult question.
> 2. A problem hard to solve.

This comes from *paskanen a shayle* ("deciding a problem in religious law").

To say "There is a real *charley!*" means "That is a very tough question to answer!"

Young Bronxites or Brooklynites or Lower East Siders liked to cry, "Hey, have I got a *charley* for you!" I never heard the phrase in Chicago, Washington or Los Angeles.

△ △ △

Even his widow, Malka Finsterman, could not deny that her late husband had been very unpopular. Friends he had none; critics he had everywhere. So it was with special feeling that she asked Rabbi Podovnik: "Doesn't even a *momzer* deserve a kind word after he dies? This is a *shayle.* Don't we Jews believe in the utmost compassion in—"

"Stop already!" said the rabbi. "I'll make for your Benny a sermon no one will ever forget."

And he did. To a huge audience who had come to hear how Rabbi Podovnik, known far and wide as a severe judge of men, would frame a funeral oration for the notorious Benny Finsterman, Rabbi Podovnik declaimed:

"We are here to say goodbye to a man known to us all as Benny Finsterman. He was known to us all as a cheapskate, a *paskudnyak* who never helped a friend, never paid a debt, never gave a cent to charity. But one thing I can tell you with a full heart: compared to his brother Louie, Benny was an angel!"

Chasid

Chasidim

> See HASID.

chassen

chazzen

> See KHAZEN.

cheder

> See HEDER.

Chelm

> Rattle the *ch* into a Scottish *kh*.

The mythical town inhabited by simpletons.

Why Chelm was stigmatized as the archetype of foolishness, I do not know, nor do I know who does. (There were, in fact, three real towns in Eastern Europe called Chelm.)

I think that the prototype of Chelmish reasoning is this: "Sleep faster: we need the pillows!"

△ △ △

After misfortunes accumulated in Chelm, the elders decided to replenish the community's funds by—making beer. Having never made beer, they assumed, as true Chelmniks, that it was easy.

After a week of experiment and testing, they produced a liquid which all pronounced *geshmok*—and they sent a quart to a world-famous brewery in Munich, Germany, with this note:

> O Famed and Worthy Brewmasters:
>
> We, the elders of Chelm, seeking to help our poor, our widows, our orphans, have produced a beer that we can produce and sell for a healthy profit. But since we are humble folk, not known to the larger world, it would greatly help our cause if a famous and distinguished brewer such as you appraised our potion and attested to its taste, healthfulness and other qualities.
>
> May the Holy One, blessed be His name, speed your answer to the hopeful, thankful
>
> Elders of Chelm

A week later came the answer from Munich:

> Your horse has diabetes.

△ △ △

In Chelm, the best cobbler, among all the tailors, is Chaim Yudel, the baker.

chozzer

See KHAZER.

chutzpa
hutzpa (standard)
khutspe

Pronounce that *ch* with a potent *yech*ing, as if expelling a silicon chip from the roof of your palate. Hebrew: audacity, insolence, gall.

Ultra-brazenness; shamelessness; hard-to-believe effrontery, presumption or gall.

This quintessential word, too arrogant to synonymize, has been accepted (and gratefully) in English. It will be found in a considerable number of legal briefs and judicial rulings. (They are gleefully mailed to me by lawyers, with marginal notes like *Mazel tov!*, Wow! or *Mon Dieu!*) I received such a U.S. Court of Appeals decision, sent to me from a professor of constitutional law in (believe me) Corpus Christi.

Definitions of *chutzpa* spring up like weeds: the classic, of course, goes: *Chutzpa* is the quality shown by the man who murders his mother and father, then asks the judge to forgive a poor orphan.

A more recent description: A *chutzpanik* is a mugger who, as he runs away from his victim, points ahead and hollers: "Thief! Thief! Stop! Thief!"

△ △ △

"You want an example of *chutzpa*? How about Hymie the Gonef? He broke the Eighth Commandment—by stealing the Bible."

△ △ △

Steiner came running into the office of his partner. "Al! Al! We're ruined!"

"Davey, calm down. What happened?"

"We just received a huge crate of returned merchandise! Brassieres. Black. Two hundred and ten *dozen* brassieres! Al, what can we do?!"

"What we can do," said Al, "is cut off the straps and sell them for *yarmulkes.*"

cockamamy

cockamamie

Yinglish, and *sui generis.* Pronounced cock-a-may-me.

1. Confused, mixed up.
2. Implausible, ludicrous.
3. Far-fetched, offensive to credulity.
4. Imitation; fraudulent.
5. Cheap, not worth much.
6. (As an epithet) Silly! Absurd!

The number of definitions suggests the utility of this admirable concoction, a linguistic gem from the Lower East Side, cherished in Brooklyn, pampered in the Bronx, and now indispensable to the argot of urban life. I, for one, have found no pejorative synonym so pungent. (Neither did S. J. Perelman.) I never encountered *cockamamy* in the Midwest, South, Southwest, or California.

> 7. Decalcomanias: dye pictures transferred to the back of the hand, after wetting, rubbing and peeling off the paper.

The slang coinage seems inevitable: How many children on Broome Street or Flatbush Avenue could pronounce, much less spell, the forbidding "decalcomania"? True, the word became shortened to "decal"; but can "decal" hold a candle to *cockamamy?* Never.

Wentworth and Flexner's *Dictionary of American Slang* defines *cockamanie (sic!)* as "quixotic, crazy . . ." and cites a first use as occurring in 1931. But I heard it almost a decade earlier in New York City.

I should add, in the interest of cultural pluralism, that I do not for a moment doubt that the Italian, Irish and Slavic kids who were brought up in the Bronx or the Lower East Side cried *Cockamamy!* too.

△ △ △

The movie colony in Hollywood was once captivated by a *cockamamy* spiritualist who held costly séances during which he displayed his "supernatural" powers. Some friends of Groucho Marx, a notorious skeptic (I may even say he was a pluperfect cynic), challenged Groucho to appraise the psychic's wizardry for himself.

Marx went. He sat, silent and baleful, as the spiritualist summoned long-dead parents, relayed messages to and from the dead, made astonishing predictions, confidently answered questions about life after death.

After two hours of mumbo-jumbo, the seer intoned, "Now Melchimedzer, my medium angel, is getting tired. I have time for only one more question . . ."

Marx asked it: "What's the capital of North Dakota?"

△ △ △

In the lobby of the Excelsior Park Hotel, Mr. Atron beheld a man smoking a very large—and very smelly—cigar. Said Mr. Atron, "That's some *cockamamy* cigar! It must cost all of five cents."

"It cost sixty."

"Sixty cents! How many do you smoke a day?"

"Ten, fifteen."

"And how many years have you been smoking?"

"Fifty."

"Well, did you ever stop to think that if you hadn't thrown away all that money on cigars, you could own a hotel as big as this!"

The stranger paused. "Do *you* smoke?"

"Absolutely not!"

"So do you own this hotel?"
Said Mr. Atron, "Certainly."

colboy

kolboy (standard)

colboynik

colboynitse (f.)

> Recommended for Yinglish. From Hebrew and English (see below).

> 1. Cowboy.
> 2. Hot shot, *shtarker.*
> 3. Smart aleck; a posturer.

One of the temptations (and booby-traps) of linguistics is present here: for despite the seemingly obvious connection of *colboy*-cowboy, the former is not the child of the latter: *kolboy* is a Hebrew word (from *kolbo*) for:

> 4. A compendium of "all rules" or "all prayers."
> 5. A rabbi who also serves as cantor, scribe, *moyl, shochet,* i.e., one who can perform all religious functions.
> 6. A scoundrel: an exemplar of bad character traits, capable of committing anything.

Since the same phonetics make up *colboy* (the Yinglish pronunciation of "cowboy") and *kolboy,* the homophones were pounced upon with delight by immigrant Jews.

The cowboy was as intriguing to immigrant Jews as he was to others. All immigrants loved the silent movies, since a knowledge of English was not needed to understand them. (Subtitles were read aloud by a son, daughter, nephew.) The movies were the cheapest and best form of entertainment in a slum or working-class neighborhood. The cowboys (notably the great William S. Hart and Dustin Farnum) were archetypes of courage and valor.

The silents to which I was taken as a child, by my parents or my uncle, still glow in my memory. Even at the age of six or seven, I felt a kinship with those in a mythical kingdom called Hollywood who made the magical movies.

△ △ △

Ike Orgel, a loyal new Texan, and a strutting *colboy,* visiting New York, boasted to a relative: "Alvin, did you know I have three hundred cattle!"

"So? I'll bet a lot of Texans own three hundred cattle."

"In the *freezer?*" asked Ike.

Columbus' medina

Rhyme *medina* with "Katrina." Hebrew: country.

The United States.

This laudatory metaphor was also uttered in bitterness by those immigrants who had come to the New World under the illusion that the streets were lined with silver, if not gold, and ended up in filthy tenements and sweatshops, and sometimes lived in ratty cellars and coal bins.

See AMERICA GONEF!

△ △ △

This may be the place to examine the question raised before: Was Columbus a Jew? Here is a nosegay of tantalizing data:

● The name Colón (Columbus) was common among the Jews and Marranos of Portugal and Spain.

● Columbus' son, who was his secretary, said that his father was "of the royal blood of Jerusalem," a phrase favored by crypto-Jews.

● A Marrano, Santangel, convinced Queen Isabella to ignore her Christian savants (who called Columbus' plan a pipe dream) and approve the expedition westward.

● As royal comptroller, Santangel advanced Columbus over a million *maravedi*. The rest of the money was raised by Isaac Abravanel.

● Columbus delayed sailing until the day of the royal edict expelling all Jews from Spain; and that day turned out to be Tish Abov, the darkest day on a Jewish calendar. (It commemorates the destruction of both the First and the Second Temple.)

● The names of the crew on Columbus' first voyage show at least six to ten Marranos (crypto-Jews); and land was sighted, in that historic landfall, by one: Rodrigo de Triana. (Triana was baptized just before the ships sailed away.)

● Columbus showed a striking affinity for Jews—as friends, confidants, advisers and company.

Do I think Columbus was Jewish? No. His behavior in the Caribbean attests to his being a zealous, proselytizing Christian; his conduct in Spain, after his imprisonment, was that of a Christian martyr, clinging to his crucifix and his chains, forever Catholic in his prayers.

Do I think Columbus was a Marrano? As the Yiddish goes, *Vayr vayst?* ("Who knows?" Or, better, "*Who* knows?").

Do I think Columbus came from Marrano parents or grandparents? Yes.

This will be all I have to say on this subject.*

△ △ △

computernik

> Someone who is mad about computers, large or small; a gadget nut.

△ △ △

The mathematical wizards crowded before the great computer at the Technion Institute. "It's a mistake!" exclaimed one scientist. "No question of it. The computer made a mistake!"

The assembled *meyvinim* passed the read-out tapes around, calculating, frowning, scrutinizing.

And after a full hour of communal bafflement, the chief of the laboratory, observing the dismay on the faces of his colleagues, exclaimed: "Gentlemen, don't be discouraged. Do you realize it would take 4,200 mathematicians, working 12 hours a day, over 363 *years* to make a mistake like this?"

Contempt via reiteration, plus the scathing "sh–" gambit

"Who says she's not clean? Clean–shmean, let her shave off her mustache."

"Honest–shmonest, he sings like a frog."

"Nice–shmice, did they give a penny to U.J.A.?"

△ △ △

In an elegant suite of law offices, the phone rings. It is answered: "Zecker, Zecker, Zecker and *Zeck*–er."

---

* The story I have pieced together comes from S. D. Goitein, *A Mediterranean Society;* Joshua Starr, *The Jews in the Byzantine Empire;* Jacob R. Marcus, *The Jew in the Medieval World;* James Parkes, *The Jew in the Medieval Community;* Marcus Arkin, *Aspects of Jewish Economic History;* and Cecil Roth, *The Jewish Contribution to Civilisation.* Samuel Eliot Morison's *Admiral of the Ocean Sea* attributes small credibility to stories about Columbus' Jewish origins; but the latest edition of the *Encyclopaedia Britannica* says: "One explanation of all these facts is that Columbus came from a Spanish-Jewish family settled in Genoa."

"Hello, may I talk to Mr. Zecker?"
"I'm sorry, but Mr. Zecker is out of town."
"Well . . . can I speak to Mr. Zecker?"
"No, Mr. Zecker is in court today."
"Then how about connecting me to Mr. Zecker?"
"Mr. Zecker won't be back until six."
Sigh. "Okay, then can you connect me to Mr. Zecker?"
"Spea–king."

Could be

From Yiddish: *Es ken zayn,* pronounced *'s ken zyn.*

1. It may be; it may come to pass.
2. But maybe not.
3. Time will tell.
4. Anything is possible.
5. Wait and see.
6. *Who* knows?

I suggest—no, I maintain—that "Could be" might not have come into wide English usage (aside from Use 1, above) were it not for its persistent use by Jews. English, to be sure, has no problem with "*It* could be . . ." or "It could (might) be that . . ." But that's the point: "It could be that . . ." is very far from "Could be."

When not used as a neutral statement "Could be" contains innuendos beyond the boundaries of "It could be that . . ." The latter is straightforward. "Could be" is tentative: a doubt, a hint, a caveat about probability, a droll reminder of the surprising events that may occur to transform the unlikely into the actual, a skeptical disclaimer of commitment.

The Jewish propensity for skepticism is beautifully served by this truncated form of "Perhaps that's so—but don't forget: perhaps it isn't." Sagacity is attributed to the doubters, that is, to those who (in a world profusely populated by *fonfers, ploshers, k'nakers, shacher-machers, trombeniks, et alia*) don't take things at face value, don't fall for exaggerated asseverations, don't believe every promise and, in general, use so many grains of salt per annum that they might as well buy it by the barrel.

The following illustrate the denotations numbered in the definition above.

1.

A: Darwin said that man is descended from animals.
B: Could be.

2.

A: Do you think Pfaumbach is telling the truth?
B: Could be.
A: You don't sound confident.
B: I'm not.

3.

A: I wonder if Schultz will pay that bill.
B: Could be. . . . How long do you expect to live?

4.

A: Will Dora really marry a man forty years older?
B: Could be.
A: It's hard to believe.
B: With *Dora?*

5.

A: I don't think Mishkin will have the *nerve* to show up. What
   do you think?
B: Could be.
A: Could be what: Yes or no?
B: Neither.

6.

A: You think *she* was the one who tipped off the police?
B: Could be.
A: Or do you think *he* did?
B: Also, could be.
A: You certainly like to straddle the fence!
B: I know how to say, *Who* knows?

crazy-doctor

Note the all-important hyphen.

A psychiatrist or psychoanalyst.

A "crazy-doctor" is not a doctor who is demented; he is a doctor who
treats crazy people.

Jews are quite at home with ideas of insanity, hallucinations, schizo-
phrenia, paranoia. Jewish history is studded with dramatic instances of
one *meshuggener* or another. The Bible itself is surely a chronicle in
which extraordinary irrationality of one sort or another possesses many
characters. And in the history of psychiatry and psychoanalysis, Jews
have played a conspicuous, often commanding, role.

Remember the old, well-known, unchallenged folk saying: "Everyone has his own *meshugas*."

△ △ △

A psychoanalyst is a Jewish doctor who hates the sight of blood.

A psychotic thinks that 2 plus 2 equal 9; a neurotic knows that 2 plus 2 equal 4—but he just can't *stand* it.

A neurotic builds castles in the air; a psychotic thinks he lives in them; the psychoanalyst collects rent from both.

The depressed person builds dungeons in the air.

A hysteric knows the secret of perpetual emotion.

Anyone who goes to a psychiatrist ought to have his head examined.

—SAMUEL GOLDWYN

△ △ △

Anecdotes to treasure:

Two psychoanalysts meet while strolling on Park Avenue. It's a matter of choice which one will greet the other thusly: "You're fine; how am I?"

△ △ △

Two psychiatrists enter an elevator.

The attendant calls, "*Good* morning, gentlemen."

After the psychiatrists get off on their floor, one asks the other: "What do you think he meant by that?"

△ △ △

Mrs. Savitch phoned a famous psychiatrist, "Hello, is this the crazy-doctor?"

"Madam, I am a psychiatrist, a neurologist and an M.D."

"Listen, Doctor, I have some terrible thing driving me *meshugge*. But before I come to you, I have to know: How much is a visit?"

"I charge seventy dollars a visit, madam."

"Seventy—" Mrs. Savitch gasped. "Goodbye. *That* crazy I'm not."

curses

Among Jews, swearing is rare, but cursing common. I mean that venting anger or frustration in obscene phrases which are directed at no one in particular ("*Damn* this weather!") is less common among Jews than the invocation of one or another calamity (fire, flood, pain, death) upon someone specific.

I suspect that one reason for this is that fighting or physical contention was despised in Jewish ethics and mores; hence, *verbalized* hostility tends to be compensatory—and admired.

Examples: If you break my jaw (or leg or arm) you do no more than demonstrate your muscular power—which any ignoramus, barbarian or animal can probably do better. But if you hurl a juicy, literate, flamboyant execration, you act as no animal or savage can, for you use the brain and wit and eloquence God gave you, a gift reserved to man, of all the creatures in creation, a talent—indeed, a resource—more precious than fists, feet, fangs or claws.

Curses also offer a special swift, sweet catharsis. Words are swifter than sparring, more exact than blows, more surgical than violence.

If it is possible to talk of doting curses, of heraldic curses, of obligatory curses, of curses that bring sweet relief to both cursor and cursee, the Jews of yesteryear were masters of the genre. Sholom Aleichem's tales are garnished with curses of great color and eloquence, curses in which tension or terror are at last discharged: when Menachem Mendel, for instance, returns to his home from some misadventure, his wife and mother-in-law blister his ears with curses—then burst into tears of joy. I. L. Peretz's story, "A Woman's Fury," is a shattering tale in which maledictions erupt from unbearable poverty. (You can find it in Joachim Neugroschel's *The Shtetl*, published by Richard Marek.)

For several dozen specimens of Yiddish contumely, see the entry "Curses" in my *Treasury of Jewish Quotations*. Here are a few:

> May your insides churn like a music box.
>
> and
>
> May all his teeth fall out—except one (so he can have a permanent toothache).
>
> and
>
> Like a beet he should grow—with his head in the earth.

The most authoritative collection and analysis (however suffocating the jargon) is James Matisoff's *Blessings, Curses, Hopes, and Fears* (Ishi Press).

△ △ △

My favorite story about cursing is this:

Cecil (né Sidney) B. de Millstein, the most imaginative moviemaker in Israel, was finishing his spectacular *The Triumph of King David*. On the desert near Beersheba three high towers had been erected, each crowned with cameras, cameramen, sound equipment. These towers, plus his own, were de Millstein's way of insuring that the climactic scene, a battle that used 3,000 extras, 400 camels, 2,000 spears, etc., would be photographed *in toto*.

"Action!" called de Millstein over the loudspeakers.

What action it was! Never had a filmed battle raged with such authenticity. And when, after fourteen uninterrupted minutes, de Millstein cried "Cut!" the crews burst into cheers.

Into his telephone hookup to Tower Number 1, Cecil B. de Millstein barked, "You got it all, Moishe?"

An anguished voice cried, "Our power went off! We couldn't shoot a single frame!"

"May the Lord plant beets in your stomach!" fumed de Millstein. "May they name a disease after you!" He flipped the intercom to Tower Number 2. "Cha-im! You caught it all?"

"Mr. de Millstein, *please* don't get mad. The cameraman forgot to reload! I ran out of film after three minutes!"

"Idiot! Murderer! May your tapeworm develop constipation! May all your teeth fall out—except one!" De Millstein snapped to Tower Number 3. "Sol? Sol?"

"Mr. de Millstein, *never* was there such a scene! You are a genius—"

"Okay. Rush the film to the lab."

"The film?" echoed Sol. "I thought it was a rehearsal!"

"Moron!" roared de Millstein. "May trolley cars invade your stomach! May the *moyl* circumcise your first son and bless the wrong piece!" The great de Millstein slammed down the phone, and turned to his own cameraman. "Thank God you're here, Nate! I'm sure everything was okay with *our* setup."

"Absolutely!" chortled Nate.

"Enough film in the camera?"

"Plenty!"

"The sound okay?"

"The sound is perfect."

"Thank God!"

"We're ready whenever you are, Mr. de Millstein."

customer

As used here, this is not a synonym for purchaser or prospective buyer.

1. Person.
2. Type, member of a category or group.

I know that "customer" is used in colloquial English, as described above. But when so used, "customer" is usually preceded by a qualifier! "He's a tough customer," "She's a smart customer."

In Yinglish, "customer" has been altered to mean a person whose characteristics are not spelled out but are implied, or take meaning from the preceding conversation.

"To preside? She's not your customer."

"Does he have a temper? You named the right customer."

"You want to complain to me about my son? You chose the wrong customer!"

△ △ △

Dr. Leon Feuermann, one of the leading cardiologists in Munich, who was being considered for a professorship at the medical school, was rejected. A member of the faculty told him, "You didn't get the appointment because—well, you're a Jew. The committee is searching for another cardiologist."

Dr. Feuermann sat down and composed the following:

> To the Faculty of the University of Munich:
>
> May I recommend for the Chair of Cardiology Herr Hans Granauer? I have known this excellent man for 14 years. He is honest, hardworking, and does not drink.
>
> Herr Granauer, you should understand, is not a doctor. But he certainly is your customer: he is a *goy*.
>
> Yours,
> LEON FEUERMANN, M.D.
>
> P.S. Grenauer is the janitor at 26 Waldstrasse, where I live.

D

dairy

Dairy foods.

The conversion of an adjective to a noun is a familiar propensity of Yinglish: in New York, for one, "Danish" has become an acceptable way of asking for a Danish pastry (unknown, incidentally, in Denmark, where such confections are called Vienna buns).

△ △ △

SCENE: *A Dairy Restaurant*

"Waiter, waiter!" called a customer. "This fish is awful!"
"But you ate here last week and said the fish was delicious."
"That was last week."
"I give you my word," said the waiter, "this is the same fish."

△ △ △

Mr. Isadore Steinman appeared before the gates of Heaven, where the admitting angel, consulting his records, said, "Steinman . . . Steinman . . . Isadore Steinman . . . from Far Rockaway . . . Lifelong vegetarian. Ate mostly dairy . . . How do you like that?" He looked up. "You're not due for six weeks yet! Steinman, who's your doctor?"

daven

davenen

Pronounce it DAH-ven and DAHV-nen. Origin: uncertain.

To pray.

One of the surprising things about *daven* is that no other Hebrew or Yiddish word exists for the same denotation. The nearest ("I shall pray") means to pray for someone else. But how can you do someone else's praying for him?

Maurice Samuel, in his elegant *In Praise of Yiddish*, confesses that the etymology of *davenen* ("to pray") remains a mystery. It is neither Hebraic nor Romance; and it has a Germanic suffix (*nen*). *Davenen* has even been traced, rather fancifully, to the Persian *divan:* a collection of poetry. But Max Weinrich flatly declares, after examination of several "pseudo-etymologies," that *daven* is of uncertain origin. *(History of the Yiddish Language,* page 680.) I would be the last man on earth to argue with him.

An excellent, authoritative guide to all aspects of Jewish prayer is Hayim H. Donin's *To Pray as a Jew* (Basic).

△ △ △

My mother told me a story, when I was very young, that has never left my memory:

An old Jew found himself in a strange place, and when it was time for him to say *mayrev* he found that he had lost his prayer book. So he addressed the Lord: "Dear, sweet God, I have bad news for You. I don't have my prayer book. Even worse, I am getting old and forgetful, and I never had much of a memory, so I cannot recite the evening prayer (*mayrev*) by heart. But I have a solution, Almighty One, and I hope it meets with Your approval: I will just call out all the letters in the alphabet, and You, please, put them together in the right way."

△ △ △

Oh Lord of the Universe: please take a real look at Your world!

When I pray, I pray quickly, because I am talking to God: but when I read the Torah, I read slowly, because God is talking to me.

If praying did any good, they would hire men to do it.

—FOLK SAYINGS

Prayer is the service of the heart.

—TALMUD: *Ta'anith,* 2:1

Even when the gates of Heaven are closed to prayer, they are open to tears.

—TALMUD: *Berakoth,* 32a

Pray only in a room with windows (to remember the world outside).

—TALMUD: *Berakoth,* 34b

I love to pray at sunrise—before the world becomes polluted with vanity and hatred.

—THE KORETSER RABBI

△ △ △

Said Milton Peskin to the rabbi: "My wife—we're going to have a baby."

"*Mazel tov!*"

"It's our first child, *Rebbe*. And my Goldie isn't so young. When she goes into labor, at our home, would you make a special prayer for her?"

"I'll do more than that, Peskin! I'll bring along a *minyen!*"

When the labor pains began, Mr. Peskin telephoned the doctor—and the rabbi: "*Rebbe!* The delivery has started!"

The rabbi arrived with nine alerted, cheerful males. The prayers began. And loud, vigorous prayers they were!

Outside the bedroom, Milton Peskin paced and paced. Soon the cry of a baby was heard. The doctor stuck his head out the door: "It's a boy!"

"A boy!" Peskin ran to the head of the stairs and announced to the swaying bodies below, "It's a boy!"

"*Mazel tov!*" yelled the *minyen.*

"Praised be the Lord of Israel!" cried the rabbi.

Back to the bedroom door ran Peskin. It opened. "A girl!" called the doctor.

Peskin sped to the stairway. "Twins. A girl. I have *twins!*"

Now the *Mazel tovs* shook the very rafters.

Back to the bedroom raced Peskin.

Out popped the head of the doctor. "Another girl!"

"*Another* girl?!"

"Triplets!"

Peskin fairly flew to the stairway, down which he now bellowed, "For God's sake, down there: stop praying!"

deli

> Truncated form of "delicatessen," which is from German via French via Latin: *delicatus:* giving pleasure—plus German: *essen:* to eat. French: *delicatesse:* delicacy. Yinglish.
>
> 1. Cooked meat, fish, relishes, salads, cheeses.
> 2. The store where such foods are featured.

Need I extol the glories of this urban institution, never more popular than today—where there seems to be a delicatessen in the most rural places?

The length of the word, difficult to get on a small sign or window, caused some unknown genius to invent *deli.*

△ △ △

On Saturday nights, after I was eleven years old, while my parents' sweater store was open on Kedzie Avenue, I was given a quarter and allowed to get my dinner at the corner delicatessen. A quarter bought me two corned-beef sandwiches on rye (bologna was a nickel) and a *shpritz* (soda) drink. I still remember the *haute cuisine*.

△ △ △

SCENE: *A Deli Supreme*

CUSTOMER: Waiter! Look!

WAITER: I'm looking.

CUSTOMER: What's that *fly* doing in my soup?!

WAITER: Uh—it looks like the breast stroke.

△ △ △

Solly Motz went into Fishbein and Klamins Deli on Amsterdam Ave, chose a nice, plump whitefish at the Appetizing, picked up a bialy and sat down at a table. But when he picked up his knife and fork, the eye of the whitefish stared at him in so direct and accusatory a fashion that Solly could not bear it. Solly laid down his knife and fork, and left.

A week later, Solly went into Fishbein and Klamins again and from the delicacies displayed behind the glass at the Appetizing, Solly chose a plump whitefish. And again, as he sat down, the reproving glare from the plate drove all hunger from Solly, who left the fish uncut, unboned, uneaten.

It was a month later that Solly found himself on Houston Street, where he went into Yosha Kimmel's. He sat down at a table and ordered, "Your famous bagels and cream cheese, a glass tea, and a nice whitefish."

When the waiter placed the items on the table, a glaring, cold fish eye transfixed poor Solly as in an icy tone the whitefish murmured, "What's the matter, mister? You gave up Fishbein and Klamins?"

dentnist

Yinglish, and not *ippy-pippy (q.v.)*.

Dentist.

"Dentist" deserves your affection, if not your approval. A starchy Jew of Germanic (geographic, not genetic) lineage often cited "dentnist . . . carpentner . . . paintner . . ." to me as horrid examples of the linguistic perversity of Jews from Eastern Europe: "They know perfectly well how to pronounce 'dentist' or 'painter.' How do you account for their stubborn solecisms?" Here is what I told Wolfgang:

    1. *-ner* is a Yiddish suffix which, with *-er*, designates a doer of something: *redner* (speaker).

2. -*ist* is also used, as in English, to designate a performer of something: *kompanist* (accompanist), *sopranist* (soprano).

So the phonetic confusion of -*ist* with -*nist*, albeit undesirable, is hardly ground for elevated dudgeon.

Immigrant Jews also say "salesslady" and "salessmon" because— well, look up those entries; it's worth it.

△ △ △

Dr. Abel Grutman, a very deft *dentnist*, was a compulsive wit. He asked a new patient, "Open wide . . . *Gevalt!* Lady, you have the biggest cavity I ever saw in my practice! . . . Lady, *you have the biggest cavity I ever saw in my—*"

"I heard you, Doctor! You don't have to repeat yourself."

"Who's repeating?" blinked Dr. Grutman. "That was an echo."

Diaspora

From Greek: *diaspora:* scattering. The Hebrew equivalent is *galuth:* exile; the Yiddish is *golus.*

The dispersion of Jews around the world.*

See COLUMBUS' MEDINA.

Among the descriptions of ghastly episodes in the Diaspora, I give

---

* In 721 B.C.E., the Assyrian King Sargon II crushed the northern Israelite kingdom of Samaria (*i.e.,* the kingdom of ten of Israel's twelve tribes), and exiled the inhabitants, who vanished.

In 701 B.C.E., Sennacherib crushed the army of Judah, then recorded in cuneiform: "200,150 people, small and large, male and female [did I bring] out of their midst as booty." He transported them to Babylonia with halters around their necks.

In 586 B.C.E., Nebuchadnezzar destroyed Solomon's Temple in Jerusalem and deported huge numbers of Hebrews to serve as slaves in Armenia, Georgia, the Caucasus.

King Cyrus of Persia defeated Nebuchadnezzar's son in Babylon in 538 B.C.E.; and under a historic proclamation allowed all Jews to return to Judea from exile. Some did, and rebuilt the Temple. Most of the exiles did not return.

I mention these events only to counteract the impression that the Diaspora, or exile, of the Jews began when the Romans, in 70 C.E., tore down the Temple.

There are data (but they are questionable) indicating that Jews visited China as long ago as the tenth or eighth century B.C.E. Experts seem to agree that Jews certainly reached China after the Roman destruction of the Temple in 70 C.E. (see Michael Pollak's careful *Mandarins, Jews, and Missionaries,* Jewish Publication Society). For an extraordinary assemblage of diaries, letters and contemporary documents concerning famous Jewish travelers such as Benjamin of Tudela, Rabbi Samuel ben Samson, Judah al-Harizi, the great charlatan David Reubeni, *et alia,* see Elkan Adler, *Jewish Travellers* (Hermon Press).

you W. E. H. Lecky's masterful and restrained account of one occurrence in the fifteenth century:

> History relates very few measures that produced so vast an amount
> of calamity. In three short months, all unconverted Jews were obliged,
> under pain of death, to abandon the Spanish soil. Multitudes, falling
> into the hands of the pirates who swarmed around the coast, were
> plundered of all they possessed* and reduced to slavery; multitudes
> died of famine or of plague, or were murdered or tortured with hor-
> rible cruelty by the African savages.
>
> About 80,000 [Jews] took refuge in Portugal, relying on the prom-
> ise of the king. Spanish priests lashed the Portuguese into fury, and the
> king was persuaded to issue an edict which threw even that of Isabella
> into the shade. All the adult Jews were banished from Portugal; but
> first all their children below the age of fourteen were taken from them
> to be educated as Christians. Then, indeed, the cup of bitterness was
> filled to the brim. The serene fortitude with which the exiled people
> had borne so many and such grievous calamities gave way, and was
> replaced by the wildest paroxysms of despair.
>
> When at last, childless and broken-hearted, they sought to leave
> the land, they found that the ships had been purposely detained, and
> the allotted time having expired, they were reduced to slavery and
> baptized by force. A great peal of rejoicing filled the Peninsula, and
> proclaimed that the triumph of the Spanish priests was complete.
>
> —*History of Rationalism in Europe*, Vol. II

dibitzer

Yinglish: 100 percent so, and inspired. Origin: obvious.

The man or woman who advises a *kibitzer*.

Let us pause in our daily rounds to salute the unknown genius who saw
the obvious need for this neologism; after all, if there is a word for the
nudnik with a college education *(phudnik)* there should certainly be a
word for the intrepid soul who kibitzes a kibitzer. English, one of the
most energetic of word-borrowers from other tongues, offers a welcome
home to the inventive.

△ △ △

The cardplayers at the retirement home were cursed by a *dibitzer* of
such persistence that they met to decide how they could put an end to
his *dibitzing*.

"Let's tell him once and for all," said Mr. Sidel, "he should mind his
own business! We already have a kibitzer!"

---

* Not only pirates took their money: the captains and crews of the boats, hired at scandalous rates, robbed them too.

"You think you can insult a *nudnik* like that?" asked Mr. Yuri.

"We shouldn't play in the game room where he waits for us," suggested Mr. Berkowitz.

"So where should we play? In the laundry?" scoffed Mr. Donberg.

"Aha!" That was Saul Weinberger. "Let's make up a game. Any cockamamy way of bidding—a game so crazy he won't be able to figure it out. That will shut him up!"

The others applauded this idea.

That afternoon the four men appeared in the game room as usual; and, as usual, Morris, the kibitzer, pulled up a chair—and soon, leaning over him, hovered Hymie, the *dibitzer*.

"How's about today we play Pitznik and Blitznik?" sang Mr. Weinberger. "A penny a point."

Said Mr. Yuri, "I *love* Pitznik and Blitznik! Deal."

Mr. Berkowitz divided the deck into four parts, handed one part to each of the other players, picked up his portion and tossed a card before Mr. Berkowitz. "Iffle!"

"Jiffle!" retorted Berkowitz. "Plus ten cents."

"I have a Knotch!" exclaimed Mr. Sidel. "So I raise you!"

"Oh, boy!" chortled Mr. Yuri, "I have a red Shmatzer! So I raise you both—"

"Psst!" the *dibitzer* hissed to the kibitzer. "Tell him not to be a fool!"

"What do you mean?" demanded Mr. Yuri.

"You can't beat a Knotch with a lousy red Shmatzer!"

Dismissal via repetition

An effective rejection lies in the repetition, either blandly or bluntly, of an offer. Thus:

> Q. Will you take ten dollars for it?
> A. Will I take ten dollars for it?

The answer means, "Of course I won't! That's a preposterous offer."

The answer may also run:

"Would *you* take ten dollars for it?"

But that *tu quoque* is more contentious, therefore less ironic, than the steely echo, "Will I take ten dollars for it?"

Readers who wish to challenge my attribution of Yinglishness to this ploy of repetition are requested to see RIDICULE THROUGH REPETITION.

Do me (him, her) something

Yinglish. From Yiddish: *Tu (ti) mir eppes.*

I know of no language other than Yiddish from which this awkward but expressive phrase could have come. It is often given with extra energy as "*Go* do me something."

1. There's not a thing you can do.
2. I don't care what you feel or say.
3. It's done, and that's that.
4. I know you disapprove, and I knew you would disapprove, but that's what I wanted to do, and I did—so accept it.

△ △ △

Mr. Spitalny told his new secretary, "Please check these sales figures. And to be sure, add up the column three times."

At 4:30, the secretary said, "Here you are, Mr. Spitalny."

"Did you check your results?"

"Yes, sir. Three times—"

"Thank—"

"—and here are the answers."

(Go do her something.)

See SO SUE ME; GO FIGHT CITY HALL.

donstairsikeh (f.)

donstairsiker (m.)

The neighbor downstairs.

Donstairsiker is a fine example of the Jewish penchant for adapting an English word to a simple immigrant's simple needs. Surely "the man (woman) who lives downstairs" is a cumbersome form of *donstairsiker.*

Donstairsiker opened the door to *nexdooriker* and *opstairsiker;* but I have never heard any neologist venture so far as to say *across-the-street-i-ker.* Mind you, I do not question that someone, sometime, hit upon that compound synonym; I just never heard it.

△ △ △

We had a *donstairsiker* who once exclaimed that he greatly enjoyed a radio presentation of that marvelous opera *Madman Butterfly.*

And I knew a *nexdooriker* who was attending night school and became such an enthusiast about American history that he even knew that Washington's Farewell Address was Mount Vernon.

Don't ask!

From Yiddish: *Freg nit* (or *nisht*). "Don't ask *me*" is English; "Don't ask" (or "Dun't esk!") is Yinglish.

1. Things are bad.
2. The answer would be so disheartening I prefer not to give it to you.
3. The answer is obvious.
4. Absolutely!

This laconic imperative contains a symphony of signals:

"Don't ask me to tell you (whatever it was you asked me) because I would rather not even *mouth* the answer."

Or: "Were I to answer your question instead of putting you off with a 'Don't ask!,' it would depress you so much you'd be sorry you inquired!"

Or: "Take a hint: do me a favor; desist."

△ △ △

"How's your wife?"
"Don't ask." (She's in bad shape.)

△ △ △

"It will be the best party of the year! Are you coming?"
"Don't ask." (Absolutely!)

△ △ △

"You look terrible, Joe. How's business?"
"Don't ask!"
"Ah . . . Listen, for this time of year, that's not so bad."

△ △ △

"*Shalom,* Teddy. How's your wife?"
"Still sick."
"And your children?"
"*They,* thank God, are fine."
"And your *gesheft?*"
"I can't complain. Excuse me, Henry, I have to go—"
"Wait a minute. Has it ever occurred to you, Teddy, that in all the years we've known each other, it's always *I* who asks the questions—never you. Have you even *once* asked how I am, how's my Shirley, my job?"
"Migod, Henry, you're right. How thoughtless have I been! From today on— Henry! How are things with you?"
Sighed Henry: "Don't ask."

Don't knock a teapot

From Yiddish: *Hok nit kayn tshaynik. Tshaynik* is from *tchay,* which means "tea" in many Slavic languages. Chinese, originally.

1. Don't talk nonsense.
2. Don't talk my ears off.
3. You confuse me with so much yammering.
4. You give me a headache!

This picturesque admonition may have come from the meaningless whistles of the steam in a kettle. Or, I prefer to think, it originated in some *shtetl* kitchen where a child banged away on a discarded teapot. Toys, in our sense, were very rare among the poor, who gave children ordinary objects which could be adapted to play: an old pan became a drum, a wooden spoon a gun, a broken cup a sand scoop. A discarded, leaky teakettle made an enchanting toy. And "to knock a teapot" became a vivid way of describing chatter, meaningless yak-yak-yakking.

"Did *he* knock me a teapot!"

"She drives me up the wall, the way she *hoks a tshaynik.*"

Don't mix in

> From Yiddish: *Mish zikh nisht (nit) arayn:* "Don't mix yourself into [that]."
>
> Don't butt in.

"Don't mix in" is the precise equivalent of "Don't butt in." The latter is used in English slang (instead of "Don't interfere"); the former is a Yinglish invocation.

Jews of earlier generations would translate directly from the Yiddish to exclaim, "Don't mix yourself in!" But the reflexive "yourself" of Yiddish sounds, in English, like the object of the verb "mix"; this amusing relationship is the comic basis upon which vaudeville performers once used to get laughs in German or Yiddish dialect routines. (The Amish of Pennsylvania, I am told, say "Throw the cow over the fence some hay.")*

doppess

> Rhymes with "stop us." Possibly from German: *doppig.*
>
> A commiserator, thoroughly useless, who does nothing but offer oral sympathy.

---

* Reflexive verbs are mandatory in Yiddish. They were once obligatory in English. After all, "I wash" (without "myself") can mean "I run a laundry."

This admirable coinage describes a personality type known in all cultures and everywhere held in scorn. The word comes from New York's garment district, a cauldron of linguistic alchemy.

A *doppess* is a special variant of *shlemiel, shmegegge, klutz,* or dope. I particularly call "dope" to your attention, because (Hans Rosenhaupt of the Woodrow Wilson Foundation wrote me) the natives of Frankfurt, Mainz and the surrounding terrain used the German slang *doppess* to describe a clumsy *(doppig)* person. Dutch Jews used *doppess* to describe a fumbler or groper.

But the *doppess* I cherish is something else again. It is best described in the words of a Seventh Avenue Mencken:

> So think about a loft in the garment center. There stand a dozen men before the ironing boards, pushing their big, heavy steam irons. Okay? But every so often, one man runs his iron right off the board. He—is a *shlemiel.* The iron lands on the big toe of the next man. *He* is a *shlemazl.* And who is the *doppess?* The *doppess* is the *shmuck* who goes *Tsk! Tsk! Tsk!*

That is a penetrating description of a human type: the man or woman who goes through life clucking sympathy. That's *all* they do. They don't help; they don't call for help; they never offer an idea or a solution. They just go *Tsk! Tsk! Tsk!*

See TSITSER, SHMEGEGGE.

dotso

1. That is true.
2. Is that so?
3. Can you believe it?
4. I'll be darned!

My father, who had a peerless ear, believed his ears when he heard, all around him:

1.
"My son just finished high school."
"Is *dotso?*"

2.
"You know who wrote me? Tarshawer!"
"Is *dotso?*"

3.
"Did you say you're going to L.A.?"
"Uh-huh. *Dotso!*"

How much clearer, I must say, is *Dotso?* than "Is that so?"

△ △ △

Place: *A Community Chest Reception*

Mr. Thornycroft Peabody, somewhat tipsy, exclaimed, "I'll have you know, Mr. Podovitz, that I come from one of the first families of Boston. In fact one of my ancestors signed the Declaration of Independence."

"Is *dot*so?" murmured Podovitz. "One of mine signed the Ten Commandments."

△ △ △

In the deli on lower Third Avenue, Simon Colstein called a waiter over. "What kind of sandwich am I eating?"

"What you ordered: pastrami on rye."

"Is *dot*so? I'm half through and haven't hit any pastrami."

"So take another bite."

Mr. Colstein took a bite. "Still no pastrami!"

Said the waiter, "You went right past it."

dreck

From the German: dung; excrement.

(Vulgar)
1. (Literally) Excrement.
2. Cheap, worthless, trash.

Dreck is a well-known, widely used epithet in colloquial English. Why that is so, I am not sure; the vocabulary of contumelious judgment is scarcely sparse in conventional English: "junk . . . garbage . . . trash." And in English slang, epithets are many and colorful: "baloney . . . bull . . . crap."

Perhaps it is the driving *dr* and the emphatic *k* that appeal to our indignation. "The play was *dreck!*" is much stronger than "The play was lousy." And *dreck* seems to purge the feelings more than does "junk." *Dreck* is, in fact, just and barely this side of taboo.

△ △ △

scene: *Art gallery*
Trabinsky: Is that a painting? It says "Night Scene."
Sakorski: It should say "*Dreck* by Moonlight."
Trabinsky: Why do they hang stuff like that?
Sakorski: Because they couldn't find the artist.

dreml

drem'l (standard)

driml

> Rhymes with "trem(b)le" or "Friml." Slavic: to doze.

> A sweet, pleasant catnap.

I had always assumed that *dreml* is the Yinglish version of "dream" (pronounced *drim* by Jewish immigrants), rendered more affectionate by adding the suffix for the diminutive that is so dear to Jewish hearts. The assumption was feckless. Max Weinreich's magisterial *History of the Yiddish Language* (University of Chicago Press) informs me that *dremlen* is Slavic; in Polish: *drzemac*.

I list the word in an effort to make it part of Yinglish.

△ △ △

My father was an accomplished *dremler*. More interesting, he sometimes sang in his sleep. He was fond of operatic arias. Usually, he hummed the melodies in his slumber, rather politely; but when the fervor of remembered music carried him away, he would let fly with a passage from *Aïda*.

Between my father's songs and the fact that my sister occasionally walked in her sleep, the night hours on Douglas Boulevard were bewitched.

dresske

> A little dress.

But the "little" does not stand for (or only for) "small." *Dresske* is obligatory modesty; it tells you that the lady did not pay much for it. A *dresske* comes off a rack; it is hardly *haute couture;* it may have been "Marked Down Drastically!" It surely did not come from Nieman-Marcus.

But if *dresske* does not represent the diminutive, what does?

I'm glad you asked. The diminutive, or the affectionately referred to, is *dresskeleh*. One of the characteristics that admits Yiddish words into English parlance is this virtuosity in diminutization.

△ △ △

The classic throwaway use of *dresske* was immortalized in Palm Beach, when the mother of a famous radio tycoon, complimented on her new frock, replied, "*This* little *dresske*? It's nothing. I use it only for street walking."

Drop dead!

Yiddish: *Ver derharget:* "Get yourself killed."

1. Go to hell.
2. I wish you would die on the spot.

This locution is a vigorous version of the English "F—— you!" and the more useful because its component words, if not its affective point, are perfectly respectable.

The phrase was used with enormous effect by Garson Kanin as the second-act curtain line in *Born Yesterday.* No one who saw that play will forget the impact of the phrase as enunciated by Judy Holliday: "Du–rop du–ead." The slow, sweet, studied rendition was stupendous. Waspish ladies have been tossing "Drop dead!" into their phones (to obscene callers) and as retorts (to abusive cabbies) ever since.

E

Eat a little something

Yinglish, absolutely.

Do not for a moment think that the "little" is a hint for you to restrain your appetite: *au contraire*, the host's table may be sagging under the weight of comestibles. "Eat a little something" is the obligatory apology for the supposed inadequacy of the food.

△ △ △

Is there anyone who has not heard the by-now-hoary exchange:

HOSTESS: So have some cookies, homemade.
GUEST: They're delicious! But thanks, no. I already ate four.
HOSTESS: You already ate five—but who's counting?

Eat fruit

Yinglish to a fare-thee-well.

A Jewish mother or hostess characteristically sang out, "Eat fruit!" to family and guests alike. Ever since the early plays of Clifford Odets, this invitation has identified the giver as a Jewish woman, but Odets was not the first to employ the locution. I heard it in vaudeville skits in the early twenties.

"Eat fruit!" is not merely a form of politesse. One must remember that, to Ashkenazim, fruit was a rare luxury. The only time my mother ate an orange, when she was a girl, was on her birthday.

The healthfulness and low price of fruit in America made immigrants dizzy with pleasure. And the lesson drummed into Jews about the necessity, the *mitzve*, of generous hospitality created a steady flow of invitations to "have a piece fruit already."

. . . eat your heart out

From Yiddish: *Es dir oys s'harts.*

Be consumed by envy, or by grief.

This phrase is used for gloating: "He won the contest, so eat your heart out!"

In Yiddish, the original meaning is less taunting and more descriptive, albeit exaggerated: "Her children's conduct is so terrible, she's eating her heart out." "Your jealousy will make you eat your heart out one of these days."

△ △ △

Boris Solter taught his dog, Moishe, to stand on his hind legs for twenty minutes at a time. Then he taught the dog to wear a *yarmulke.* Then he taught him how to *daven.* Soon Solter got a prayer shawl and taught Moisheleh not to shrug it off his shoulders. And then, when the high holidays came around, Boris Solter took the dog with him to the synagogue. Boris had bought two tickets, and Moishe sat between Boris on one side and old Mr. Wolkoff on the other.

And at the right time, Moishe rose to pray—along with the whole congregation. True, his praying was not very clear, and was punctuated by muffled yips and heartfelt wails—but there could be no doubt about it: the dog was praying.

This led Mr. Wolkoff to exclaim, "Boris! Do my ears play tricks on me—or is your *hintele* actually *davening?*"

"He's *davening* alright."

"Boris!" cried Mr. Wolkoff. "You can make a fortune. This dog belongs on television!"

Sighed Boris, "Don't eat your heart out. *He* wants to be a bookkeeper!"

Echoing a question to maximize indignation (without stressing so much as a syllable)

The critical point in this ploy lies in echoing the words without their interrogative upbeat; repeat the question as a declaration —ironic, accusatory, even embittered.

1.

Q. Did you visit Shapiro?
A. Did I visit Shapiro.
(Meaning: "Am I made of stone *not* to visit a friend whose wife just died?")

2.

Q. Did you visit Shapiro?
A. Did I visit Shapiro.
   (Meaning: "I spent practically all night with him!")

3.

Q. Did you visit Shapiro?
A. Did I visit Shapiro.
   (Meaning: "How can you insult me by even asking?")

△ △ △

WAITER: Did you call me?
MR. ABT: Did I call you.
WAITER: So what do you want?
MR. ABT: I want to know my offense.
WAITER: What do you mean "offense"?
MR. ABT: I've been on bread and water ever since I came in.

-el

Suffix which diminutizes a noun—in Yinglish.

"Such a pretty *boxel*."

"Who will notice this *spotel?*"

When a noun ends in *el*, the suffix for diminutization becomes—*eleh*.

△ △ △

Regardez this dialectical ballet:

MRS. APTER: How much is that pickle?
GROCER: That pickle is a nickel.
MRS. APTER: Eh—and how much is this *pickeleh?*
GROCER: This *pickeleh* is—a *nickeleh*.

Enjoy!

Yinglish à la mode.

Enjoy! (Complete sentence.)

This extraordinary transformation of a transitive to an intransitive verb, dropping the hitherto essential "yourself," has long been popular among American Jews. It has become familiar English usage, especially in advertisements. (Harry Golden's book *Enjoy, Enjoy!* was widely read when published in 1965.)

Americans enjoy abbreviating words and truncating phrases: "Have a happy"; "Order of ham and"; "A Danish."

I happen to dislike "Enjoy!" I *never* use the verb bereft of object: Go do me something.

△ △ △

Velvel Soporin, the greenhorn, having heard so much about the wonders of Coney Island, got up enough courage to ask a girl to go there with him.

The next morning a friend asked, "So, Velvel? Did you enjoy?"

"Y–yeah. But the Tunnel of Love was some disappointment. We got so wet I caught a cold."

"That's strange. Your boat leaked that much?"

The greenhorn blinked. "You mean there's a *boat?*"

△ △ △

Nate ("Nails") Koslovsky, a no-goodnik, was gunned down by hit men of the O'Callahan mob. Bleeding from bullet holes, Nails staggered up the stairs. "Mama!" he cried. "Mama!"

His mother flung open the door. "Nateleh!"

Nails clutched his bleeding abdomen: "Mama—I—"

"Don't talk," beamed Mama. "First eat; enjoy! Later, you'll talk."

Enough already

> Yinglish, *con brio*. From Yiddish: *Genug shoyn*.

> Stop! Say no more.

This once indigenous (to Brooklyn, the Lower East Side, the Bronx) phrase has infiltrated colloquial English and, although still anything but proper, seems to be growing within the American vernacular. It is used widely, albeit with a sense of amusement, in show business and in literary and journalistic circles. I have heard it tossed out, with full awareness of its *infra dig* onus, in London's Mayfair.

△ △ △

Haravitz got a job as a bus driver in Manhattan. His first day, his box took in $80. The next day, his box held $85. But the third day, his box coughed out over $450!

The supervisor said, "Hey, this is funny. How come?"

Answered Haravitz: "After two days on your route, I figure it's a dog. So I said, 'Enough already!' and I drove over to Forty-second Street. Mister, *that* route is a gold mine!"

Enough with . . .

From Yiddish: *Genug mit.*

That's enough about . . .

This imperative form is widely used by Bronxians and Brooklynites. It is deployed by others for jocular effect. I do not recommend it.

△ △ △

Philippe Doran, interior decorator, said to the Julius Grobniks: "I have gone through the apartment you just bought. Now, how would you like me to furnish it?"

"With nothing but the best!" said Mrs. Grobnik.

"I understand. What period do you favor?"

"Period?" blinked Mr. Grobnik. "What's punctuation got to do with it?"

"I mean the *style*," said Philippe. "Would you like—say, French?"

"I don't like the French."

"Then—perhaps Regency?"

"Regency-shmegency."

"Then—modern?"

"Modrin?" echoed Mr. Grobnik. "Every Sam, Dick and Larry has modrin."

Exclaimed Philippe Doran, "You simply must decide on a period."

Said Mrs. Grobnik, "Enough with discussing. I just want that my friends should walk in, take one look, and drop dead—period."

See AGAIN WITH . . .

entitled

The remainder ("to that"; "to the privilege") is ignored. As in the Yinglish "Enjoy," transitive verbs are converted to intransitive colloquialisms:

How I need a vacation! I'm entitled.

Let her use the washing machine now; she's entitled.

From now on, call him "Doctor." He's entitled.

△ △ △

EMPLOYEE: My wife insisted I should ask you for a raise. She says I'm entitled.

EMPLOYER: So I'll ask my wife if I should give it to you.

eppes

epes (standard)

> For humorous effect. From the Yiddish: *eppes,* via German: *etwas.**

Eppes has such economy, variety and aptness that it is widely used in Yiddish; now it is being transferred, right and left, to English. And for good reasons.

1. Something.
2. A bit.
3. Not much.

> *Eppes* smells in Denmark.
>
> He is *eppes* peculiar. ("He is a bit peculiar.")
>
> Give them *eppes* a contribution. ("Give them a minimum.")

But *eppes* also means:

4. Large, notable.

> Did *he* make *eppes* a contribution! ("He donated a very large sum.")
>
> Is he *eppes* stubborn! ("His stubbornness passeth endurance.")

5. Remarkable; prodigious.

Recent American slang uses the irritating (to me) "some kind of" to mean "extraordinary" ("She is some kind of singer!"). The Yiddish *eppes* does that more subtly:

"There is *eppes* a cook!" ("There is a cook whose merits are so many that it would be foolhardy for me to try to describe them in detail.")

"If ever I saw *eppes* a faker, that guy is one." ("I don't exactly know in what ways that man is a faker, but he is.")

6. Perhaps; maybe.

> You think he is *eppes* sober?
>
> I think she is *eppes* a hot number.

---

* The *tw* (pronounced *tv*) of *etwas* became the phonetic *p* of *eppes; t,* a dental voiceless explosive, fused with *v,* a labial voiced fricative.

7. For some reason; inexplicable.

All of a sudden, I am *eppes* not hungry.

8. Unsatisfactory; debatable.

You call that *eppes* lucky?

That's *eppes* not kosher.

9. Sort of; some sort of.

We've got to do something! Who has *eppes* an idea?

She was wearing *eppes* a costume from the Salvation Army.

△ △ △

MRS. RUBOFF: Did my husband give me *eppes* a birthday surprise! Two weeks in Aruba.
MRS. CANTOR: A*ru*ba? Where is that?
MRS. RUBOFF: I don't know. We flew.

Eskimo

American slang for Jew.

Why? I don't know. Perhaps because of the last syllable in "Eskimo." Moe, Ike and Abe seemed to be the most common names used in America to ridicule Jews. On the West Side of Chicago, "Abey" or "Ikey" was more commonly jeered at us than "kike" or "sheeny." Not that the latter were in short supply.

Eve

From Hebrew: *havvah,* or *havah.*

The first woman, created by the Lord out of Adam's rib.

You may be asking, "What is Eve doing in a book about Yinglish?" That is a fair question. Eve is here because I want her here—and I am writing this book. Besides, I have run into some fascinating data about our common mother; enjoy!

The first mention of Eve, in the Masoretic text, calls her *ishah* (Genesis 3:20) which is translated as "woman" because she was taken from man: *ish.* Adam is reported as having called his mate "woman" or "wife." No name. Adam also calls her *havvah* (or *havah*), to mean "the mother of all the living."*

Considering the everlasting brouhaha around the name and role of Eve, it is surprising that Genesis allots her so few lines. The *Encyclopedia of the Jewish Religion,* edited by Werblonsky and Wigoder, disposes of Eve in nine lines.

△ △ △

My favorite story about Eve is this: "Adam," said Eve, "after we eat the apple, we're going to do *what?*"

Every Monday and Thursday

Yinglish, and not essential.

1. Repeatedly.
2. Very often.
3. Surprisingly.

The reason these two days are singled out for purposes of illustrative emphasis is that Mondays and Thursdays are the days on which the Torah is read aloud in *shuls* and temples. (Those were the market days in ancient Judea.)

"That boy will drive me crazy! Every Monday and Thursday he has to have the car."

"What's gotten into that girl? Every Monday and Thursday it's a new boy!"

excuse the expression

No instance of Bronxian, Brooklynian or Lower East Sidean is more genteel (and grating) than this gratuitous apology. Purists say that "excuse the expression" marks the user as (excuse the expression) *déclassé.*

△ △ △

In a crowded bus in Tel Aviv, Lottie Avada kept groping for her purse. "Miss," sighed an old man next to her, "I'll pay for you."

---

* But *havah* raises prickly questions. See *Dictionary of the Bible,* James Hastings, revised edition by Grant and Rowley (Scribners, pages 266–267); and *The Torah: a new translation according to the masoretic text* (Jewish Publication Society, Philadelphia).

"No, thanks," said Lottie, and fumbled some more.

"Lady, *please!* Let me pay—"

"No. I'll get my purse open—"

"But till you get it open, you already unbuttoned three buttons on my—excuse the expression—fly."

F

fancy-shmancy

100 percent pure Yinglish.

1. Overly ornate.
   "Did you ever see such a fancy-shmancy reception?"
2. Pretentious, affected.
   "That fancy-shmancy Maurice Vermont. I knew him when he was Morris Greenberg."
3. Attempt at style that fails, hence is vulgar.
   "Their decorator is classy, but their furniture is fancy-shmancy."

The employment of the sardonic *shm (q.v.)* must have been among the earliest reduplications adopted by Lower East Side Jews. "Fancy-shmancy" came to the attention of cosmopolitan New York when it appeared in the very popular vaudeville sketches of Potash and Perlmutter, Smith and Dale, *et alia.* The mocking phrase then graced the fastidious pages of *The New Yorker* in essays by S. J. Perelman and stories by Arthur Kober.

farfufket

farfyufket

I recommend these with pleasure for robust Yinglish. Pronounced far-FUF-ket or far-FYUF-ket. Origin: uncertain (but the word is engagingly echoic).

1. Befuddled.
2. Discombobulated.
3. Taken aback, disoriented, unhinged.

If you are fond of the *farfufketer* or the *farfufketeh,* employ the playful *farfyufket.* The liquid *y* adds affection to accuracy.

See FARMISHT, FARTUMELT, FARTUTST, GEFUTZEVIT, TSEDREYT, TSE-DUDLT.

△ △ △

Little Joey was over an hour late coming home from school.

"Joey!" cried his mother. "What happened?"

"I was appointed Traffic Guard. I have white gloves and a white band across my chest. And I am supposed to stop traffic and let the kids cross the street."

"So—o? You got so *farfufket* you're over an hour late?"

"No, Ma; but you can't imagine how long I had to wait before a car came along I could stop!"

farmisht

farmishter (noun, m.)

farmishteh (noun, f.)

> Yiddish: mixed up. From German: *vermisch:* mix . . . mingle . . . cross.

> Confused; all balled up.

"I'm so *farmisht* I don't know whether I'm coming or going."
  "A *farmishter* like that shouldn't go for accountant."
△ △ △
"Mr. Rockefeller, you should move to our neighborhood!"
  "Really? Why?"
  "Because no rich man ever died there."
  See FARTUTST, GEFUTZEVIT, TSEDREYT, TSEDUDLT.

farpatshket

> Yinglish with scorn. Pronounced far-POTCH-k't. From Russian: *patchkaty:* sloppy. Yiddish, *patshken:* to soil; to dawdle.

> All messed up.

There is an echoic splash to *farpatshket* that I admire. Words like this should be treasured. "You call it art? *I* call it *farpatchket!*"

See ONGEPATCHKET.

farshtinkener

Pronounced far-SHTINK-en-er. From the German: *vershtinken:* to stink up.

1. All stunk up.
2. Disgusting, abominable.

This word may be spurned by Oxonian keepers of the flame, but it certainly serves its function pungently.

△ △ △

A *farshtinkener* anti-Semite, recounting his trip to Africa at a posh dinner, said, "It was wonderful. Our group didn't see one pig or Jew."

Ghastly silence.

Then the voice of Zvi Rodinsky was heard: "The two of us could have corrected that. We should have gone together."

fartumelt

Pronounced far-TOOM-elt. From German: *tummeln:* to rush around. Enrich your Yinglish with this adjective.

1. Bewildered.
2. Dizzy, confused.

See FARFUFKET, FARMISHT, TSEDUDLT.

△ △ △

Shepsel, in the following story, and Yunich, in the next, were undeniably *fartumelt*.

Ezer and Shepsel were taking a walk. Suddenly the heavens opened and the rain poured down.

"Shepsel, open your umbrella!"

Scoffed Shepsel, "My umbrella's not worth *bobkes*. It's full of holes."

"Full of—then why did you bring it?"

"Did *I* know it was going to rain?"

△ △ △

"Battling Ike" Yunich went into the ring for the first time. In the second round he took a terrific blow to the jaw that sent him to the mat flat on his back. As he tried to wobble up, his manager yelled, "No, no! Stay down until nine!"

Ike nodded, dazed. "What time is it now?"

See FARFUFKET, TSEDUDLT.

fartutst

Pronounced far-TUTST, with the *u* sounded as *oo* in "foot." From German: *verdutzt:* confused.

The state of being mixed up, bewildered.

When used as a noun, *fartutst* becomes *fartutster* (masculine) and *fartut-steh* (feminine). I commend both to your vocabulary.

△ △ △

"Your bill is two months overdue."

"What? Didn't you receive my check?"

"No."

"I'll put it in the mail immediately."

(This man was not *fartutst*.)

See FARFUFKET, FARMISHT, TSEDUDLT.

△ △ △

"Doctor, I have this terrible delusion that I am two people—two separate, independent people! I'm so *fartutst!* Do you think I need medicine? Do you think I—?"

"Hold it," said the doctor. "One at a time."

feh!

Yinglish, and priceless. From Polish/Slavic. This expletive can hardly be blurted without exclamatory emotion. In the Yiddish spoken in the Austrian empire, the same expletive, derived from German, was *fui* or *phui*. But *feh!* has a nastier, nose-wrinkling connotation.

1. Expression of disgust.
2. Epithet for indignant disapproval.
3. Forceful epithet to signify rejection.

I recommend the expletive as cathartic when:

Emerging from a porno film.

Stepping into dog-do.

Smelling a rotten egg.

Mentioning the candidate you voted against.

Describing the creeps who infest Forty-second Street.

Appraising certain works of modern art.

Experiencing any sight, or reliving any event, that arouses revulsion.

Railing against fate, misfortune or the inevitable.

△ △ △

"Old age! *Feh!*" snorted Mr. Binder. "So far, I found only one good thing about it."

"What's that?"

"While I'm singing, I can brush my teeth."

△ △ △

Sam Persky was walking along Broadway one night. As he approached Seventy-fourth Street he realized he had not seen his friend Herschel Bienstock for six months—in fact, not since Mrs. Bienstock had passed away. Persky hastened to Bienstock's apartment. "So how are you doing?"

"Oh, Sammy," quavered Bienstock, "I barely get along."

"Listen, Hersch, would you like a nice game pinochle?"

"I would love it."

And so the two friends played pinochle, until Persky shot a look at his wristwatch. "*Feh!*" he grunted.

"What's the *feh!* for?"

"My watch stopped. Herschel, what time is it?"

"Who knows?"

"I have to know. Give a look at your *zager*."

"I don't have a *zager*."

"So look at the clock in your kitchen."

"I don't have in the kitchen a clock."

"So the bedroom, Hersch! Your bedside table."

"On my bedside table I don't have a clock neider."

Persky's jaw dropped. "You mean to tell me that in this whole apartment you don't have one single watch or clock? For God's sake, don't you ever want to know what time it is?"

"Sure. When I want to know what time it is, I pick up my bugle."

"Your what?!"

"My bugle." Bienstock leaned over and from the floor lifted a shiny bugle. "I'll show you." Bienstock went to a window, put the bugle to his lips, and blared a forceful "Ra-ta-ta-ta-*tah!*"

And from a dozen flats in the courtyard came: "What's the matter with you, you crazy, playing the bugle at a quarter to eleven at night?!"

feygele (standard)

faygele

Pronounced FAY-geh-leh. Diminutive of Yiddish *foygl:* little bird.

1. A little bird.
2. A jailbird.
3. An unruly young rascal who may end up as a *foygl.*
4. A young man of great delicacy, great sensitivity, or effeminate manners.
5. A homosexual, plain and simple.

This euphemism was common in Jewish circles long before the English word "gay." In the Talmud there is a descriptive term, *tum-tum,* which gives you the general idea. *Tum-tum* more accurately referred to a shy, beardless adolescent or a hermaphrodite.

△ △ △

"Mrs. Yastrow, is it true what I hear about your son?"
"What do you hear about my son, Mrs. Beckman?"
"That he announced he's a practicing homosexual."
Mrs. Yastrow moaned. "It's true."
"So where is his office?"

△ △ △

A Jewish *feygele* ordered the following inscription on his tombstone:

GAY IN DRERD*

fifer

fayfer (standard)

Rhymes with "lifer." From German: *Pfeifer:* whistler.

1. A man who whistles a lot, often unconsciously.
2. A shrill, noisy person.
3. A boaster.
4. Someone who talks adenoidally.

A *fifer* is not necessarily a *fonfer;* the latter will talk your ears off.

△ △ △

Sherman Toffel had just moved into his new office. On the door gleamed:

TRIUMPH INVESTMENT COUNSELORS
Pres. SHERMAN TOFFEL

Sherman, a *fifer,* was president of nothing but himself, and he had no secretary, so when there was a knock on the door, Sherman called,

---

* If you are puzzled: in Yiddish, *gai* means "go," *in drerd* means "into the earth."

"Come in," and lifted the phone, into which he briskly said, "Mr. Morgan, we bought you ten thousand." He waved the visitor to a chair. "After discussing it with the Merrill Lynch people, I advise selling the potash and going into manganese. How much? Four million? Thank you, Mr. Morgan!" Sherman scribbled a note and put the phone down. "Now, sir, can I help you?"

"Well," said the visitor, "I came to hook up your telephone."

fin

American slang. From Yiddish: *fin(i)f.*

1. Five.
2. Hand (five-fingered).
3. A five-dollar bill.
4. (Criminal cant) A jail sentence of five years.

Fin is widely used, and known, in the vernacular—especially among sports fans, gamblers, Broadway types, gossip columnists. The slang word appears in Damon Runyon's world, in stories by John O'Hara and S. J. Perelman, and in detective fiction.

I do not support H. L. Mencken's attribution: that *fin* is derived from the German *fünf* (five), which is pronounced "foonf." But in Yiddish the word for "five" is *finif*, pronounced FIN-if. I believe English speakers adopted the Yiddish, not the German, pronunciation because the effort of Anglo-Saxons to vocalize an umlaut results in ear-bending renditions: *Führer* becomes "furore," "fyoorer," "fooroar," "furrer." But no one can mispronounce *finif*.

fonfer (noun)

fonfet (verb—in Yinglish, *fonfes*)

Pronounced FUN-fur. From Slavic: to speak through the nose. A worthy candidate for Yinglish.

1. Someone who habitually talks through his nose: "I ab sorry"; "He bay (may) buy it." (Sholom Aleichem has a very funny character like that.)
2. A double-talker, a deceiver, a cheat. "That *fonfer* will talk you out of your shirt."
3. A procrastinator.
4. A lazy worker who wastes time in palaver: "She *fonfes* more than she works."

5. One quick to promise, who does not deliver: "He *fonfes* promises."
6. A braggart. A *fonfer* capitalizes on "the patter of little feats." (Leonard Levinson)

See PLOSHER, TROMBENIK.

△ △ △

BOMBERG: Did *I* get an order! From the J. C. Penney stores. For three hundred thousand dollars!

FLAMBERG: Stop with the *fonfing*.

BOMBERG: You don't believe me? I'll show you the cancellation.

△ △ △

"I come from a famous fighting family!" *fonfed* Mrs. Roger Donaldson. "My great-great-grandfather fought the rebels at Gettysburg. My great-grandfather fought the Germans at Verdun. My grandfather fought the Japs on Guadalcanal. And my father fought the North Koreans—"

"*Mein Gott!*" exclaimed Mrs. Cooperman. "Can't your people get along with anybody?!"

Forbearance (via the repetition of a question without any comment whatsoever)

The nobility that spurns a response that would expose the idiocy of the questioner for asking such a question is packed into the interstices of the word units that make up a sentence coolly repeated:

Q. Will you accept a fee of twenty dollars?
A. Will I accept a fee of twenty dollars?

The answer means, "Can I believe my ears? Let me make sure—by repeating the question for you to hear—that I actually heard you ask me if I would accept a fee of twen–ty dollars. . . ." (Meaning: "Preposterous!")

The answer can, however, also connote enthusiasm:

Q. Will you take a thousand?
A. Will I take a thousand?

Meaning: "Wow! Will I!"

for free

Yinglish: From Yiddish: *far gornit (gornisht).*

For nothing; at no cost.

The placing of the superfluous "for" before the adjective is Jewish usage.

> A: I wouldn't go to a rock concert if it was for free.
> B: *I* wouldn't go if they paid me.

for-instance

> As a noun: pronounced "f'rinstance." From the English.

> 1. An example.
> 2. Be specific (preceded by "give a").

This usage, however inelegant, is making headway on the colloquial frontiers of English:
> "I think I know what you mean, but give me a *f'rinstance*."
> "Here are several *f'rinstances*."
> "The reviewers *praised* the book? Give me a *f'rinstance*."

Remember that the rabbis and the participants in the making of the Talmud constantly employed the device of seeking clarification via specific examples. (The Hebrew word *mashal* and the Yiddish *moshel* mean "example"—and both are heavily sprinkled throughout the two languages.)

Why *f'rinstance* should replace "example," for which it is an exact synonym, I cannot say—except that Yinglish expressions often strike Americans (and Englishmen) as striking, amusing or beguiling.

Even Secretary of State Dean Rusk once replied to a reporter: "About that question, can you be more specific? Can you give a *for-instance?*"

"from" instead of "of"

> From German: *von*, via Yiddish: *fun*.

In English, the use of "from" in place of "of" is incorrect, indefensible, ungrammatical—so you should never ever use solecisms like:
> "Who knows from vacations?"
> "My son doesn't know from barbers."
> "He's the King from Jordan."
—unless, of course, you are a pip at parody.

Damon Runyon forged a wonderfully colorful dialect, Broadwayese, an amalgam of baseball, gambling, racing, pugilist lingo. What is marked is the explicit influence of Jews upon all of them.

Frank Loesser's *Guys and Dolls* magically captured the Runyonesque characters and their startling Yinglish. (Consider the influence of writers Jo Swerling, Abe Burrows and George S. Kaufman, who also directed that tour de force.) The character Nathan Detroit produces a cascade of Yiddishized English whenever he opens his mouth; thus, "I could die from shame," etc., etc.

△ △ △

HUSBAND: Who are you mailing that to?

WIFE: The manager from my bank. I'm sending them a check for twenty dollars and sixty cents.

HUSBAND: Why?

WIFE: That's how much he said I'm overdrawn.

△ △ △

To celebrate his mother's eightieth birthday, her son sent her a bottle of champagne and a jar of caviar. That afternoon he telephoned. "*Mazel tov,* Mama!"

"Oh, thank you, Seymour! And thank you for the fine present!"

"You liked it?"

"The ginger ale I *loved,* dollink; but tell the store those little black berries taste from herring!"

From (that, this) he makes a living?

Yinglish, and nothing can be done about it.

"Do you mean to say that *that's* what he does to make a living?"

△ △ △

This is the climactic line from a famous joke:

A Jew asked his son, "Exactly what did Einstein do that was so smart?"

"Einstein revolutionized physics. He proved that matter is energy. That when light goes past the sun, it *bends.* That—"

"Awright, awright," said the old man. "But tell me: from that he makes a living?"

△ △ △

"What does your son-in-law do?"

"At the circus, twice a day, they shoot him out of a cannon."

"My! But from what does he make a living?"

From that, you could faint

From this, you could die

Why is "From this, you could die" funnier than "You could die from this"? Because placing the phrase "from this" in front defers the revelation of the consequence and thereby heightens curiosity (or dread) through the prolongation of tension.

△ △ △

For two weeks, Mr. and Mrs. Ziven had been waiting for word from their son Joseph, away at summer camp for the first time. At last, a precious postcard arrived. "From Joey! From Joey!" cried Mrs. Ziven. Her eyes raced across the written words. Then she passed the card to her husband, moaning, "From this, a person could *bust!*"

Here is the message on the card, *in toto:*

> DEAR MAMA AND PAPA,
>   They are making everyone write home.
>   JOEY

G

Galitzianer

Pronounced goll-ITZ-ee-ON-er.

A Jew from Galicia.

I have received a raft of inquiries about where Galicia (from which *Galitzianer* Jews came) actually is. It has nothing to do with the Galicia of Spain; it is in Central Europe, north of the Carpathians. It once was part of the Austro-Hungarian empire. Since 1919 Galicia has been annexed to Poland.

Jewish settlements in Galicia date back to the ninth century. Galicia was famed as a seat of Jewish learning. Its yeshivas produced great scholars and noted rabbis.

Rivalry between Galitzianer and Litvak (a Jew from Lithuania) was pronounced; Polish Jews were condescending to both; Russian Jews derided all three; and German Jews (Deutsche Yehudim) shuddered at all four.

In the United States, first-generation Jews envied second-generation Jews; and German Jewish families—Warburgs, Kahns, Schiffs, Lehmanns—formed an elite of noteworthy cohesiveness. The "pecking order" of this Establishment and its Pecksniffian patronage (of Russian and Polish Jews) is described by Stephen Birmingham in *Our Crowd: The Great Jewish Families of New York.* San Francisco's Jews were a distinguished group of descendants of settlers dating back to the Gold Rush.*

See LITVAK.

---

* For an illuminating inquiry into the values and conflicts within the Jewish communities in America, see Nathan Glazer's *American Judaism* (University of Chicago Press); Moses Rischin's *The Promised Land: New York's Jews: 1870–1914* (Corinth Books); articles in *The Jews: Their History, Culture and Religion*, Vol. II, third edition, Louis Finkelstein, editor (Harper); and *The Jews: Social Patterns of an American Group*, Marshall Sklare, editor (Free Press).

△ △ △

A Litvak friend of mine claims that the following advertisement must have been written by a Galitzianer:

FRIEDLANDER BRASSIERES, INC.

announces

a new line

of

ULTRA-LITE FALSIES

Beware of Imitations!

△ △ △

And a Galitzianer friend tells me about the young Litvak who paid court to Sooky Chammish. He finally went to her father and formally asked for Sooky's hand.

The old man said, "You're a nice young man, and my wife and I like you. But we have to be practical. Tell me, can you support a family?"

The Litvak blinked. "Who wants to marry the family? I only want to marry Sooky."

gefutzevit

Yinglish gloss of English slang "futz up." "Futz" is, of course, the vivid euphemism for the most explicit four-letter word in English. Euphemism or not, "futz" is itself taboo. Whether *gefutzevit,* which insulates "futz" at both ends with sonic padding, is also taboo, depends on the confidence or amusement with which it is deployed.

As an expletive:
1. All screwed up!
2. I've been screwed!

The exclamation is heard in blackjack when a player draws a card over 21, or in dice when a player rolls a 7 in mid-series to crap out, or in poker when a player gets a card that renders a hand useless.

As an adjective:
3. Confused, discombobulated.
4. Thrown for a loop.
5. Unfairly defeated.

△ △ △

The men's store of Chartog and Blitstein was very successful. Mr. Chartog liked to have a customer try on suit after suit, turning the man around and around before triple mirrors to see the garment from every angle.

Then Mr. Blitstein would say, "Let *me* show this gentleman the number that's best for him." And Blitstein usually made the sale. He would boast, "See what a salesman I am? *I* sold him on the very first try!"

Mr. Chartog would retort, "But who got him *gefutzevit?*"

See FARFUFKET, FARMISHT, TSEDUDLT, etc.

gelt

From German: *Geld:* money.

Money.

Roman law held that a monetary debt was personal (promissory notes could not become claims against an estate). In Germany a debt died when the creditor died. In England, up to the middle of the nineteenth century, some debts were not transferable.* But the Talmud ruled that for Jews *all debts must be honored*—even after the debtor or creditor died.

Popes, kings and noblemen enlisted (or preempted) the aid of Jews to finance their cathedrals, armies, palaces, estates—in this way transferring the medieval sin of usury to those outside the Christian fold, to souls already so obviously doomed to perdition that extra transgression did not matter. Jews were forced to become moneylenders (they were forbidden to own land, or join certain guilds)—and then were despised for the hateful occupation. Oh, Shylock . . .

The stereotype of Jews as good businessmen (they are certainly not better than Chinese, Arabs or Greeks) is not lessened by the delight Jews take in telling stories such as this:

Mr. Jacobs is drowning. "Help! Help!"

The lifeguard swims to his rescue and shoves him toward shallow water. "Now—can you float alone?"

"Migod," gasps Jacobs, "is this a time to talk business?"

△ △ △

INSURANCE SALESMAN: Mr. Langer, how much life insurance are you carrying?

LANGER: Ten thousand dollars.

---

* In Eastern Europe, Jews were often murdered, in ones or twos, or in the *en masse* orgy of a pogrom, to "cancel" debts owed them by pious noblemen.

SALESMAN: How long do you think you can stay dead on that kind of *gelt?*

△ △ △

Sign in the window of a pawnshop:

Come in! Don't be shy!
Borrow your way out of debt!

△ △ △

"Why is it," an English snob asked Chaim Weizmann, "that you Jews are said to be so mercenary?"

"For the same reason," replied Dr. Weizmann, "that you English are said to be gentlemen."

△ △ △

SCENE: *Garment Center, New York City*

PROSKOFF: Komer?!

KOMER: Don't get excited.

PROSKOFF: Five months already you didn't pay my bill! Where's my *gelt?*

KOMER: I was in the hospital! . .This afternoon, be*lie*ve me, I'll—

PROSKOFF: Believe you? I should kill you! (grabbing Komer by his lapels) Every time a new excuse—(stops) Komer, *this* you call a buttonhole?!

Get lost!

Yinglish. From Yiddish: *Ver farvalgert!* (Get lost), *Farlir zikh!* (Go lose yourself), *Ver farfallen!* (Go into hiding).

1. Go away fast.
2. Move on; don't hang around here.
3. Disappear!

One group of linguists think "Get lost" is an Americanism, and not of Yiddish origin: I maintain they are wrong. Sidewalk hawkers were a common sight in Jewish neighborhoods. These hustlers were gifted in gab, tireless in their "sell," and hated to be watched by the gawking kids who gathered to hear the pitch. To this undesired audience, a spieler would mutter, "Beat it!" or "Why don't you go home?" When none of these sufficed, the thwarted salesman might snarl, *"Farlir zikh!"* ("Go lose yourself!"). I was one of the urchins advised to get *farvalgert.*

Another datum from my experience: In Chicago during the 1920s, when Prohibition nurtured gangsters and violence galore, I sometimes heard the ominous "Get lost!" (to mean "Get away from here!"). The command was used by hoodlums who wanted no witness to their shenanigans. The striking phrase spread into street talk. One of my panelists was distinctly told "Get lost!" in New York back in the 1920s.

I believe that a Warner Brothers gangster movie—either with James Cagney or Edward G. Robinson—brought "Get lost!" to popular attention.

Gevalt!

Gevald!

> Pronounced ge-VOLLT! From German: *Gewalt:* powers; force. *Höhere Gewalt* is an "act of providence," or violence.

> 1. An exclamation of fear, astonishment, terror. "*Gevalt!* Fire!"
> 2. A cry for help. "*Gevalt!* Burglars!"
> 3. A desperate expression of protest. "*Gevalt,* Lord: enough already!"

Gevalt is both an expletive and a noun.

He took one look and cried, *"Gevalt!"*

"Now take it easy, don't make a *gevalt.*"

△ △ △

Man comes into the world with an *Oy!*—and leaves with a *Gevalt!*

△ △ △

A historic account of *Gevalt!* involves Countess Rothschild, part French, part English, who lay in childbirth in the magnificent bedroom of her mansion, moaning and wailing. Downstairs, her husband, the Count, wrung his hands anxiously.

"She's not ready to deliver," said the obstetrician. "Let's play cards."

They played cards.

Came the shrill cry from the Countess: *"Mon Dieu! Mon Dieu!"*

Up leaped the Count.

"No, no," said the doctor. "Not yet."

They played on.

Soon the Countess screamed, "Oh, God, oh, *God!*"

Up leaped the husband.

"No," said the doctor. "Not yet. Deal."

The husband dealt. . . .

A mighty *"Gevalt!"* was heard. The obstetrician leaped to his feet. "Now."

△ △ △

Mandel Nifkovitz made a fortune and decided to move to Oyster Bay. "Before we do that," said his wife, "we must change our name."

So it was as Mr. and Mrs. Manders Northridge that the once Nifkovitzes appeared on the social scene.

Their friendliness and hospitality won them many friends. They were even invited to join a country club.

And there, at a large dinner party, the servant serving Mrs. Northridge spilled a bowl of soup in her lap.

"*Gevalt!*" exclaimed Mrs. Northridge—"whatever *that* means!"

△ △ △

On the fairway of the Cedars of Lebanon golf course, Mr. Paslov was ambling along with his caddy when a ball struck him on the back of the head.

"*Gevalt!*" cried Paslov, clutching his dome.

Mr. Schonberg, the golfer who had teed off, hurried up with apologies.

Paslov cried, "You call yourself a golfer? You should be barred from this club! My head is *bleed*ing. I'll call my lawyer! I'll sue you for five thousand dollars!"

"B–but didn't you hear me?" protested Schonberg. "I yelled 'Fore!' "

Paslov said, "I'll take it."

Gezunthayt!

Yinglish. From German/Yiddish: health.

1. (Felicitation to one who has sneezed) *Gezunthayt!*
2. (Farewell greeting) Go in health! *(Gai gezunterhayt!)*
3. Health; good health (without the exclamation mark).

The English phrase used after someone has sneezed is, of course, "God bless you." The creator of this custom, in the West, was St. Gregory.

In our anthropologically oriented time, it is banal to remind readers that in many primitive societies, sneezing is believed to be the expulsion of one or another evil spirit. This belief is strong among the Zoroastrian Parsees, Indian tribes of the Americas and countless peoples in Africa and Polynesia. If you remember your Aristotle, sneezing was more empirically regarded: as a symptom of a pestilence.

The Romans did not cry God bless you! but *Absit omen!* ("Flee, omen!"). And the Spaniards, beholding the Cacique Indians of Florida in *Kachoo!*s, raised their arms to heaven and begged the sun to intervene against so evil an augury.

The range of Jewish sayings about health may be worth sampling:

Too much is unhealthy.

Your health comes first—you can always hang yourself later.

What a fat belly cost, I wish I had; what it does, I wish on my
enemies.

When there's a cure, it was only half a disease.

—FOLK SAYINGS

Eat a third, drink a third, but leave a third of your stomach
empty; for then, if anger overtakes you, there will be room for
your rage.

—TALMUD: *Gittin,* 70a

ghetto

Several etymologies are offered for "ghetto"; none is entirely
satisfactory to experts. The most common traces "ghetto" to the
Italian *barghetto:* part of a city. In Venice, the *barghetto* was the
foundry or arsenal section, to which Jews were confined.

1. The section of a city to which Jews were officially confined.
2. That part of a city in which Jews live as a self-segregated
   group.
3. (As an adjective) Coarse, whining, too meek.

The noxious idea of segregating Jews antedates the infamous Venetian
decree of 1517. The Lateran Councils of 1179 and 1215 issued fiats
which forbade Jews from having close or continued contact with Christians.

In Spain, from the thirteenth century on, Hebrews lived in *juderías*
that were gated and walled in—for their protection, it was said. In 1555,
Pope Paul IV ordered that the Jews in the several papal states be com-
pelled to live in quarters separated from Catholics. In Germany, laws
forced the Jews to wear a special badge, or a special (and funny) hat.
Other laws, in Germany, Spain, the Ukraine, Austria, *et alia,* at one time
or another forced Jews to attend "conversion" exhortations in churches;
and torture preceded enforced baptism.

It is worth noting that in Germany from the thirteenth to the mid-
nineteenth century, although Jews had to live in a separate area assigned to them, which they were not permitted to leave after dark, no
use was made of the word *ghetto.* A partition divided the Jewish from
the non-Jewish part of town. The Jewish section was called *Judengasse*
(Jews' street). But among Jews, the segregated area was called The
Street or The Place. Yet there was considerable concourse between Jews
and Gentiles: servants and maids often came into Jewish homes—as did
Gentile merchants, scholars, preachers.

Until the Nazis, of course.

... give!

Yinglish.

Slang imperative for:
1. Talk!
2. Tell!
3. Open up!

This colloquial command is familiar to any movie-goer:
"Who paid you, Lefty? C'mon, *give*."
"Who killed her, pal? . . . *Give!*"

... give a ...

Directly from Yiddish: *geb a* (familiar) or *get a* (formal).

Where Americans say "Take a look" and the English say "Have a look," speakers of Yinglish say "Give a look." (In Yiddish: *geb a kuk*.) Never say "Give a . . . " except for jocular effect.

1. Give, make.
"If anyone bothers you, give a scream!"
In this case, "give a" is superfluous; "scream" would be enough.
"Give a . . . " also serves to eliminate prepositions which are obligatory in English:
2. Give (me).
"If you want to chat, give a call."*

△ △ △

Captain Uriz of the Israeli navy asked the new lookout, "Markavy, suppose a man falls into the sea. What would you do?"
"I would give a holler, Man overboard! Man overboard!"
"Good. And suppose an *officer* falls overboard?"
Markavy hesitated. "Which one?"

glatt kosher

glat kosh'r (standard)

Often seen on Jewish stores. Hebrew: *glat:* smooth; *kasher:* clean.

---

* Modern Hebrew has adopted the Yiddish locution.

Wholly, truly, certified kosher.

You will see the sign *Glatt Kosher* on the windows of butcher shops or restaurants that strictly observe the dietary laws.

The reason for using *glatt* (smooth) is interesting: the *shochets (q.v.)* must carefully examine every slaughtered animal. If lungs show any sign of disease, notably tuberculosis (evidenced by nodules), the meat is declared unkosher *(trayf).* When lungs are totally free of any sign of disease, the meat is certified as *glatt* (smooth, free of any residue of serious ailment).

It should be noted that meat with nodules of a certain type may still be kosher, if a rabbi declared it kosher. *Glatt kosher* means meat unquestionably kosher. Only very pious Jews insist upon the *glatt:* to orthodox Jews, *kosher* is sufficient.

glitsh

German: *glitschen:* slip.

1. (Originally) A slide; to slide or skid on a slippery surface.
2. A risky undertaking or enterprise. "Be careful. It could be a *glitsh.*"
3. (In engineering, aircraft and computer circles) A mechanical defect.

During World War Two, two delightful neologisms for a mishap entered the language: "gremlin," from England, and *glitsh,* from aerodynamics wizards from the California Institute of Technology. The one I knew was Jewish.

Go

Yinglish.

Verb used without the conjunction "and." In English, one says, "Go *and* (see, look, ask, tell . . .)."

The imperative without a link to a conjunction is pure Yiddish: it is derived from the Biblical phrase, translated literally: "Go tell . . . " "Go praise the Lord . . . " (In English, these become "come": "Come, let us praise the Lord.")

"Go see who's at the door."

"Go give him a hand."

Please note that in this Yinglish construction there is no comma or oral pause after the verb, as there might be in English where a conjunction would be absent but understood, as in

"Go, tell him the bad news."

"Go, see if she's the one we want."

△ △ △

Molly Altman was delighted to hear what her cousin Minnie told her about the big penny scale. "Go step on it. I'll drop the penny. You'll see."

So Molly got on the scale. She watched the needle rise, then stop, leaned closer, then studied the chart. "Minnie. Go look: I should be five inches taller!"

Go fight City Hall

Yinglish (I think). Origin: uncertain.

1. What can one do?
2. What's done is done (the law is the law).
3. It's hopeless to try to change that.
4. Don't waste your time.

This expression can be used philosophically or bitterly, in resignation or in disgust. Prolonged usage may provide you with further nuances.

Where does this eloquent locution come from? The best possible explanation I have unearthed is this: The conclusion of a Yom Kippur hymn, forcefully exclaimed, goes *Gey shray khay v'kayom*, which literally means "Go cry out (to the living Lord)," but is taken to mean, with a certain skepticism, "Go *complain* to God: What good will it do?"

go for (instead of "going to be"; "going to be a")

Yinglish, and deplorable.

1. Studying to be. ("Are you going for lawyer?")
2. Aiming toward. ("Is she going for marriage?")

This transliteration from Yiddish scrapes my eardrums: never use it in my presence. (Or, to employ a classic Bronxism, "Don't fail to avoid it if you can.")

△ △ △

Louis B. Mayer was trying to get Marlene Dietrich to do a picture at MGM, on whose lot she had not worked for twenty years. "We'll give you anything you want, Miss Dietrich."

So persistent was Mayer, one of the most persuasive enthusiasts in Hollywood, that Miss Dietrich finally said, "Mr. Mayer, I'll do a test—if the cameraman is Joe Ruttenberg. He lighted me so magnificently when I was at Metro—he knows my face, my moods . . . "

"You'll have Ruttenberg," said Mayer.

The screen test was made. . . . Now Mayer, Ruttenberg and the incomparable Dietrich were in a projection room. When the test was finished and the lights flashed on, Miss Dietrich cried, "I—look—awful! My skin, my neckline—" She turned to Ruttenberg. "Joe, what's *happened* to you? Remember how gorgeously you lighted me before?"

Ruttenberg said, "Miss Dietrich, at that time I was twenty years younger. . . . "

(As a Hollywoodnik remarked: "Joe should of gone for diplomat.")

Go know . . .

Yinglish. From Yiddish: *Gey vays.*

1. How could I know?
2. How could you *expect* me to know?
3. How could *anyone* know?

"Go know that beautiful girl was an undertaker."

This vivid disclaimer shifts blame from one's self to the universe; it is matchless as a stratagem of self-exculpation: "Go know my line was tapped."

4. Don't be a fool and . . .

"Go teach a dog how to bark."
"Go show Picasso how to paint."

△ △ △

SCENE: *Hotel in Tel Aviv*

Mr. Harbash picked up the phone. "I would like some Seven-Up."

"Seven-Up? Yes, *sir!*"

The Seven-Up never arrived. But the next morning Mr. Harbash was awakened—at precisely seven.

(Go know he had talked to the night operator, not room service.)

△ △ △

"Mrs. Fein," frowned the doctor, "do you realize you're running a temperature of 103 point 4?"

"Go know; what's the record?"

gonef

gonif

ganev (standard)

> Rhyme with "Don if." Hebrew: *ganov:* thief.
>
> 1. Thief.
> 2. A clever person.
> 3. An ingenious child.
> 4. A dishonest, tricky character it would be wise not to trust.
> 5. A prankster.

The expression that accompanies the word reveals which meaning is intended:

> 1. If uttered with a grin, or an admiring raise of the hands, *gonef* is clearly laudatory. (A grandparent will say of a clever child, "Oh, is that a *gonef!*")
> 2. If uttered with dismay ("A *gonef* like that shouldn't be allowed among respectable citizens!"), the meaning is derogatory.
> 3. Uttered in steely detachment ("That one is a *gonef*"), the word describes a crook.
> 4. Said in admiration, with a cluck ("I tell you, there is a *gonef!*"), the phrasing is equivalent to "There's a clever man!"
> 5. The usage I find most interesting is *America gonef!* (*q.v.*).

Eric Partridge avers that *gonef* has been used in England since 1835. H. L. Mencken spells *gonef* as *ganov* and *gonov* and attributes *gun* (to mean a gunman) to it. This is absurd.

My favorite folk saying in this zone: "A man is not honest just because he never had a chance to steal."

△ △ △

The speaker, known for the sharpness of his tongue, ended his speech in the Knesset, Israel's parliament: "How can one have faith in this body —when half the members are idiots?"

The newspapers rang with denunciations of so harsh an observation.

The next day, the speaker rose. "I have been denounced for the statement I made before this body yesterday. I have been urged to apologize." He hesitated. "I apologize. I am happy to correct my observation: half the members here are not idiots."

(Now there was a *gonef.*)

Go talk to the wall

> From Yiddish: *Red tsu der vant.*
>
> 1. It won't do a bit of good.

2. You can't get through to him (her).
3. Don't waste your time.

Gotenyu!

Used accidentally or in reflex to stress despair or excitement. Pronounced GAWT (not *Gott*)–en–yew.

Exclamation:
1. Dear God!
2. Dear, sweet Lord!
3. How *else* can I describe how I feel?!

Please note that *Gotenyu!* is not uttered to ask God's help: it is a declamatory outburst that may simply signify joy, affection, misery, apostrophization. It adds emotion to entreaty, passion to supplication, and vigor to catharsis.

One reason *Gotenyu!* is used so often by Jews is that the word is not Hebrew, not "holy." The taboos about using a sacred word in secular situations continues to this day among the orthodox.

"Was I excited! *Gotenyu!*"

"Oh, *Gotenyu!* Are *you* in trouble!"

There is a saying that when in trouble, a Jew cries, "Oh, *Mamanyu!*" When afraid, he cries: "Oh, *Tatenyu!*" And when things are *really* black, she (I am no sexist) exclaims, *"Oy, Gotenyu!"*

Who can quarrel with such a stratification of might?

△ △ △

Teddy Somash came back from his trip abroad to announce, "Mama, Papa, I'm engaged. Look. Isn't she *wonder*ful?" Proudly, he showed his parents a snapshot.

"Teddy," asked his mother, "is she that—uh—fat?"

"N–no. She isn't *thin,* but . . . "

"And is she that tall?" asked Teddy's father.

"Well, she's a *little* on the tall side, but . . . "

"Is she Jewish?"

"No, Mama."

"Migod, Teddy, doesn't she have even *one* good thing—?"

"Papa, she's a baroness!"

Mama sank to the sofa. *"Oy, Gotenyu!* She can't even have children!"

✡ goy

goyim (pl.)

Hebrew: nation.

Gentile.

The Hebrew *goy* includes the nation of the Jews, whom Biblical text calls a *goy kadosh:* "a holy nation." The plural, *goyim,* was frequently used in ellipsis—a shortened reference with words omitted: thus "(other) nations (than we are)," therefore non-Jews. In time, and by the well-known linguistic process of extension, a Jew who was not a practicing Jew was called a *goy.*

Goy is generally used to mean "Christian," but the name long precedes Christianity. The Hebrews considered heathens, pagans, Egyptians, Assyrians, Greeks, Romans *goyim.*

A male *goy* is a *sheygets,* a female a *shikse (q.v.).*

Gentiles are not used to Jewish problems.

—FOLK SAYING

Never let it be slighted that the Talmud commands Jews to help the Gentile, no less than the Jew, to succor the poor *goy* and visit the Gentile sick, and bury their dead. The Psalms let no Jew forget that the mercy of the Lord embraced *all* of His creatures. The *Sefer Hasidim* ("Book of the Pious") says: "If a Jew attempts to kill a non-Jew, help the non-Jew."

△ △ △

God says: "Both the Gentiles and the Israelites are My handiwork: Can I let the former perish on account of the latter?"

—TALMUD: *Sanhedrin,* 98b

△ △ △

You are of course familiar with the witty and condescending quatrain created by (I believe) W. N. Ewer, although credited to Hilaire Belloc, who made no secret of his anti-Semitism:

How odd
Of God
To choose
The Jews.

The jingle was answered by some unknown wag:

Not news,
Not odd.
The Jews
Chose God.

To which some humble Jew responded:

Not odd
Of God:

Goyim
Annoy 'im.

△ △ △

Harry Abramovitz wanted to join the Greenvale Country Club, a club known never to have had a Jewish member. This deterred Harry not at all. First, he went to court and had his name changed from Harry Moses Abramovitz to Howard Trevelyan Frobisher. Then he flew to a plastic surgeon in Switzerland, who transformed his Semitic profile into a Nordic one. Then he hired a tutor from England to change his Hester Street accent to the mellifluous modality of Regent Street. Then Harry worked his way into the graces of several members of the Greenvale Country Club. . . .

Two years after launching upon his project, Howard Frobisher, né Harry Abramovitz, appeared before the membership committee.

The chairman said, "Please state your name."

In plummy Oxonian accents, Harry said, "Howard Trevelyan Frobisher."

"And where were you educated, Mr. Frobisher?"

"The usual places: Eton . . . Oxford . . ."

The chairman beamed. "And what is your religious affiliation?"

"*Goy.*"

greeneh (f.)

greener (m.)

grine (standard)

> Pronounced GREEN-eh and GREEN-air.
>
> 1. A greenhorn.
> 2. A newcomer to America.
> 3. Someone not yet Americanized.

I doubt whether a day went by in a Jewish neighborhood without the words *greeneh* or *greener* being heard. No family I knew failed to "bring over" a relative from the Old Country. Often, the very first money saved was sent as transportation fare to a relative who had been left behind.

It is impossible for us today to appreciate the enormity of the decision to leave one's home and family to emigrate, no doubt forever, to a very strange land 5,000 miles away.

Stories about immigrants are endless. The trials, sagas, laughter and tribulations of the Jewish *greener* are masterfully depicted in the pages of the *Jewish Daily Forward.* Not the least remarkable stories appeared in the "Letters" column known as *A Bintel Brief.**

Read *The Old East Side,* an anthology edited by Milton Hindus (Jewish Publication Society), which has superb chapters by Abraham Cahan, Henry James (!), Jacob Riis, Lincoln Steffens. A trail-blazing book is *The Spirit of the Ghetto,* by Hutchins Hapgood (1902), recently reprinted. *World of Our Fathers,* by Irving Howe (with the assistance of Kenneth Libo), is a warehouse of valuable information.

See CASTLE GARDEN.

△ △ △

The *greener* ran down the slip at the Staten Island ferry and flung himself into space, across the patch of water, landing on the boat with a terrific crash. He picked himself up, breathing hard, dusting off his trousers. "I made it!"

"So what was your hurry?" asked a passenger. "We're coming *in.*"

△ △ △

GREENEH MOTHER (registering her daughter in elementary school): Her name is Rachel.

TEACHER: How old is Rachel?

MOTHER: Seven.

TEACHER: Father's name?

MOTHER: Herschel.

TEACHER: What language do you use at home?

MOTHER: Clean! Always! Never bad words.

△ △ △

The story is told about a strictly kosher restaurant on the Lower East Side in which the waiter was—Chinese. Even more astonishing, the *Chinaziker* rattled off the menu in effortless Yiddish and took all the orders in Yiddish. He even uttered the obligatory sarcasm of *vaiduhs* (*q.v.*) in Yiddish.

One night, as a customer was paying his bill, the *balebos* asked him, "Your foist time here, ha?"

"Yeah."

"So—my food—did you enjoy?"

"I enjoyed. But the best part of the meal, I have to tell you, was meeting a Chinaman who speaks such foist-class Yiddish."

"Shh!" hissed the proprietor. "He thinks I have been teaching him English!"

---

* A collection translated by Isaac Metzker was recently published by Doubleday.

gunsel

gendzl (standard)

gunzel (English slang)

> Pronounced GUN-z'l or GON-z'l. Origin: fascinating but not proved. From Yiddish: *gendzl:* gosling.

In American slang and underworld cant, *gunsel* was used to characterize an inexperienced young man. It has been drastically transformed to designate:

1. A drifter or hobo.
2. A homosexual's love object.

In 1915 or so, *gonzil* or *gunsel* came into use among prisoners (and bums) to mean what I just said it means.

3. A young hoodlum.

The first time I encountered *this* usage was in a piece in *The New Yorker* by S. J. Perelman: "Scores of hoodlums, gunsels, informers, shysters . . . "

4. A young thief or criminal.

A movie advertisement for *The Mob* (1951) described the protagonist (I can hardly dignify the bum by calling him a "hero") as "a run-of-the-mob gunsel."

5. A young gunman—not in the West, but in urban criminal circles.

You may remember this usage in the movie *The Maltese Falcon.* Humphrey Bogart derisively called the icky gun-toter Wilmer (memorably played by Elisha Cook, Jr.) employed by Gutman (immortally created by Sydney Greenstreet) his *gunsel.*

It is not clear whether pronouncing the word as *gunsel* conveyed the image of a gunman. Was *gunsel* or *gunzel* used in American slang independently of *gendzl?* In Yiddish, *gandz* (goose) is a colorful synonym for "fool," and *gendzl* (little goose) means a young fool; in German *Gänschen* is used for a foolish girl.

Gut Shabbes

Gut Shabes (standard)

Used as Yinglish for certain effects. Pronounced goot ꜱʜᴏʙ-bes. From German *gut* and Hebrew *Shabbat:* "the Sabbath."

1. The customary greeting, freely and widely used by Jews, on Friday eve and Saturday; both a salutation and the expression of a hope to the one greeted. If you want to hear a fusillade of *"Gut Shabbes!"*'s just stand at the entrance to any synagogue or temple. The greetings are delivered both on entering and leaving.
2. The climactic comment in an anecdote or joke.

An amusing adaptation of the traditional salutation occurs in many stories, to mean "That did it!" or "You can't top that!" or "Would you be*lieve* it?"

△ △ △

The mayor of a certain town in Romania was a notorious anti-Semite. It astonished bystanders, therefore, when the mayor's auto caught fire and old man Stolovich ran over with a bucket, emptied the bucket, ran back into a store, filled the bucket, came out, emptied it again, started to run back, panting and sweating. . . .

A woman tapped Stolovich on the shoulder. "Slow down. You'll get a heart attack. Anyway, do you think a couple of pails of water can do any good?"

Said Stolovich: "Who said it's water? It's kerosene. *Gut Shabbes.*"

△ △ △

"Mrs. Bolinsky," said the judge, "this case hinges on your testimony, and you have described what you saw on a dark night a whole block away from the accident, so I must ask you: How old are you?"

"I," said Mrs. Bolinsky, "am fifty-four—plus a few months."

"Mmh . . . how many months?"

Mrs. Bolinsky pondered. "A hundred and two."

"Gut Shabbes!"

△ △ △

Sign:

Sᴀᴍ Sʟᴀɴꜱᴋʏ

ʜɪ-ᴄʟᴀꜱꜱ ᴛᴀɪʟᴏʀ

I will mend for you.

I will press for you.

I will even dye for you.

Gut Shabbes.

H

Hadayadoodle?

"How do you do?"

This is a mischievization of "How do you do?" The coinage simply testifies to the fact that some people get tired of clichés. Linguistic play, not to say inventiveness, is prized by Jews.

△ △ △

SCENE: *Maslinsky's Delicious Restaurant*

MASLINSKY: *Hadayadoodle.* Are you enjoying?

CUSTOMER: What?

MASLINSKY: My food.

CUSTOMER: I could get more nourishment biting my lips.

Hagadah

Hagode (standard)

Pronounced ha-GOD-da. Hebrew: tale.

The narrative read aloud at the Passover Seder that recounts the story of Israel's bondage and flight from Egypt.

The *Hagadah* contains psalms, prayers, hymns—even amusing jingles to hold the interest of the children, who must sit through a very long ceremony.

Do not confuse *Hagadah* with *Agada,* which comprises all of the Talmud's allegorical material: fables, folklore, parables, anecdotes. The legal and theological portions of the Talmud constitute *Halakhe (q.v.).*

✡ Halakhe (standard)

Halakha

Halakah

> Pronounced ha-LOKH-a in Yiddish, using the guttural *kh*. He-brew: law.
>
> 1. Jewish law, including all of the accumulated decisions of the sages.
> 2. That portion of the Talmud which comes from the Oral Law as distinguished from the Written Law, which is the Torah plus all legalisms from the rest of Holy Scripture.

The Talmud consists of *Halakhe* (law) and *Agada* (fables, folklore, anec-dotes, etc.).

Halakhe is the codification of the orally transmitted commentary and interpretation of the Written Law. Example: the Pentateuch (Torah) forbids "all manner of work on the Sabbath," illustrating work with five or six examples. But in the Talmud, two huge tractates (*Shabbat* and *Eyruvin*, or *Eyrubin*) expatiate upon, dissect and embroider the meaning of "work."

The oral tradition was believed to be contemporaneous with the Written Law. What is crucial to remember is that Jews were originally forbidden to recite (or "read from memory") the Written Law, *or* to fix Oral Law by writing it down. The danger this presented—*i.e.*, the ulti-mate loss or misconstruction of passages—was magnified by repeated persecutions, which interfered with the considerable time required for the massive amount of memorization. Rabbi Judah ha-Nasi ("the Prince"), so revered in rabbinical literature that he is called simply "Rabbi," decided to codify the oral tradition in the third century C.E. That codification, in six "orders," is the *Mishna,* the first part of an entry in the Talmud.

The *Halakhe* also performed the historic task of adapting the laws of Moses to post-Biblical problems.

Hallelujah

> From Hebrew: Praise ye Yah (the Lord).
>
> The joyous expression used in liturgy and religious hymns, sometimes to signal the end of a psalm or hymn.

The *Yah* is probably the abbreviation of JHVH (YHVH).

In the 1611 English authorized (King James) version of the Bible, the "Alleluia" of the Latin Vulgate was used. (The Vulgate, for a thousand years the Bible of England and Germany, is still used in Spain, Italy and France.) *

halva

halvah

> Pronounced holl-VAH. From Turkish: *helva,* and Arabic: *halwa.*

> A very sweet flaky confection made of honey and sesame seeds.

Halva is a *nosh (q.v.)* or dessert. Contrary to myth, it is not a Jewish goody. It was unknown to the Jews of Eastern Europe. They first encountered it in New York, where it was sold by Turkish, Syrian and Armenian vendors. (I, too, find this hard to believe.)

✡ Hasid

Hasidic (adjective)

Hasidim (pl.)

Chasid

> Pronounced KHA-sid; the *kh* must be rattled as if clearing fishbones out of your palate. Hebrew: pious one.

> 1. A follower of the Hasidic sect. The men are fully bearded, with *peyes (q.v.),* usually wearing a broad-brimmed black hat, a white shirt, no necktie, and a long black coat.
> 2. A revered, idolized, often self-ordained mystic leader, treated by his disciples as a saint and a prophet.

The Hasidic movement, strongly opposed by many rabbis and other Jews as too fundamentalist, mystical, reactionary, was founded by Israel ben Eliezer (called the *Baal Shem, q.v.*) in the mid-eighteenth century.

---

* Neither Greek nor imperial Latin used the letter *j:* the vowel *i* served as a consonant when it appeared before a vowel (not unlike the Hebrew letter *yod*). *J* was a medieval variant of *i,* used to begin a word. Until the eleventh century, both *j* and *i* were pronounced as *y* when they preceded a vowel; then the *y* of *foreign* words was rendered in English with the Anglo-French *dz* sound. The earlier pronunciation of the *j* as *y* is, of course, preserved in *Hallelujah.*

His teachings emerged from intense absorption in cabalistic works. He derogated Talmudic casuistry, formal services in synagogues and doom-laden preaching. He preached a gospel of joy and ecstasy, happy dancing and hand-clapping to celebrate the Lord. See *The Hasidic Anthology*, edited by Louis Newman, and the classic two-volume *Tales of the Hasidim*, by Martin Buber. Elie Wiesel's *Souls on Fire* (Random House) is a gallery of moving, vivid portraits of the charismatic leaders of the Hasidic movement.

A negative view is Arthur Cohen's:

> Hasidism is generally regarded as a happy, joyful, life-affirming teaching, manifest in wise sayings, marked by exuberant song and unconstrained prayer. This notion owes its longevity to the misemphases characteristic of Martin Buber's rendition of Hasidic literature. . . .
>
> The corrective to this mistaken view has been the life work of Gershom Scholem, who has shown in an impressive series of studies that the Kabbalah continues to counter the settled assumptions of traditional orthodoxy. Hasidism emerges from the Scholem reconstruction as a multivalent religious phenomenon, not at all as univocal and coherent as the Buber fabrication would have it.
>
> —*New York Times*, January 13, 1980

In justice to the Hasidim, I should mention that Gershom Scholem has, in turn, been severely denounced by Rabbi Chaim Liberman, follower of the famous Lubavitsher *Rebbe*.

△ △ △

Critics of the Hasidim remark that their excessive piety often turns into fanaticism. In the Williamsburg section of Brooklyn, bloody riots periodically break out when hundreds of Hasidim hurl eggs, bottles and rocks at a rival Hasidic group. Recently, five or six hundred loyal Satmars attacked equally orthodox Belzers; the former are passionately anti-Zionist; the Belzers are just as vehemently Zionist. A police officer later said: "It's like the Hatfields and the McCoys." A departing Satmar said, "We're going to drive them out [of Brooklyn]!" A departing Belzer said, "These are terrible people. They terrorize everyone!" (See *New York Times*, March 2, 1981, page 3, section B.)

△ △ △

The old cobbler blinked as he read the salutation in the note from the Hasid, delivered with a pair of shoes by one of the holy man's disciples:

> O, Shining Light of Israel! O, Sentinel of Our Faith! O, Tower of Learning! O, Ocean of Wisdom:
> Please mend these shoes.

The cobbler hurried to the Hasid's home. "*Rebbe*, I am only a cobbler so I do not understand your note to me: such a—a lofty greeting!"

"Lofty?" echoed the holy man. "I was not aware . . ."

"Oh, *Rebbe!* You called me the Shining Light of Israel, the Sentinel of Our Faith, a Tower of Learning—"

With a puzzled frown the Hasid said, "But that's the way people always address me."

✡ Haskala

Rhymes with "La Scala." Hebrew: knowledge, education.

The movement of enlightenment and secular education among Jews: the forerunner of Reform Judaism.

Haskala was launched by Moses Mendelssohn (1729–1786) and was bitterly denounced by orthodox Jews, who recognized the threat that secular education, Western rationalism and philosophy posed to traditional faith. Those who followed the *Haskala* called themselves "enlightened ones" or *Maskilim.*

Hau boy!

1. Oh, boy!
2. Oh, Lord!

One of the songs the late Allen Sherman wrote and sang in his very popular record *My Son, the Folk Singer* contained a marvelous set of phonetic-affective plays upon the pitch, intonation and stress of "Oh, boy"—excited, querulous, sad, triumphant. . . . Mr. Sherman's ear was acute, his mimicry faultless.

△ △ △

The celebrated Weizmann Institute perfected a robot that could answer questions never before programmed into electronic devices. At the first demonstration of this marvel, lines four blocks long formed. Scientists, tourists, journalists, laymen, poured questions at the astonishing I-Can-Answer-Any-Question Robot. The most memorable feat of all, in my judgment, was this:

SCHNECKER: Where, at this very moment, is my father?

ROBOT: Your father is sunning . . . with a beautiful blonde . . . on the beach . . . in front of the Sheraton hotel . . . in Tel Aviv.

SCHNECKER: Wrong! Wrong! (laughing) My father is Mr. Harry O. Schnecker and I just spoke to him on the phone. He's with my mother in their apartment in Haifa. What do you say to that?

ROBOT: Harry O. Schnecker *is* . . . with your mother . . . in their apartment . . . in Haifa. But your *father* is on the beach . . . with a beautiful blonde . . . in front of the Sheraton . . . in Tel Aviv.

SCHNECKER: *Hau boy!*

healthnik

A health nut.

△ △ △

SCENE: *Doctor's Office: Park Avenue*

"Mr. Esner," said Dr. Pokrass as he completed his physical examination, "you're in *terrible* shape! You simply must start taking exercise!"

"I hate exercise."

"You must begin jogging!"

"Jogging?" wailed Esner.

"Slow, sensible jogging. Your first week, jog five blocks a day. The next week, jog ten. The week after that, fifteen . . . and so on. And after you've reached the point where you can run two-three miles every day you'll be a new man! Call me in a month. Goodbye."

The days passed. The weeks passed. Then Dr. Pokrass' phone rang. "Hello?"

A voice puffed, "Heh . . . heh . . . this—is—Esner. . . ."

"How's the jogging?"

"Doc—you're—talking to a dead man! Arches? No more. Spine? Like a needle! Head? Like a boiler! Every *inch* of my whole body is on fire—"

"Mr. Esner, don't panic. Jump in a cab and come over."

"Cab?" echoed Esner. "I'm in *Albany!*"

Hebe

Pejorative abbreviation of "Hebrew."

Jew (offensive).

I give you a jingle I heard at the University of London:

> Roses are reddish,
> Violets, bluish:
> If it wasn't for Christmas,
> We'd all be Jewish.

△ △ △

Said Albert Einstein when his astounding theory had not yet been confirmed: "If my theory is proved, Germany will claim me as a German, and France will declare me a 'citizen of the world.' If my theory is proved wrong, the French will say I am a German, and the Germans will say I'm a Jew."

heder

cheder

> Rhymes with "braider." Rattle the *h;* it's a *kh.*

1. Hebrew school.
2. A room where Hebrew is taught.

At the end of a boy's first day in the *heder,* it was the custom for his mother to embrace and enfold him as she prayed that he "fulfull his years" with three things: the study of Torah, marriage, and *mitzves* (good deeds).

Let historians and educators, sociologists and anthropologists note that when 90 percent of humankind was illiterate, every Jewish male over five or six (unless mentally deficient) was learning to read and write. I would make the point more strongly: when 90 percent of the human race could not read or write, a great many Jews could handle at least *three* languages: Hebrew (for prayer, Talmudic study and discourse); Yiddish or Dzhudesmo (the "mother's language," spoken in the home); and the language of the nation in which they lived: Russian, Polish, English, Italian, Spanish, French, German, Czech, Greek, Turkish, etc. . . . It surprises me that so little has been made of this phenomenon by culturologists.

△ △ △

On a Jewish boy's first day in Hebrew school the teacher would show the child the alphabet on a chart, and before (or after) the lad repeated the teacher's *aleph* a drop of honey was placed on his tongue. "How does that taste?" the teacher would ask.

"Sweet."

"The study of Torah," was the response, "is sweeter."

Sometimes the boy's mother would give him honey cakes shaped in the letters of the alphabet before he went off to *heder,* or when he returned, to make him remember: "Learning is sweet."

And after the boy's first day in the *heder,* some parents would hide a coin under his pillow or drop a coin before him. "Ah, an angel dropped that from heaven—to tell you how pleased is God that you have learned your first lesson."

△ △ △

When the new boy came to *heder,* the *melamed* asked, "Can you read Hebrew?"

"Read Hebrew?" the lad blinked. "I haven't even been here two minutes!"

△ △ △

Deborah, age ten, returned from her Bible class at the Temple.

"So darling," beamed her mother, "what did you learn today?"

"The children of Israel, the children of Israel!" griped Deborah. "Mama, didn't the grownups ever do *anything*?"

hok

hak (standard)

> From Yiddish/German: to hit.
>
> 1. To yak-yak-yak.
> 2. To criticize interminably.
> 3. To nag.

The most potent retort to anyone *hoking* you is the celebrated Yiddish saying *Hok mir nit kayn chainik* ("Don't knock me a teapot"). This robust complaint/plea has been shortened to the verb alone.

> "I'll go, I'll go: don't *hok* me anymore."

> "Stop *hoking!* I'll think it over."

△ △ △

"So how's business?"

"Terrible."

"I hear your season was disappointing."

"It was a disaster!"

"They say you were ready to sell out and move to Arizona."

"Maybe further!"

"But then Korngold came to you with a fantastic offer."

"Better than fantastic!"

"And now—"

"Wait a minute. You seem to know the whole story—"

"That's true."

"—So why are you *hoking* me?"

"This is my first chance to get all the *de*tails."

hole in the head

> Accepted from Alaska to the Hebrides. Directly from the Yiddish: *loch in kop* (pronounced LAUKH-in-kup).

> I need it like a hole in the head.

This is pure Yinglish, widely heard in the United States and the United Kingdom. It frequently appears in newspapers, movies, television shows. It was propelled into our vernacular by the play *A Hole in the Head,* by Arnold Schulman, and more forcibly impressed upon mass consciousness by the Frank Sinatra movie. ("Movie" is a word so American it does not appear in the great thirteen-volume *Oxford Dictionary of the English Language.*) "Hole in the head" was used with vigor, in Yiddish/English/Yinglish, for a century B.S. (Before Sinatra).

homentash (standard)

hamantash

> The sweet pastry, stuffed with prune jam or poppy seeds, eaten to celebrate Purim. The name means "Haman's pocket," after the hideous Haman who wanted to murder all the Jews in Persia.

See PURIM.

hoo-ha

hu-ha (standard)

1. An exclamatory flourish that accentuates sentiments ranging from aspirated admiration to hoarse scorn. (See below.)

2. A big to-do; confusion, complexity.
   "That was some *hoo-ha* in Times Square!"
   "What was I supposed to do in the middle of such a *hoo-ha?!*"

3. A fuss, "stink," a stir, an issue magnified.
   "Did she make a *hoo-ha* about the service!"
   "I'll give them a *hoo-ha* they'll never forget!"

As an expletive, this immensely versatile declamation serves to express:
1. Admiration: "His new wife? *Hoo-ha!*"
2. Envy: "Is he well off? *Hoo-ha.*"
3. Deflation: "That you call an actor? *Hoo-ha.*"
4. Skepticism: "It's a foolproof deal? *Hoo-ha.*"
5. Astonishment: "He joined the Navy? *Hoo-ha!*"
6. Scorn: "Does she gossip? *Hoo-ha.*"

Do not for a moment think that this sextet exhausts the affective possibilities of this hyphenate. Facial and vocal counterpoint will register other sentiments with distinctive piquancy or dubiety:

7. You can't mean it! ("You'll leave home? *Hoo-ha!*")
8. Imagine! ("He moved to Japan? *Hoo-ha.*")
9. Wow! ("The party? *Hoo-ha!*")
10. Like hell. ("I should donate to his campaign? *Hoo-ha.*")
11. Who do you think you're fooling? ("Do I believe you? Every syllable, *hoo-ha.*")
12. Well, I'll be damned! ("In the chapel, in the middle of the eulogy, she just stood up—*hoo-ha*—and walked out!")
13. I'd like to live long enough to see that! ("He's going to win the Kentucky Derby? *Hoo-ha.*")

△ △ △

DISCIPLE: Master, do you believe that money isn't everything?
SAGE: *Hoo-ha.* It isn't even enough.

△ △ △

SCENE: *Post Office*

CLERK: This package—you'll have to put more stamps on it.
ITKOV: Why?
CLERK: It's too heavy.
ITKOV: *Hoo-ha.* And will more stamps make it lighter?

How come?

How come you . . . ?

> From Yiddish: *Vi kumt es . . . ?* "How come [is] it . . . ?"

The conventional English interrogative runs, of course, "How is it that you . . . ?" Yinglish reduces "is it that" to one word: "come," the exact calque for *kumt.*

"How come you didn't show up?"

"She's late. How come?"

The steady way in which alien words and phrases cross linguistic frontiers to infiltrate a language, all the while behaving as if they were citizens from way back, is nicely illustrated by this phrase. It sounds like perfectly acceptable, albeit colloquial, English.

△ △ △

Mr. Shenker met Mr. Jossel on Essex Street. *"Sholem aleichem."*

"Gey in drerd (go to hell)!" replied Jossel.

"Hanh? Are you crazy?! How come to my polite *Sholem aleichem* you answer 'Drop dead'?"

Mr. Jossel shrugged. "I'll explain. Suppose I answer '*Aleichem sholem.*' You naturally ask where I am going. I say I'm going to the *shul* on Avenue A. You say the *shul* on Avenue B is nicer. I say I never liked the *shul* on Avenue B. You holler, 'Any man who prefers the *shul* on Avenue A to the *shul* on Avenue B must have a hole in the head!' So I give you: 'Any man who chooses the big, cold *shul* on Avenue B to the darling little *shul* on Avenue A must be *meshugge!*' So you call me a dumb *Chaim Yankel!* So I cry, 'Ha? Insults? From *you* yet? *Gey in drerd!*' . . . Shenker, instead of going through such a *hoo-ha*, I answer right away, 'Drop dead!' That stops the discussion. . . . *Now* I say '*Aleichem sholem.*'" And off he went.

How's by you?

Yinglish, and unattractive. From Yiddish: *Vos iz mit dir?* ("What's wrong with you?" "Are you angry?" "Are you crazy?") or *Vi geyts bei dir?* ("How goes it with [by] you?").

1. "How are things?"
2. "What's new with you?"

I think the phrase improper except when deliberately used for humorous purposes, or by an immigrant, or to someone familiar with Yiddish.

The late Allen Sherman created a memorable Yinglish version of the French nursery song *Frère Jacques.* It began:

Sarah Jackman, Sarah Jackman,
How's by you, how's by you?

△ △ △

Mr. Kronen had moved to the suburbs. On the commuter train to Penn Station one morning, a neighbor, Mr. Ginzburg, asked, "So, Mr. Kronen. How is everything by you?"

"Now, it's okay. But it wasn't easy for me, living out in the country. In fact I was very, very discouraged until I got myself a paramour. What a difference that's made!"

"A *paramour*? . . . Uh—does your wife know?"

"Sure she knows."

"And she doesn't *mind?*"

"Why should she mind? She doesn't care *how* I cut the grass."

I

icky

> Possibly from the Yiddish *eklen* or *iklen:* to make nauseated, or *ekeldig:* disgusting.
>
> 1. Unpleasant.
> 2. Nauseating.

Icky is popular slang among teen-agers and young adults. No one seems to know where it came from: some believe it a clone of the *yeccch!* made so trendy by *Mad* magazine. I see no reason why Jewish children did not pick *yekh!* up from their parents' frequent use of the uvular fricative *kh.* From that to the unvoiced stop consonant *ck* is a breeze: indeed, it is much easier said than explained.

△ △ △

You want an icky story? Here's an icky story:

Old Mr. Charkin was taking his first trip by air. Just as the plane was ready for takeoff, a swarthy Arab in the traditional *kaffiyeh* (head-dress) and *jellaba* (robe) took the seat next to Mr. Charkin. He looked at the old man, buckled on his seat belt, and deliberately spat on Charkin's shoes.

Up went the plane. The Arab put his head back and dozed off. Soon the aircraft ran into a terrible storm: tremendous bouncings up and droppings down. Poor Mr. Charkin grabbed for his handkerchief —too late. All over the sleeping Arab's robes, Mr. Charkin threw up.

The old man closed his eyes and prayed to the Lord. With pounding heart he waited for his seatmate to awaken. . . .

And when the Arab yawned and opened his eyes, Mr. Charkin leaned forward and asked, "Are you feeling better now?"

I could bust from (aggravation, anger, envy)

Yiddish: *Men ken platsn* ("One can burst").

"Bust" is, of course, simply slang for "burst." But "bust" is the better English word for *plats*, which is Yiddish. The idea of someone actually exploding from emotional pressures is Yiddish to the core, and the core is precisely where such explosions originate.

△ △ △

Mendel and Morris, old pals, came out of a big wedding in a state of alcoholic euphoria. As they staggered home, Mendel stopped short. "Look! On the sidewalk. What *is* that?"

Morris focused carefully. "A ladybug."

"A *lady* bug? My God, Morrie, I could bust! Have you got eyesight!"

See FROM THAT, YOU COULD . . .

If my bubbe had wheels, she would be a wagon (a trolley car, a bus)

If my uncle had wings, he would fly

If my mother had a beard, she would be my father

The fanciful hypotheses presented above are used whenever an annihilating *reductio ad absurdum* is appropriate: whenever someone lingers over an "iffy" conjecture, or clings to a preposterous hope.

△ △ △

"If that *plosher* only stopped talking so much, he would win more arguments."

"And if his grandmother had wheels, she would be a wagon."

△ △ △

"If your sister had any sense she would drop that phoney like a hot potato!"

"And if your mother had a beard, she would be your father."

I'm telling you (that) . . .

Stuart Berg Flexner, co-author of *The Dictionary of American Slang*, flatly attributes this expression to the influence of American Jews (*I Hear America Talking*, Van Nostrand Reinhold).

In my opinion, we must distinguish between "I tell you . . ." and "*I'm* telling you." The former is, of course, straightforward English; it is, indeed, elegant, when used in the hortatory mode; it is the phrase which takes on majesty in the numberless admonitions of the New Testament.

In contrast, "*I'm* telling you . . ." is quintessential (translated) Yiddish: it uses the present participle dear to Jewish hearts; it calls attention beforehand to the fact that the speaker, and no lesser authority, is the source of the information to be revealed; and it places the self of the annunciator in the very center of the substance to be communicated.

△ △ △

I'm telling you: the best blurb I ever read was Groucho Marx's: "From the moment I picked this book up until the moment I put it down, I could not stop laughing. Someday I hope to read it."

. . . in good health

> From German via Yiddish: *gezunterhayt.*

This phrase is common amongst the children and grandchildren of Jewish immigrants, who often uttered obligatory phrases such as:
Go in good health.
Wear it in good health.
Use it in good health.
Take it in good health.
Travel in good health.
Sleep in good health.

Note that *gezunterhayt* does not only mean "in good health." The expression is also employed to register the favorable feelings of the speaker; "Borrow it *gezunterhayt*" does not mean "Borrow it in good health," but "I'm *glad* to lend it to you."

△ △ △

SCENE: *Fogel's Famous Fur Fair*
WOMAN: It's beautiful. I'll take it.
FOGEL: Thank you. Wear it in good health!
WOMAN: Thank you. I—I just hope it won't be damaged if I wear it in the rain!
FOGEL: Lady, did you ever hear of a mink carrying an umbrella?

ippy-pippy

ipsy-pipsy

Playful and amusing. Derivation: unknown (and who cares?).*

1. Everything is dandy!
2. Very fancy.

This exclamation, which I find enchanting, may be used derisively or with amusement, not unlike "fancy-shmancy."

△ △ △

HUSBAND (on phone): Darling, I have good news. You know that play you've been dying to see? I just got two tickets!

WIFE: *Ipsy-pipsy!* I'll start dressing!

HUSBAND: Good. They're for tomorrow night.

See NIFTER-PIFTER.

△ △ △

To the astonishment of his friends, Mendel Polstoker, a building contractor, won the competitive bidding for the digging of a tunnel under the English Channel.

"Mendel, how in the world do you plan to build a tunnel twenty-five miles long?"

"What's the problem?" asked Mendel. "I'll start a crew digging on the English side, and my son Howard will start on the French side. We dig and dig—until we meet."

"But, Mendel," said a civil engineer, "one of the toughest problems in all of engineering is plotting underground directions. You'll start digging in England, and your son in France—and those tunnels must meet *exactly!* Did you ever think of that?"

"Certainly. And if the tunnels *don't* meet? *Ipsy-pipsy:* My clients will get two tunnels for the price of one."

ish kabibble

Derivation: unknown; possibly a corruption of the Yiddish *nit gefidlt* (or *nisht gefidlt*).

1. I should care.
2. I don't care.
3. Why worry about it?

This extraordinary slang phrase, uttered with a shrug, was often heard from 1917 to 1947 to mean "So what?" or "It doesn't bother me," or (in current cant) "I couldn't care less."

---

* One expert rashly guesses that *ipsy-pipsy* is descended from *ipse dixit*—i.e., in approval of a dogma not really understood. In the same way, "hocus-pocus" became the demotic clone of *hoc est corpus*.

Fanny Brice, the Ziegfeld *Follies* comedienne and radio star ("Baby Snooks"), seems to have introduced "ish kabibble!" meaning "Why worry?" The phrase caught the attention of the "dean of cartoonists," Harry Hershfield, who launched a syndicated comic strip, *Abie the Agent,* about the adventures of one Abe Kabibble. It was called "the first adult comic strip" in the American press, and was immensely popular from 1914 to 1932 (*Editor and Publisher,* October 17, 1970).

A jazz song, "Ish Kabibble . . . (I don't care)," became the staple of a trumpet player in Kay Kyser's band (21,000,000 radio listeners weekly), who adopted the name, a *shlemiel's* manner, a funny haircut, nonsensical logic, and performed as a comic. He was a great favorite when touring U.S. army camps, and for a decade on NBC. He brought "Ish Kabibble" to millions of American children.

△ △ △

The Technion Institute in Israel developed an electronic machine for translating English into Russian. The machine was returned to the laboratory for improvement when this sentence was fed into it:

"The spirit is willing, but the flesh is weak."

—and this answer, in Russian, popped up:

"The vodka agrees, but the meat smells."

Shrugged the Chief of Translation, "Ish kabibble!"

I (you, he, she) should live so long!

I (you, he, they) should only live so long!

> Note the Yinglish "so" to replace the English "that."

The declamatory "You should live so long!" (or "You should only live so long!") is far from a petitionary benediction. It is an ironic invocation in which the irony accentuates the absurdity of the behest:

1. May I live as long as that will take!
2. That'll be the day!
3. He will take so long in delivering on that promise that I only wish I live long enough to see it, which I doubt.
4. I don't think you or I will live long enough to see *that* happen.
5. Don't believe it!

△ △ △

"Did you hear? Engelman pledged five thousand dollars to the Red Cross!"

"I should only live so long." (Engelman will never cough up five thousand dollars.)

△ △ △

"She said she'll sign the petition!"

"She should live so long!" (Who can believe her?)

△ △ △

"I hear that your wife . . . ran away with another man."

"I should only live so long!" (Who could ask for anything more?)

I should worry . . .

> Yinglish. Origin: uncertain. Several panelists think it related to *mayn bubbe's dayge:* my grandma's worry (concern, problem).
>
> 1. I won't worry (about that).
> 2. I would be a fool to worry about that.

If you question whether this locution is Yinglish, or if you believe it to be demotic English, you must ask yourself whether Americans ever used the phrase for inverse meaning before it appeared in the Jewish sectors of New York. The answer, to my mind, is No. The Yiddish equivalent, *mayn bubbe's dayge,* was used to mean, "Let my grandmother worry about that; I don't."

The phrase is uttered with a shrug, for (as noted) its meaning is opposite to its wording.

When I was young, the girls would chant:

> I should worry,
> I should care,
> I should marry a millionaire.
>
> He should die,
> I should cry,
> I should marry another guy.

In this doggerel, the meaning is:

> I don't worry,
> I don't care,
> I hope to marry a millionaire.
>
> Should he die,
> I may cry,
> But I'll marry another guy.

See ISH KABIBBLE.

✡ Israel

> Hebrew: Champion of God.

1. Precisionists used *Israel* only to name the people of the Northern Kingdom, where the ancient Ten Tribes of Israel dwelt.
2. The name of the state created on May 14, 1948.
3. Jewry as a whole.
4. Popular Jewish first name.

△ △ △

A Texan, visiting Israel, fell to boasting. "When you've been born and raised in the U.S.A., you just can't help feeling sorry for other people. Just think of the *heroes* I was brought up on: George Washington, Patrick Henry, Paul Revere . . ."

"Paul Revere? Isn't he the one who ran for help?"

△ △ △

Leonard Dubin, from Mount Vernon, was visiting Israel. One day he was taken by a guide to the unveiling of the Tomb of the Unknown Soldier. After much ceremony, speeches and fanfare, to the roll of drums and the blare of bugles, the covering tarpaulin was pulled aside. There stood a simple marble tomb. On the front, in fine Hebraic characters, was chiseled:

MORDECAI ABBA KASSELBAUM
Born: Kishinev, 1920
Died: Negev, Israel, 1980

Leonard Dubin frowned. "I thought this was the Tomb of the Unknown Soldier!"

"It is," said the guide.

"But that's absurd! 'Unknown'? Why, there's his name, his birth date, his—"

"Mister Dubin, don't get excited. You don't understand. As a *soldier*, Kasselbaum was unknown, but as a tailor—!"

Is the bride too beautiful?

> From Yiddish: *Di kale iz tsu shayn?* ("What's wrong? Is the bride too beautiful?")

Greater scorn is hard to imagine. To complain about the beauty of a bride is like carping about the colors in a sunset. A beloved folk saying, based on a passage in Talmud (*Kethubot,* 17a), runs, "All brides are beautiful."

△ △ △

When Yehudi Menuhin made his astounding debut in New York, musicians flocked to Carnegie Hall to hear the very young genius. Every famous violinist was there, among them Mischa Elman, with his friend, an equally famous pianist.

The boy Menuhin brought the house down with his wizardry. During one astounding display of virtuosity, Elman mopped his neck, whispering, "God, it's hot in here!"

His companion murmured, "Not for pianists."

Is the whole world crazy?

You mean the whole world is crazy?

> From the Yiddish: The *whole* world is not crazy.

> Sarcastic rebuke meaning, "Is everyone in the world wrong— except you?" or, "Cut it out! You can't be right; everyone else cannot be wrong!"

It can't (wouldn't) hurt!

> From Yiddish: *Es ken nisht (nit) shatn.*

The most famous use of this idiom occurred (I suspect the occurrence was fictitious) during a dramatic performance in a Second Avenue theater, when a star, at the climax of his great scene, collapsed.

"Doctor! Get a doctor!" cried an actress.

"Is there a doctor in the house?" cried another.

In the second row a man shouted, "I'm a doctor!" and hurried up the stairs to the stage. He bent over the prostrate actor, pried open an eyelid, felt the recumbent's pulse.

"Give—him—an—enema!" came a resounding shout from an old lady in the gallery.

The doctor leaned over and placed his ear against the fallen one's breast.

"Give—him—an—enema!" trumpeted the gallerian.

The doctor straightened up. "Lady, the man is dead! An enema won't help!"

"It vouldn't *hoit!*"

It shouldn't happen to a dog!

I heard this heartfelt invocation in various Yiddish and Yinglish accents:

"It shouldn't happen to a *hunt* (dog)!"

"It shouldn't heppen to a dug!"

"It shouldn't hoppen to a duck!"

Whatever changes were rung on the tune, the central meaning was clear.

Dogs, incidentally, were very rare in our neighborhoods (they take feeding). Jews always speak about animals with kindness: rest on the Sabbath applies to animals, and the Torah is full of instances of God's displeasure with any who are unkind to dumb beasts (Deuteronomy 22:4). Jews neither hunted nor patronized cruel sports.

What I find most admirable are the rabbinical injunctions to Jews that they must feed an animal before feeding themselves; that an animal may not be gelded; that any beast that falls under the weight of its burden must be helped up. "It shouldn't happen to a dog!" carries overtones not apparent to those unfamiliar with Jewish traditions.

J

J.A.P.

Pronounced "Jap." Acronym for "Jewish American Princess."

This is an "in" word used by young American Jews to describe a rich, spoiled, or nubile Jewess.

△ △ △

Zelda Feibush, aspiring pianist and heiress, wrote to the celebrated Leopold Mankovski: "You are my idol. It will mean everything for me to hear your honest opinion of my talent."

The impresario, famed for his kindness, invited Zelda to his studio. There she played for him. She played Beethoven, Debussy, Chopin. . . . Mankovski sat silent, his eyes closed.

Finally, Zelda blurted, "Maestro, please—what should I do now?"

The maestro opened one eye. "Get married."

△ △ △

BERNIE: Mr. Batzel, I—I want to marry your daughter.
MR. BATZEL: My! And have you seen my wife yet?
BERNIE: Oh, yes. But I prefer your daughter.

△ △ △

Q. What do J.A.P.s most often make for dinner?
A. Reservations.

△ △ △

J.A.P.: This meat—you call this *meat?* It's a disgrace!
WAITER: What's wrong with it?
J.A.P.: What's *wrong* with it? It—tastes funny!
WAITER: So laugh.

Jehovah

The name of God, quite incorrect, which first appeared in Christian texts in 1516.

Some unknown papal scribe, a German (who probably would have rendered YHVH orally as "Yahveh" and written the *Y* as a *J*), attached the diacritical marks meant for Elohim to the sacred four letters: YHVH, thus: JeHoVaH. You may be sure that no Hebrew—priest or rabbi or layman—ever pronounced the awesome four letters as "Jehovah." (See YHVH.)

The first pronunciation of YHVH may have been "Yahveh." This was replaced, after several thousand years, by "Jehovah," the version of the divine Name used in virtually all Protestant Bibles. (The sound of *ya* in Hallelujah is thought to be a short version of YHVH.) The illustrious editors of the Standard Edition of the New English Bible (Oxford and Cambridge Presses) retained "this incorrect but customary form," offering a footnote of correction each time the name Jehovah appears:

"The Hebrew consonants are YHVH, probably pronounced *Yahiveh*, but traditionally read *Jehovah*."

There is a tantalizing aspect to all this: The Name was pronounced only in the ancient Temple in Jerusalem. But whenever that supersacrosanct secret (which the Hebrew priests did not confide to laymen) was enunciated, the musical part of the service was designed to swell up so as to drown it!

See ADOSHEM, YAHVEH.

△ △ △

Old Mr. Lobitch was knocked down by a hit-and-run driver just outside St. Patrick's Cathedral. A priest, coming out of the church, hurried over, kneeled, and automatically asked, "Do you believe in God the Father, God the Son, and God the Holy Ghost?"

Dazed Mr. Lobitch blinked and murmured, "Here I am dying, and this fellow asks me riddles!"

△ △ △

The story is told of the great pianist Leopold Godowski, who was having a suit made for a national tour.

Driven to desperation by the endless delays of the tailor, Godowski finally cried, "Tailor, in the name of heaven! It has already taken you six *weeks*."

"So?"

"So? Six weeks for a pair of pants? It took God only six days to create the universe!"

"*Nu*," sighed the tailor, "look at it."

Jew

Jew in Hebrew is *Yehudi* (after Judah, son of Jacob); in Aramaic, *Yehudai;* in Greek, *Ioudais;* in Latin, *Judaeus;* in German, *Jude* (pronounced YOU-deh); in French, *Juif;* in Spanish, *Judío;* in Italian, *Guideo;* in Portuguese, *Judeu.* (I must tell you that the Japanese *judo* has nothing to do with Jews: *judo* means "soft art," more or less.) In Anglo-French, the word for *Jew* was *Iew* or *Geu.* Chaucer referred to Jewry as *Iewerie.*

The English word, says Max Weinreich (*History of the Yiddish Language*), is the Old French *Giu;* like the German *Jude,* the name comes from Latin: *Judaeus,* which was the Romans' way of translating the Hebrew *Yehudah,* the name of the Jewish commonwealth during the time of the Second Temple. *Yehudah,* in English, is "Judah." (Judah's descendants, of course, made up one of the tribes of Israel; they settled in Canaan and westward from Jericho to the Mediterannean.)

References for one or another aspect of Jewish history are strewn through this book. A most original and insightful work is the slender rumination by Arland Ussher: *The Magic People: An Irishman appraises the Jews* (Devin-Adair).

△ △ △

Dear God, if you really loved the Jews why did you make them the chosen people?

The happiness of Jews is never entirely free from fear.

Calamity may be blind, but it has a remarkable talent for locating Jews.

—FOLK SAYINGS

What was their crime? Only that they were born. . . . That is why the Portuguese burnt them.

—VOLTAIRE, *Sermon du Rabi Akib*

The study of the history of Europe teaches [this] lesson: the nations which dealt fairly with the Jew have prospered; the nations that tortured and oppressed him wrote out their own curse.

—OLIVE SCHREINER

The Jews are not hated because they have evil qualities; evil qualities are sought for in them, because they are hated.

—MAX NORDAU

jokenik

1. A compulsive teller of jokes.
2. One addicted to collecting or consuming jokes.
3. One who is jocular in inappropriate situations.

△ △ △

At the Hillcrest Country Club, in West Los Angeles, one large round table is a special preserve for comedians. Around this board I have seen, at one time or another, the likes of Milton Berle, George Burns, Danny Kaye, Henny Youngman, Phil Silvers, et cetera. The jokes cascade here; the repartee is swift; the anecdotes never run out. But comedians listen with but one ear, for they are usually primed to "top" a rival.

At one luncheon, a jokenik sat down. He looked haggard.

"What's wrong?" someone asked.

"What's not wrong? Last month, my brother died. Last week, they put my wife's leg in a cast. Yesterday, my son went skiing and broke his nose, jaw and two ribs. And this morning, coming here, I accidentally hit an old jalopy, driven by a lady must be eighty.years old. She's going to sue me for a million dollars. . . ."

From across the table came: "You think *that's* funny? Let me tell you about the Arab and the Irishman. One day . . ."

K

kabtsen

kabts'n (standard)

kabtsonim (pl.)

> Rhyme this with "Hobson" or "Hopson." From Hebrew: *kabotz:*
> to collect.
>
> 1. A poor man.
> 2. A ne'er-do-well.
> 3. A cheapskate; a stingy person.

I recommend *kabtsen* for Yinglish: uses 2 and 3 contain a quality of moral judgment that is lacking in the English "pauper." I mean that *kabtsen!* is a sneer, an epithet, directed against a man or woman not because he or she is impecunious, but because she or he is stingy: "That *kabtsen!* The last time he picked up a restaurant check was—does anyone remember when he picked up a check?"

△ △ △

The elders decided to give Yissel the *Kabtsen* a face-saving job. "Yissel, we will pay you a ruble a day. Sit on the hill outside our *shtetl* every day, from dawn to sunset."

"Wh—what do you want me to do?"

"We want you to be our lookout—for the approach of the *Meshiakh* (Messiah)."

"Pssh!" cried the *kabtsen*, slapping himself on the cheek. "The *Meshiakh*—and if I see him coming, what should I do?"

"When you see him you run back to the *shtetl* as fast as you can, shouting 'The *Meshiakh!* He is coming!' "

Yissel's face lighted up just thinking of the glory. . . .

One day, a year later, a traveler approached the little village and noticed a figure sitting on a hill. *"Sholem aleichem,"* called the traveler. "What are you doing on this hill?"

"I am waiting for the *Meshiakh.* It's my job. I sit here every day."

The traveler suppressed a smile. "Confidentially, how do you like this job?"

"Ssssh!" Yissel looked about. "It doesn't pay much, but I think it's steady!"

✡ Kaddish

Kadish (standard)

> Pronounced ᴋᴏᴅ-ish. From Aramaic: *kadosh:* holy.
>
> 1. The solemn prayer, glorifying God's name, that closes synagogue prayers.
> 2. The prayer of mourners for the dead.
> 3. A son is sometimes affectionately called *Kaddishel* or *My Kaddish.*

The *Kaddish* is a doxology that glorifies God's name, affirms faith in the establishment of His kingdom and expresses hope for peace. The language is not Hebrew but Aramaic, which the Jews used in their Babylonian exile and during the days of the Commonwealth.

The *Kaddish* has become known (and is used) as the "mourner's prayer," even though it contains no reference to death or resurrection. The prayer is not, in fact, a prayer for the dead at all. It is an affirmation of the virtues of the deceased, and a pledge of loyalty to the tenets of Judaism. Far back in the mist of history, the idea grew that praises of God (or the gods) would help the souls of the departed find eternal peace.

The fact that the mourner, in the depth of his suffering, glorifies God is thought to be the highest affirmation of God's righteousness and the strongest statement of the mourner's resignation to His will. But many a Jew would follow the remarkable example of the Berditshever Rabbi, who wrote a poem in which he refuses to say *Kaddish* when he gets to Heaven, because of the Holocaust.

△ △ △

May I give you my favorite prayer for the dead?

> When you gaze upon the dead, remember this: You have been shown more than you can understand. Search not for what has been hidden from you. Seek not to understand what is so difficult to bear.
>
> Mourn the dead, and hide not your grief; but fear not death, for we share it with all who ever lived and with all who ever will be. The

good things in life last but limited days, but a good name will endure forever.

O God, forsake us not in the days of our desolation. . . . Now, help us to live on, for we have placed all our hope in Thee.*

△ △ △

With the humor so characteristic of him, Sholom Aleichem described the prayer of mourning that he and his five brothers recited for their departed mother.

You should have heard us deliver that *Kaddish!* All our relatives beamed with pride, and strangers envied us. One of our relatives . . . exclaimed, "When a woman has six sons like that to say *Kaddish* after her, she will surely go straight to paradise. Either that or the world is coming to an end!"

△ △ △

"Rebbe," complained Mr. Flockman. "It's over a month my Joel has been going to your *cheder*. And he doesn't know five words in Hebrew!"

"I know."

"So why are you already teaching him the *Kaddish?* Do I look like a dying man?!"

"No, no, Mr. Flockman," exclaimed the rabbi. "You should only live as long as it will take your boy to learn the *Kaddish!*"

kaiser

1. A German or Austrian emperor (Caesar)—but that is not why the entry is here.
2. A breakfast roll: high, fluffy, often sprinkled with poppy seeds.

These delicious rolls were called "kaiser rolls" either because they were favored by some Austrian monarch (no mean distinction, considering the exalted art of Viennese baking) or because to poor Jews a light, airy, white-flour roll was thought to be fit for a kaiser.

The name "kaiser rolls" seems to have been used in Chicago, not New York: when I first asked for the goody in New York, the counter-men looked buffaloed. New Yorkers say "seeded roll."

kalyike

Pronounced KOLL-yi-keh. From Russian: cripple.

1. A crippled person.

---

* Freely adapted from *Ecclesiasticus*, by Jeshua (or Jesus) ben Sirach (*fl.* around 180 B.C.E.).

2. A clumsy or inept type.
3. A talentless performer.

"He has all the social polish of a *kalyike*."
"She walks like a queen, but she dances like a *kalyike*."

△ △ △

Barney Statz went to a cheap clothier on Twenty-fourth Street. A salesman took him in tow. "I have a suit *made* for you! Here. Just try it on!"

Barney got into the garment and surveyed himself in the mirror. "The right sleeve is too long."

"So stick out your elbow," said the salesman. "See? That takes up the length."

"The collar is way up—"

"So raise your head! See? The collar goes down."

"But now the left shoulder is wider than—"

"So *bend!* This way. Look how it evens out!"

And Barney Statz left the store right elbow stuck out, head back, left shoulder tilted. . . . A stranger accosted him. "Excuse me. I'm looking for a suit. Please tell me—who is your tailor?"

"My tailor?" groaned Barney. "Are you nuts?"

"No, *sir!* Any man who can fit a *kalyike* like you must be a genius!"

See KLUTZ.

kayn ayn hore

kayn ayen hore (standard)

kayne horeh

> Rhymes with "Dinah Cora." Hebrew: *eyn ha-ra:* no evil eye.
>
> 1. A phrase, more colorful than "knock wood," employed to ward off the evil eye: "My baby? In perfect health, *kayn ayn hore.*"
> 2. A gnomic phrase used in the hope of continuing a presently favorable state: "He should only go on growing, *kayn ayn hore.*"
> 3. The magic phrases uttered to demonstrate that your praise is genuine and not tainted with envy: "He is an angel, *kayn ayn hore.*"

All our forebears were afraid of offending the gods, and it was widely believed that jealous mortals cast an evil, lethal spell. To thwart the demons of the devil, phrases like *kayn ayn hore* were employed with whatever magical gesture (spitting, winking) was deemed effective.

Mothers would drop salt and a crumb into a child's pocket to feed any goblins who came along. Girls wore beads, a necklace, a bracelet. (A Greek classmate of mine always carried garlic in his pocket, to protect him from afreets.)

If you carry vestigial fears about the powers of the evil eye, comfort yourself with this passage from the Talmud:

> If a person fears the Evil Eye, let him take the thumb of his right hand in his left hand, and the thumb of his left hand in his right hand, and declare; "I, so-and-so, am of the seed of Joseph—over which the Evil Eye has no power."
>
> —*Berakhot,* 55b

I hate to complicate matters, but the powers of the evil eye were not limited to the satanic; they were sometimes entrusted to the very righteous, as an instrument of divine retribution. An exalted soul like Eliezer ben Hyrcanus could turn a sinner to bone and ashes (so it is recorded), merely by glaring at him.

It saddens me to report that in medieval Germany the evil eye was called a *Judenblick* ("a Jew's glance").

In the fourth century, a Catholic council in Spain issued a canon forbidding any Jew to stand in a field that belonged to a Christian: a Jew's mere glance could wither the crop.

△ △ △

A venerable Jew was on the witness stand.

"And, sir, how old are you?" asked the attorney for the state.

"I am, *kineahora,* seventy-eight." (Jews often pronounce the Hebrew in one compressed *kineahora.*)

"What?"

"I said I am, *kineahora,* seventy-eight."

"Just answer the question, please. Without comments. Now then, how old are you?"

"*Kineahora,* seventy-eight."

The judge intervened: "You will answer the question, and *only* the question, or I shall hold you in contempt of court!"

The counsel for the defense cleared his throat. "If it please the court, may I be permitted to ask the question? . . . Thank you." He turned to the old man. "*Kineahora,* how old are you?"

Beamed the old man: "Seventy-eight!"

khaluts (standard)

chalutz

> Hebrew. Use the guttural *kh.*

A pioneer—especially one who went to settle in what was then Palestine.

△ △ △

Mrs. Duberkind was leaving the kibbutz where she had spent ten days. A *khaluts* asked her: "Did you enjoy your stay?"

"Y–yeah."

"What didn't you like?"

"Frankly," said Mrs. Duberkind, "the food you serve is—terrible! And such small portions!"

khazen (standard)

khazonem (pl.)

Rhyme with "Tarzan." Rattle the Scottish *kh.*

A cantor.

Considering the cascade of jokes and gibes about the intellectual limitations of the professional singer who assists the rabbi in services at a synagogue or temple, it may startle you to know that in Hebrew, *khazen* means "seer."

Some temples are now using female singers as *khazonem.*

The passages of liturgy sung by cantors are not written down, but they are (despite impressions to the contrary) standardized. A cantor can be any member of the congregation—even one who sings off-key. He utters the opening words of a prayer; the congregation takes it up; the cantor sings the final verse—and starts a new prayer by singing its opening words. Some professional cantors have voices of operatic caliber, and some opera tenors (Richard Tucker was one) were descended from *khazonem.*

Music in Jewish services is thought to be a recent innovation. The thought is incorrect. There were musical instruments in the Temple— but they *were* banned for over ten centuries.

△ △ △

A *khazen* is a fool: he stands on a platform and thinks he's on a pedestal.

—JOSEPH ZABARA

Any Jew can sing better than the cantor—only at the moment he happens to have a cold.

—FOLK SAYING

"If I had that *khazen's* voice," my father used to say, "I would sing just as well as he does."

khazer (standard)

khazeray

chazzer

chozzer

> Rattle the *kh:* KHAH-z'r and khah-z'RY. Hebrew: pig.

1. Pig.
2. A greedy lout; a glutton.
3. An ungrateful type.
4. A cheap, selfish person.
5. One who takes advantage of another, through cheap tricks or cunning tactics.

Oddly enough, given the ancient taboo on the porcine, Jews rarely use *khazer* to describe someone dirty, as English speakers do when they snap "Pig!"

Khazerish, the adjective, is used (also oddly enough) with a tinge of envy: "He lives a *khazerishen tug*" means "He's living it up."

Khazeray means awful food, cheap merchandise, obscenity, or contemptible reading. I much prefer *khazeray* to its colloquial synonym, "crap." Its sonic lilt is enough to recommend it.

△ △ △

The day after Mrs. Zelkin's funeral the rabbi dropped in to console the widower. To his astonishment he beheld the bereaved on the sofa making love to a dazzling redhead.

"Zelkin!" roared the rabbi. "Your beloved wife not even cold in the grave and already you're—"

Cried the *khazer,* "In my grief should *I* know what I'm doing?!"

kibbutznik

1. A member of a *kibbutz* in Israel.
2. An enthusiast about *kibbutzim* (pl. of *kibbutz*).

△ △ △

In a certain kibbutz the house of Dov Stoller was on fire. He called the fire department. Soon a dinky fire engine roared up, so fast and so recklessly that it almost went right into the flames.

Four young firemen leaped out while the engine was still moving. . . . Soon the flames were extinguished.

Dov Stoller took out his wallet. "Here! A contribution for such truly fearless men!"

"Wow!" cried the young chief. "Hey, *kibbutzniks!* Now we can get brakes!"

kibitzer

KIB-itz-er. From German: *kiebitz:* looking over the shoulder of someone playing cards. Webster's *Third New International Dictionary* enters a second "acceptable" pronunciation: ki-BIT-zer. Not only have I never heard the word so pronounced; I would develop severe spasms if I did.

One who *kibitzes*—that is:
a. Comments from the sidelines.
b. Offers unasked-for advice.
c. Wisecracks, needles.
d. Fools around, wastes time.
e. Second-guesses nastily.
f. Distracts through irritating patter.
g. Sticks his nose into the business of others.
h. Humors others along.

I should think that by now no one needs to have *kibitzer* illustrated. *The Kibitzer,* a play by Jo Swerling (1920), made the word a byword.

△ △ △

The sign on the doctors' door read:

> DR. ROBERT LEWIN, Brain Surgery.
> DR. J. O. BANKMAN, Psychiatry.
> DR. CHARLES GOLUB, Proctology.

Under this imposing troika, a *kibitzer* scrawled:

> *We specialize in*
> *Odds and Ends.*

kike

Vulgarism. From Yiddish: *kikel:* a circle; to roll. (Before you challenge the etymology, read what follows.) Note the phrase *Ikh kikel zikh fun gelekhter:* I roll with laughter.

1. A most obnoxious synonym for Jew.
2. (As used by Jews) A cheap, unpleasant, ill-mannered, greedy, conniving, deceitful or money-grubbing Jew.

I was astounded the first time I heard a Jew use the vulgarism *kike*. The user was a scion of a wealthy German-Jewish family. Stephen Birmingham's *Our Crowd* (Harper & Row) is an illuminating record of prestige and status symbols in "the great Jewish families of New York."

My entry *kike* in *The Joys of Yiddish* started a *tararam (q.v.)* that has not abated. A reason often given for the word is that assimilated German Jews made fun of later, poor immigrants from Eastern Europe, whose names often ended in *-sky* or *-ski,* by using the mocking *ki-ki.* This strikes me as thoroughly unconvincing: *-sky* or *-ski* are always pronounced *skee;* therefore, the derogation should have been *keeks* or *kee-kees,* but in no conceivable way *kikes.*

I offered instead a striking bit of history: a letter from an immigration inspector at Ellis Island who cited the "dean" of that group, Philip Cowen, as having told him that *kike* was a contraction of *kikel*—and that Jewish immigrants from Eastern Europe who were classified as illiterate (because they used only Hebrew/Yiddish, or were otherwise not familiar with the English alphabet) were asked to sign their entry form with an X. This the Jews would not do: X was a cross, the sign under which their forebears had been slaughtered, the sign under which pogroms were still being executed. Instead of a cross, the immigrants made a circle *(kikel).*

In time, the inspectors learned to call to each other: "Don't put a cross on his card; put a circle," or "Use a *kikel,*" and, in time, "Make it a *kike,*" or "He's a *kike.*"

Lo and behold, John Ciardi, in *A Browser's Dictionary* (Harper & Row), asserts: "Rosten credits immigration officials with having derived *kike* from *keekle,* a phonetic alteration of which I cannot believe their appointed stupidities to be capable." Alas, Mr. Ciardi painted himself into a corner: the officials derived *kike* from *kikel.* (I never heard it pronounced *keekel.*) Ciardi goes on to report that children used to taunt a Jew by rhyming "Ike" (considered the typical Jewish name) with *kike,* in this chant: "Ikey-kikey, kikey-Ikey." Perfectly true. But that has no bearing on the Ellis Island datum.

Nor do I understand why far more competent Yiddishists than I thrash around to dismiss the Ellis Island circle-for-cross explanation. If Philip Cowen's testimony is inaccurate, will someone please tell me: Why would anyone have invented such an explanation?

I add another significant item: Jewish storekeepers and peddlers conducted much of their trade on credit. Many of these early merchants could not write English. They checked off a payment from a customer, in their own or the customer's account book, with a little circle ("I'll make you a *kikeleh*"). They never used a cross, as far as I know.

Some irate *mavens* (or *meyvinim*) have written me triumphantly that the Yiddish word for "circle" is either *krayz* (ring) or *tsirkl* (rod). True.

But that does not mean that *kikel* is not. Alexander Harkavy's *English-Yiddish Dictionary* lies before me: he defines "circle" as *kikel*. The date of publication: 1910. Historical datum: From 1880 to 1910, approximately one-third of all the Jews in Eastern Europe emigrated, and 90 percent or so came to the United States.

I will stand by the Cowen-Ellis Island explanation. Contrary evidence will be treated with reverent skepticism.

△ △ △

Meyer Levinsky entered a certain tony restaurant in a certain persnickety suburb. As he started for a table, the maître d' glared. "Wait! We don't serve kikes!"

"That's all right," said Levinsky. "I don't eat them."

△ △ △

Nat Chernish stopped a man on Fourteenth Street with a hearty "Bloomgarten, you son-of-a-gun! It's been *ages*. My, have you lost weight! And you're wearing a toupee! What's happened to you, Bloom—?"

"I," growled the stranger, "am not Bloomgarten. My name is Cavanaugh. Out of my way, you kike!"

"My, my," clucked Chernish. "Changed your name, too, eh?"

kind

kinder (pl.)

> This is not the antonym of "cruel." It is Yiddish, pronounced to rhyme not with "find" but with "sinned." From German.

> Child.

There is a revealing folk saying: "You can tell a Jew by how he treats his children."

Even as a child, I could not help noting the dulcet tone of voice, the beatific bliss with which the utterance of *kind* was accompanied. (For a surprising history of human attitudes to childhood read Philippe Ariès' illuminating *Centuries of Childhood*.) To Jews, having a child meant fulfilling a divine commandment: it was to perform the first *mitzve*. Not to have children was an affront to God (Genesis: *Rabbah*, 34:14).

△ △ △

Mrs. Tobash was proudly wheeling her granddaughter down the avenue when a friend stopped her, peeked into the pram and cried, "My, *my!* You got there some gorgeous baby!"

"You think *she's* gorgeous?" sniffed Mrs. Tobash. "Wait'll you see her pictures!"

△ △ △

Old Mr. Tenser desperately wanted to be close to his only grandson, Victor. But the lad seemed interested in only one thing in the world: basketball.

One night, when Victor was at a school rally, Mr. Tenser glued himself to the television set. He watched an entire game between the New York Knicks and the Los Angeles Lakers. Around midnight, Victor came home.

"Velvel!" cried Mr. Tenser. "You know what I did? I watched the game between New York and Los Angeles!"

"Oh, great. What was the score?"

"The score," said Grampa proudly, "was 99 to 106."

"Who won?"

Grampa pondered. "106."

△ △ △

The *nakhes* (pleasures) you get from children are more precious than gold.

If you must strike a child, use a string.
—TALMUD: *Baba Bathra,* 21a

Never threaten a child; either punish or forgive him.
—TALMUD: *Baba Bathra,* 21a

A child's tears move heaven itself.

It is better that children cry than that their mothers (fathers) cry.

Every child exaggerates its own importance. It has the *right* to say: "the world was created for *me*."
—TALMUD: *Sukkah,* 21a

Children without a childhood are tragic.
—MENDELE MOKHER SEFORIM

It is better not to have had children than to bury them.

And lest sentiment, much less *shmaltz,* carry the day, I give you:

Little children won't let you sleep; big children won't let you live.

One father can support ten children, but ten children don't seem to be able to support one father.

Parents once taught their children to talk; today children teach their parents to be quiet.

△ △ △

Wits in New York were quick to quip that when Israel built its first ocean liner it would be called the *S.S. Mein Kind.* (*Ess, ess* means "Eat, eat.")

kishke

Pronounced KISH-keh. From Russian: intestine.

1. Intestines.
2. A baked treat, made of meat, flour, spices stuffed into a ' casing of intestines.
3. Indelicate slang for "belly" or "guts." ("I felt that loss right in my *kishke*.")
4. To be hit in the *kishkes* is to be knocked for a loop.

△ △ △

A psychiatrist was hit in the *kishkes* by a picture postcard he received from a patient who was vacationing in Barbados:

Having wonderful time. Why?

klutz

Rhyme it with "cuts." German: a log, a clumsy person, a strong but stupid man.

1. A blockhead.
2. A graceless bungler.
3. Anyone heavy-handed, all-thumbed.
4. An insensitive clod.

A *klutz kashe* is a foolish or irrelevant question.

A "klutzy" girl is not likely to dance well, drive well, or even —well, you can go on without help from me.

△ △ △

The klutziest *klutz* on earth was the man who hurried to the hospital to announce: "Mr. Gerstein, I come with the best wishes for your recovery from the trustees of our synagogue. And that's not just a wish, Mr. Gerstein. It's an official resolution. Passed by a vote of thirteen to nine!"

△ △ △

The girl who can't dance says the orchestra can't keep time.

A *klutz* is easily seduced.

△ △ △

The doctor finished examining the homely girl and with a smile he said, "Have I got good news for you, Mrs. Karshov!"

"No, Doctor. It's *Miss* Karshov."

"Oh. Have I got bad news for you, Miss Karshov!"

See KUNYE LEML.

k'naker (standard)

k'nocker

> Rhyme it with "locker," not "lacquer." German: one who cracks a whip, or cracks nuts.

> 1. A "somebody"; a man of achievements, a big shot. "That Bienbloom—started out a nobody and now he's a real *k'naker.*"
> 2. A braggart, a show-off.

The German *knacker* contains none of the mockery which is part and parcel of the Yiddish *k'naker.* This is especially so if you realize that for sarcastic prolongation, *k'naker* is often rendered as *k'nyaker (q.v.).*

△ △ △

"We are, to be sure, at peace," said Israel's Prime Minister at a meeting of the cabinet. "But our inflation is unbearable, our foreign debt is staggering, we need more and more oil—I don't know what to do. . . . "

"Declare war," said one minister.

"War? Against whom?"

"Against the United States."

Incredulity. Snorts. Snickers. "You must be crazy. Israel against America? Such a war would last ten minutes."

"Correct. We will surrender. And immediately the United States will send us vast quantities of food, supplies, oil, give us huge grants, rebuild our roads and harbors, send us—"

"Just a minute," growled the Prime Minister. "All that is fine, and would certainly happen. But tell me, *k'naker,* what if we *win?*"

△ △ △

SCENE: *Dance Hall*

> K'NAKER: Are you dencing?
> K'NAKERKEH: Are you esking?
> K'NAKER: I'm esking.
> K'NAKERKEH: I'm dencing.

know from . . .

> From the Yiddish: *Vos vays ikh (zi, er) fun . . .*

The breezy substitution of "from" (*fun*) for "about" is a characteristic of Jewish New Yorkers' English in the 1920s and 30s. It is unacceptable. Such usage today is employed to characterize or parody:

"He's a Lehman, so what does he know from *mama-loshn?*"

"She's been married four times, so what does she know from loneliness?"

See KNOW FROM NOTHING.

△ △ △

Mrs. Abram Kolnik in Kiev sent a telegram to her husband in Zhitomir:

SAYS TO OPERATE OPERATE

Soon Mr. Kolnik sent a wire back to Kiev:

SAYS TO OPERATE OPERATE

The poor man was at once arrested by the secret police—on suspicion of treason to the state by sending coded information.

After the customary beating of the prisoner, the G.P.U.-nik in charge demanded: "If you don't decode those messages it's off to the Gulag for you!"

Quavered Abram Kolnik: "Who knows from codes? I'll *read* you the telegrams. My wife went to Kiev to consult a surgeon. So she consulted him. So she wired me his opinion—and a question:

SAYS TO OPERATE! OPERATE?

So I thought it over, and figured she has to go through with it. So I wired her:

SAYS TO OPERATE? OPERATE!"

... know from nothing ...

Yinglish. From Yiddish: *fun gornisht (gornit)*

In Yiddish, double negatives are both proper and common: *e.g., Zie hot nit keyn mon* (She has not no man). What I find even more piquant is that in Yiddish one can use a *triple* negative: *Keyner hot nit keyn vort gezugt* (No one had not no word uttered)—which in English would be "No one uttered a word."

"He knows from nothin'!" has become familiar English slang.

"He don't know from nothing" emphasizes meaning by mocking English grammar triply: 1) in using "don't" instead of "doesn't"; 2) in adding the unnecessary "from"; 3) in doubling the negatives.

△ △ △

Hy Hochstein was on the *Metsiye*, the yacht of his wholesaler, Charley Robson. Off Montauk Point, the sea got very rough. Charley Robson tripped, fell on the deck, and broke both legs. "Hy!" he gasped. "The radio! The Coast Guard! They have to bring us in!"

Into the radio phone, Hy called, "Coast Guard! Coast Guard! Here is the yacht *Metsiye*. The owner just broke his both legs! Help! Help! I know from nothing about boats!"

The speaker crackled; the Coast Guard came in: "We read you, *Metsiye*. What is your position?"

"Partner in Evergood Sofas," cried Hochstein. "But is this a time for small talk?"

k'nyaker

> Amused pronunciation of *k'naker (q.v.).*
>
> The Slavic *k'ny* is a gloss for mockery.

May I remind you that American Southerners sometimes put a playful palatal *y* into words beginning with *k* (or the *k* sound)? They may say "President C'yarter," or "C'yaptain Cook went off to the South Seas," or "y' cousin K-yate." Mark Twain describes this verbal mischief in *Life on the Mississippi*, as beautiful prose as ever was written by an American— or an Englishman, for that matter.

△ △ △

An Israeli politician who prided himself on having a phenomenal memory was pumping hands in a receiving line when a man approached him with a hearty "You don't remember me, but back in Brooklyn I made your pants—"

"Major Pantz," the politician, a *k'nyaker*, bellowed, "I'd recognize you anywhere!"

kochalayn

kokhaleyn (standard)

> Pronounce the *ch* as a Scot would: *kh*. KAUKH-a-layn. From German: *koch:* cook, and *allein:* alone.
>
> A bungalow or room, with facilities for cooking.

Hotels in the Catskills were too expensive for many a Jewish man, woman, widow, couple or family. Hence the growth of the *kochalayns*.

I first heard this admirable word in Liberty (near Monticello), when a New York friend of my mother confided: "How can my Sidney and me affoder a fancy three-meals-a-day place? We always find a *kocha-layn*."

△ △ △

Speaking of the Catskills: It is a canard, circulated I believe by Florid-ians, that a Catskill farmer named Goldstein, hoping to immortalize his name, bred a Guernsey cow with a Holstein bull. This gave him a Gold-stein. The only trouble was that the creature refused to go "Moo—moo." Instead it went "*Nu—nu?*"

Kol Nidre

Pronounced CALL (or CULL) NID-reh. Hebrew: all vows.

The awesome prayer that is chanted just before sunset on Yom Kippur eve.

Kol Nidre is actually a legal statement, not a religious importunity, which begins:

> *Kol Nidre* [all vows], obligations, oaths which we may vow or swear or pledge . . . from this Day of Atonement until the next . . . we do re-pent . . .

These words, moreover, are uttered in Aramaic, not Hebrew: not one worshipper in a hundred knows their meaning. Yet *Kol Nidre* is chanted with more feeling than any other prayer in Judaism; and the cantillation by the cantor in the twilight, and the antiphonal response by the con-gregation, and the scrolls of the Torah held aloft by three honored worshippers—these are profoundly moving. (Beethoven used part of *Kol Nidre* in his Quartet in C Sharp Minor.)

Despite its legalistic text, *Kol Nidre* has come to be regarded as a recapitulation of all the tragedies and suffering which Jews have en-dured. The confession of sins, incidentally, is collective, not individual.

✡ kosher

Used in English since 1860. Rhymes with "No, sir." From He-brew: *kasher:* prepared properly; fit to eat.

1. Fit to eat by observing Jews, because ritually fulfilling the dietary laws. (A butcher's sign *bosor kosher* means "kosher meat—and no other.")
2. Pertaining to orthodox Judaism. ("Is he a kosher Jew?" means "Does he abide by the kosher laws?")

(In slang)

3. Authentic; unadulterated; the real McCoy. ("What do you mean is it an antique? It's 100 percent kosher.")
4. Legal, lawful. ("Is the deal kosher?")
5. Trustworthy. ("Is that firm kosher?")
6. Authorized; security cleared. (At the Pentagon "Is he kosher?" means "Can I transmit classified information to him?")

For a straightforward statement of kosher laws see Samuel Dresner's *The Jewish Dietary Laws* (Burning Bush Press).

△ △ △

One day, Ari Frosch went into a fancy delicatessen. He bought some canned peaches, two bananas, an orange, and then, in an archly blasé manner, asked, "Um—how much is a quarter pound of—bacon?"

At once a tremendous clap of lightning-and-thunder shook the premises. Frosch glared at the ceiling: "I was only *ask*ing!"

kreplakh (standard)

Pronounced KREP-lokh or KREP-lekh; use a Germanic *kh*. From German: *Kreppel.* (Note French: *crêpes.*)

A dumpling, like Italian ravioli, that contains chopped meat or cheese. Usually served in soup.

Kreplakh are a much-loved delicacy, traditionally eaten on Purim and the day before Yom Kippur.

Kreplakh is plural. I never heard of the name for only one, because I never heard of anyone eating only one.

△ △ △

Old Mr. Gruskin sat down with a sigh. "Waiter . . . I don't need a menu. I know what I want. I'm from out of town. I've walked my feet off. And all I saw in New York was terrible. Filthy streets. Drivers, *murd*erers! And the people—so rude, so angry. . . . So, waiter, bring me a nice bowl of chicken soup with *kreplakh*. And just one kind word to a visitor."

The waiter brought the bowl of soup, put it down and started to leave.

"Waiter!" said Mr. Gruskin. "What about the kind word?"

The waiter bent over and whispered, "Don't eat the *kreplakh*."

Kunye Leml (standard)

Kuni Lemmel

Pronounced koo-ni LEM-mel or KUN-yeh LEM-m'l. From German: *Lummel:* bumpkin.

1. A simpleton.
2. An unsophisticated sort.
3. An awkward person.

A *Kunye Leml* is the clone of *shlemiel,* a *nebech,* a *shmendrick,* a *nayfish,* a *Chaim Yankel,* a *kalyike,* a *shmo,* a—I had better stop, so rich is Yiddish in the nomenclature of ridicule.

See YOLD.

△ △ △

Itzik, a *Kunye Leml,* came to the rabbi. "*Rebbe,* a cloud darkens my every moment. Last week my Rizeleh gave birth to a fine baby boy . . ."

"*Mazel tov!* So what's to worry?"

"*Rebbe,* it takes nine months for a baby to be born, no? And Rizeleh and I were married—only three months ago!"

"Ah . . . ah. . . ." The rabbi stroked his beard. "To such a problem we must apply the highest wisdom of Talmud. . . . *You* got married three months ago?"

"*Yaw.*"

"And your Rizeleh, *she* married you three months ago?"

"*Yaw, Rebbe.*"

"So you and Rizeleh have lived together as man and wife for three months now?"

"*Yaw, Rebbe.*"

"*Nu?* Three plus three plus three! Nine! Go home to your dear wife and baby!"

kvell

Pronounced as spelled. German: *quellen:* to gush.

1. To chortle with pride and glow with pleasure (usually over the achievement of your child or grandchild).
2. To crow over someone's misfortune. "Be charitable, don't *kvell* over his mistake."

△ △ △

Mrs. Blum met Mrs. Steen, who was pushing a pram with two little boys in it.

"Good morning, Mrs. Steen. My! Such *beautiful* little boys! How old are they?"

"The doctor," *kvelled* Mrs. Steen, "is eight months; the lawyer is two."

I know it's an old story. But so is the one about the three cross-eyed prisoners; see my INTRODUCTION.

kvetsh (standard)

kvetch

Slang usage in English. Rhyme with "fetch." German: *quetschen:* to squeeze; to press. Do not confuse with *kvitsh,* which means "scream," or *krekhts,* which means "to groan . . . moan . . . croak . . . wheeze in complaint."

As a verb:
1. To squeeze, pinch. "Don't *kvetsh* the peaches."
2. To fuss, grouse, be ineffectual. "She *kvetshes* all day long."
3. To fret, complain, sigh. "What's she *kvetshing* about now?"
4. To delay. "He's still *kvetshing* around."
5. To shrug. "He *kvetshes* his shoulders."
6. To eke out a living. "He *kvetshes* a livelihood."

As a noun: kvetsher:
1. Anyone who complains, frets, gripes. "What a congenital *kvetsher!*"
2. One who works slowly, inefficiently. "It will take forever, he's such a *kvetsh.*"
3. A wet blanket. "Don't invite them to the party; he's a *kvetsh.*"

I once saw a lapel button that read:

KAFKA
IS A
KVETCH

You could say the same about Proust.

△ △ △

In the old days (say, forty years ago), a suitor of overly long standing was called a *kishen kvetsher:* "cushion squeezer," meaning a male who spent too much time sitting in the parlor (front room) instead of taking the girl out.

L

L'chayim

L'khayim (standard)

> Pronounced with a German *kh*, to rhyme with "to fry em." Hebrew: To life.

> The toast offered with raised glass.

Some worthy *goyim* confuse *L'chayim* with *Mazel tov*. This is unnecessary. *L'chayim* is used like "Your health," or (I shudder to say) "Here's mud in your eye." But *Mazel tov (q.v.)* is used as "Congratulations" or "Hurrah!"

L'chayim is the Jewish counterpart to England's "Cheers," Sweden's *Skoal*, Spain's *Salud*.

like

> Yinglish.

> 1. Pretend, imitate, simulate.
>   I made like a detective and sat down.
>   She made like a dancer and walked through the stage door.
> 2. *(Used before an adjective, instead of "rather"):* Sort of; in the manner of.
>   He laughed it up like crazy.
>   It's like freezing outside.

These usages have exact analogues in Yiddish: *Er makht zikh vi meshugge:* "He makes (himself) like crazy."

A third use in Yinglish does not have a Yiddish analogue, but is a distinctive Jewish/Bronx/Brooklyn contribution to linguistics:

> 3. *Used to finish a sentence.*
>   He was so skinny he was a skeleton, like.

The recent vogue of "like" in teen-age jive, Harlem argot, and the counterculture (to say nothing of drug takers) should not mislead you into thinking that "like" is a recent slang innovation. It appeared in Yinglish decades ago. (See Wentworth and Flexner, *op. cit.*, page 319.)

△ △ △

CUSTOMER: Waiter! Waiter!

WAITER: What do you want?

CUSTOMER: I want you should make like a waiter! The service is terrible!

WAITER: How do *you* know? You haven't had any.

likewise

Yinglish, alas; the too genteel Bronxian response to a Bronxian introduction. From Yiddish: *mir oykh:* to me, also.

1. How do you do?
   FRIEDA: Joe, meet Hilda.
   HILDA: Glad to meet you.
   JOE: Likewise.

In this usage, "likewise" is a "classy" or "upward mobile" rubric.

2. Me, too.
   DORIS: If I don't get something to eat, I'll *faint!*
   JENNY: Likewise.

3. I feel the same way.
   ISADORE: The way I feel, those punks ought to be arrested and sent to jail!
   JACOB: Likewise.

These locutions, strictly speaking, are acceptable, but as style they are deplorable. Good taste, whether in language or luggage, is difficult to describe, though easy to label. Take my word for it: "Likewise" grates on the ear. Even worse is:

4. Likewise, I'm sure.

I'm sure this is gruesome. The *Oxford Dictionary of the English Language* asserts that "likewise" goes back to 1449, meaning "in a like wise," or "in the same way." But this is not the usage I cite. The Catskills-zone meaning is different and distinctive: "I feel the same way," or "Me, too."

I would like to exile "likewise" speechwise.

Listen

Interjection (not verb) to gain attention or stress a point.

I do not mean to suggest that "Listen" is not English; I mean to say that speakers of Yinglish use "Listen" at the beginning of a sentence with much greater frequency than do conventional speakers of conventional English, and with prolonged intonation: "Lis-sun." In Yiddish, *Hayer* or *Herr* ("hear") or *Her zikh tsu* ("Listen to what I am going to say") are very common as introductory signals. Hence, the transition into Yinglish.

△ △ △

"Did you see that movie?"

"Listen, I wouldn't go to a piece of junk like that!"

"She said you *hate* her!"

"Listen, she wasn't exactly exaggerating."

"Did you hear that Congress is going to cut taxes?"

"Listen, it's about time."

"Listen" is often preceded by "Say" or "So," depending on the speaker's enslavement to his/her early environment.

One of the most literate men I know, a speaker of perfect English prose, will often toss a "*Lis*sun" or "Say *lis*ten," or "So listen awreddy" into his speech, mimicking the intonation of the Bedford-Stuyvesant (New York City) area in which he was raised.

△ △ △

"I hear you're going to Palm Springs."

"So listen, it's about time. I need the rest."

"Did you go to C.C.N.Y.?"

"Say listen, who could afford Harvard?"

△ △ △

"Nathan, I've come to the conclusion that Adam and Eve were Communists!"

"How do you figure that?"

"Say listen: They didn't have shoes, a decent coat, a skirt, a pair of pants, their best food was an apple—and they thought they were in Paradise!"

Litvak

Yiddish: Lithuanian.

1. A Jew from Lithuania.
2. An erudite but dry, pedantic Jew (say the Polish Jews).
3. A clever, sharp or shrewd Jew.
4. A humorless Jew (say the Galitzianers).

Today, Lithuania is a Soviet republic on the Baltic Sea. Jews first settled there in the mid-fourteenth century. Jews were barred from entering Lithuania from 1495–1502. Later they were forced to wear a "Jewish badge."

Lithuania became a renowned center of Jewish traditional scholarship, and in the nineteenth century a powerful center of *Haskala* ("the Enlightenment"). Litvaks were alleged (or they claimed) to be the sharpest intelligences in world Jewry.

In 1919, the Poles took over Vilna. By 1939, the Jewish population of Lithuania was around 180,000. Shortly after World War Two broke out, the Russians deported 25,000. And the rest? They were simply murdered. By whom? By the Poles, then the Nazis, then the noble "vanguard of the proletariat" from the USSR. Today, my sources estimate, there are perhaps 8,000 Litvaks in Litvak-land.

Early on (as, following the British, we now say) I heard Sholom Aleichem's epigram: "A Litvak is so smart that he repents *before* he sins."

△ △ △

Isadore Sackstein, age twenty-four, said to a rabbi, "I must tell you, *Rebbe:* I am an atheist!"

"Do you know Talmud?"

"N–not really."

"Not even the *Pirke Abot?*"

"I never had time for it."

The rabbi stared at Sackstein. "I have news for you. You are not an atheist: you are an ignoramus."

(The rabbi was a Litvak.)

△ △ △

In a certain law office, above the water cooler, clearly visible to all the clerks and secretaries, hangs a large clock. Under the clock one of the partners, tired of the clock-watchers, and a Litvak, placed this sign:

IT'S EARLIER THAN YOU THINK!

Live a little!

1. Don't be stingy.
2. Don't skimp on your pleasures.

△ △ △

A seventy-four-year-old widower told his family, "I want to live a little yet. So I'm going to get married. To a fine young lady, a good cook, cultured—"

" 'Young'?" echoed his daughter. "How old is 'young'?"

"Nineteen."

Furor. Outrage. Astonishment. *"Gotenyu!"* exclaimed his son. "Papa, you are seventy-four! Aren't you *ashamed?*"

"Why should I be ashamed? When I married your mother, she was only eighteen."

Look who's talking

> Yinglish: analogue of the Yiddish *Kuk nor ver s'ret!* ("Just take a look at who's talking.")

This imperative is not intended to make you direct your eyes to the speaker. It is intended to announce to the world that the speaker is:
1. Utterly unqualified to make the statement.
2. Incompetent, even if qualified.
3. Shamelessly biased in the matter.
4. A well-known liar, not to be trusted in *any* matter.
5. Off his/her rocker.
6. The very person who loused everything up in the first place.
7. The pot calling the kettle black.

△ △ △

DOLLY PARTON: Look at the bust on that girl!
ANYONE: Look who's talking.

low-life

1. One who lives and acts in a low-class manner.
2. Someone who lacks character.
3. A vulgar, coarse person.
4. An untrustworthy, unreliable person.
5. A gambler, sharpie, dissembler, petty racketeer.

A low-life is a no-goodnik, plain and simple.

You may think that "low-life" is so obvious a compound noun that it must have been used in English long, long before an immigrant Jew landed in London or New York. But the magisterial *Oxford English Dictionary* does not to this day contain "low-life" or "low life" as an entry. "Low-lived" is there, as an adjective: *e.g.,* a low-lived man (but that may also mean a mortal with a low life expectancy). Like "a nothing," "a low-life" is distinct and distinctive Yinglish.

△ △ △

Eddie Gelbel was a Don Juan. Rarely did a week pass without his bedding a pretty girl, then sneaking home to his wife in the wee hours with explanations that were masterpieces of invention: He had been cajoled into a poker game with important salesmen; he had gotten a terrible toothache and the dentist gave him so much Novocain that he fell asleep for six hours; he had found a man bleeding and moaning in the street, and had to wait for the ambulance. . . .

Finally Eddie's long-suffering wife declaimed, "I'm sick and tired of this! Once more, Eddie, and I leave you!"

"Never again!" vowed Gelbel. "I promise."

He meant it. But of what avail are intentions when a man is a low-life like Eddie Gelbel? Came one afternoon when he met a particularly appetizing morsel. . . .

Not until 2 A.M. did Eddie Gelbel come to his senses. In the girl's apartment, he dressed as fast as a fireman—then held his head in his hands. What oh what could he tell Celia? . . . Inventiveness did not fail him. He picked up the phone and dialed his home. His wife answered.

Eddie panted, "C–C–Celia . . . They'll call you any minute!"

"They?"

"They'll ask ten—thousand—dollars—ransom!"

"Eddie! Migod! What hap—"

"Don't pay them a penny, Celia! I just escaped! . . . Be home in fifteen minutes."

lox

From Scandinavian via German.

Smoked salmon.

Lox has become the *sine qua non* of delicacies for Sunday brunches from Park Avenue to Nob Hill. When placed on a split bagel which has been toasted and lathered with butter and cream cheese, lox attains the gastronomic status of crêpes Suzette.

Contrary to popular belief, lox was not a feature of Ashkenazi cuisine. Lox was unknown in Eastern Europe (except for kings and barons). Lox became a luxurious staple on the Lower East Side.

△ △ △

In 1967, when the troops of Israel reached the Suez Canal, the first thing they did was confiscate all the lox.

△ △ △

A Jewish bum runs away from home—lox, stock and bagel.

L'shone toyve

Pronounced l'SHAW-neh TOY-veh; Hebrew: A happy New Year.

This is the traditional salutation for Rosh Hashanah. The whole greeting is: *Leshona toyva tikoseyvu:* "May you be inscribed for a good year." (Inscribed where? In the all-important, fateful Book of Good Deeds, by which your fate in the world to come will be determined.)

See ROSH HASHANAH.

luftmentsh

Rhymes with "put bench." German: *Luftmensch:* literally, air man, but with no connection whatever to airplanes or helicopters.

1. Someone without a trade, a skill, a job, a fixed income—or any sense about them.
2. Someone unrealistic, with his head in the clouds.
3. Someone who forever devises new but impractical schemes for making money.
4. A dreamer—poetic, sensitive, and unrealistic.
5. A naive optimist.
6. A luckless yearner; life's patsy; one inclined to end as a *shlemazl.*

The word is a German compound; its persistent use by Jews made it familiar in Yinglish.

So severe were the limits placed by Czarist authorities on Jewish residence, travel, occupations that a great many bright, ambitious Jews were condemned to try to live as *luftmentshen.* Sholom Aleichem's character Menachem Mendel is the apotheosis of the *luftmentsh.*

△ △ △

A *luftmentsh* never seems to get any older.

When a *luftmentsh* enters a shop, the merchants smile.

The *luftmentsh* forever searches for yesterday.

God protects a *luftmentsh;* no one else can.

Sholom Aleichem put it with an irony that electrifies truth: "The *luftmentsh* lives on hope—and hope is a liar."

See NAYFISH, NEBECH, SHLEMIEL, SHLEMAZL.

△ △ △

Martin Kolach, whose wife loved to ply a little straw fan as she rocked on the porch in hot weather, was examining the fans on a pushcart. "Eh . . . why are some fans a quarter, and some a dollar?"

The *balebos* said, "With a dollar fan you make like this—" he waved a fan before his brow and cheeks. "But with a quarter fan—" he picked up another— "you make like this." He held the fan still, then vigorously waved his head.

Kolach sighed, "I wonder if she'll think it's worth it."

(He was *eppes* a *luftmentsh*.)

M

Ma-and-Pa store

Mom-and-Pop store

> The designation was no doubt used by Lower East Sideans other than Jews, but it flourished in the Jewish enclaves.

> A small retail store owned and run by a man and his wife.

The traditional "corner stores" on the Lower East Side sold candy, cigarettes, newspapers, notions. The phrase picturesquely conveys the central point about size, scale and ownership.

△ △ △

The Hadassah truck stopped in front of Mendelson's corner store. The driver hopped out, singing, "Anything to contribute? Kitchenware, furniture? All proceeds go to charity. Old phonograph records—"

"I don't have old records," said Mr. Mendelson.

"Old clothes?"

"Old clothes I have—"

"Fine!"

"—but I can't give them to you."

"Why not? What will you *do* with them?"

"What I'll do with them," said Mendelson, "is every night I'll hang them up nice and neat, and every morning put them on."

mad on . . . instead of "mad at . . ."

> Yinglish, Bronxian division. Analogue of Yiddish *broygez oyf.**

---

* *Broygez* is a distinctive Yiddish word, mistranslated by the unwary as "angry," which destroys the subtle distinctions between *broygez* and *beyz* (angry) and *in kas* (furious). When

As a verb:
1. To be angry with. ("I am mad on her.")
2. Not talking to.

As a noun:
1. A grievance.
2. A complaint. ("I have a mad on her.")

I emphatically disapprove of both of these barbarisms; but my task is to record, not acclaim.

△ △ △

After his wife's cousin Tillie had spent three weeks in their spare bedroom, Mr. Goldbaum got a mad on. He went out, bought a sign, and hung it over Tillie's bed. The sign read:

> Be it ever so humble,
> There's no place like Home!

make like a . . .

From Yiddish: *makh vi . . .*

Act like; behave like.

The Yinglish aspect lies in the deplorable fact that "make" has replaced the perfectly proper "act," "behave," "imitate," or "pretend to be."

"Stop clowning; make like a gentleman."

"He's only a sergeant, but he makes like a general."

The breezy patois of television's talk shows has given this locution an immense audience and, perforce, the propriety of public usage.

△ △ △

The family was in the lawyer's office as he read the will of the late, rich Joseph N. Flockerman. "To my beloved wife Rachel . . . To my dear son, Bernard . . . To my nephew, Ralph . . . To my niece, Shirley . . . To our faithful cook, Hazel Wood . . . To my loyal chauffeur, Larry Mitchell . . ." On and on the lawyer droned. "Finally, to my nephew, Albert Kramer—"

The young man in the last row sat up.

"—who made like a son, and was always so curious to know if I would mention him in my will—"

---

you are *broygez,* you are not angry but on the outs with, and usually not talking to, someone. This was neatly translated into the Bronx idiom "mad on." "Ask her to drop in? Don't you know I'm real mad on her?"

The young man held his breath.
"Hello, Albert."

make with

Transliterated Yiddish: *mach mit.*

1. Use (verb).
2. Do.
3. Provide.

This Englishization was precious to Brooklynites and Bronxians who could find no juicy equivalent:

"I'm hungry: make with the sandwiches."

"The party's dragging: make with some jokes."

"You sing? So make with the voice."

△ △ △

SCENE: *Department Store*

TIME: 5:58 P.M.

The closing bell is ringing and ringing.

FIRST GUARD AT DOOR: It wouldn't do any good.

SECOND GUARD AT DOOR: What do you mean it won't do any good?

FIRST GUARD AT DOOR: Ring, ring. No matter how often they make with that bell, there's always someone who's the last to leave.

makhutin

Hebrew: father-in-law.

△ △ △

Lenny's *makhutin* (father-in-law) was very glum at lunch. "My new secretary. After I was sure this one would be a Godsend . . ."

"What's happened?"

"This morning she came in after ten o'clock. I said, 'Susan, you should have been here at nine-thirty!' She said, 'Why? What happened?' "

malakh (standard)

malech

Pronounced MA-lekh, with a Caledonian *kh,* not the frontal *ch* of "chickadee." From Hebrew: messenger.

Angel.

I would like to warn you that there is no point in asking angels for help by addressing them in English, or even Aramaic: angels understand only Hebrew (*Shabbat,* 12b). But Ashkenazic Jews never question that the heavenly fold is perfectly at home with Yiddish. Apart from these valuable data, let me give you some highlights of angelology:

Two angels accompany every mortal (*Ta'anith,* 11a). They are, of course, invisible.

Angels possess staggering powers: Michael tore up entire mountains; an angel lifted all of Jerusalem during Nebuchadnezzar's siege; the voice of Hadraniel, who struck Moses dumb, could penetrate 200,000 firmaments.

Johannes Kepler, a giant of science, stated that it is angels who push the planets around.

When Spinoza held *malakhem* to be no more than hallucinations, he was cast out of the Sephardic community of Amsterdam. The formal edict was drawn up by rabbis "with the judgment of the angels," surely a loaded jury.

Cabalists of the fourteenth century held that there are exactly 301,655,722 angels. They arrived at this number through *gematria.* I have not checked it.

Followers of Martin Luther, in an odd work called *Theatrum Diabolorum,* raised the number of angels to 2,500,000,000—and later four times that. As Origen solemnly concluded: "Angels multiply like flies."

I recommend to you the learned, mischievous, delightful work by Gustav Davidson: *A Dictionary of Angels* (Free Press/Macmillan).

△ △ △

Once upon a time angels walked the earth; today, they are not found even in heaven.

—FOLK SAYING

The virtue of *malakhem* is that they cannot deteriorate; their flaw is that (unlike man) they cannot improve.

—HASIDIC SAYING

Maledictions, defanged by instant cancellation—uttered as moral expediency, or possible insurance against divine wrath

"May both eyes drop out of his head, God forbid."

"A plague should seize him, may God prevent that."

"A trolley car should not run through his intestines."

"Boils—may it never come to pass!—should form on his carbuncles."

"Every bone in his body should *kholile* (God forbid) break the minute he gets here."

"Such a woman deserves the sweetest death: to be run over—softly—by a truckload of sugar."

See CURSES.

Mamale

Mamenyu

> Pronounced MA-meh-leh, MA-men-you.
>
> 1. Affectionate form of "Mama." *
> 2. Little mother; darling mother.

The Jewish use of diminutives to express fondness or concern is part and parcel of the culture. Members of the family are particularly prone —and pleased—to diminutize. So, a little brother is a *bruderel,* a little sister is a *shvesterel,* and an eighty-four-year-old aunt may be called *Tanteleh.* English, alas, does not use "motherel."

△ △ △

The patient said to his psychiatrist, Dr. Berg: "A dream. Last night. *Such* a dream . . . My mother was making my breakfast. And while I was eating it—eggs, *challa,* a Coke—a golden pigeon landed on my *mamale's* head! Doctor, what does that mean?"

"A *Coke?*" cried Dr. Berg. "*That* your mother gives you for breakfast?!"

△ △ △

The best fork is Mother's hand.

A child without a mother is like a door without a knob.

---

* Philologists (as distinguished from psychologists, psychiatrists and psychoanalysts) believe that the first syllables uttered by a baby are the whimpering or gurgling *em-em, mem-memm, ma-ma.* Jewish wits say a mother answers this call with admiring clucks: "So young —and already it knows I'm the mother!"

Baba, papa, dada, tata, nana develop later. Then come the liquid, palatalized embellishments: *dyada, tyata, nyanya,* which must fill the infant with pride over so dramatic a neologism.

A mother has glass eyes (she cannot see her children's faults).

Mothers understand what children do not say.

One mother can do more than a hundred teachers.

Mothers have big aprons—to cover the faults of their children.

△ △ △

Hearing the approaching step of his mother, Rab Joseph would rise. "I must stand, for the *Shekhinah* [Holy Spirit] enters."

—TALMUD: *Kiddushin*, 31:2

The life of the mother takes priority over the unborn child.

—MISHNAH: *Ohalot*, 7:6

mama-loshn

Rhyme *loshn* with "caution." Hebrew.

1. Mother's tongue.
2. Yiddish.
3. The "turkey" in "Let's talk turkey."

Because Hebrew was the *loshn kadosh* ("holy tongue"), Yiddish, which was spoken at home, became known as the "mother's tongue."

May I call your attention to the difference, generally ignored, between "mother's tongue" and "mother tongue"? To a Hungarian refugee's son born in, say, Trenton, New Jersey, his mother tongue will be English; his "mother's tongue" is Hungarian.

To all Ashkenazim, Yiddish was the mother's tongue. Sephardic Jews could not even understand it; nor could Ashkenazim understand Ladino, the Sephardic equivalent of Yiddish.

One of the anomalies, rarely noticed, is that whereas the sacred texts of the Jews are in Hebrew/Aramaic, the discussions thereof, in the *heder*, the *shul*, the *yeshivas*, were (and are) conducted in Yiddish! Before Yiddish existed, Jews discussed their holy texts in whatever their vernacular was. The point is made forcefully by Max Weinreich in *The History of the Yiddish Language*, Chapter 4.

△ △ △

God could not be everywhere—so he made mothers.

—FOLK SAYING

△ △ △

Perhaps the most *shmaltzy* of tributes to Mama are the Italian song *Oh My Mamma!* and the Yiddish *My Yiddishe Mama*. The moving *A Brivele der Mama* ("A little letter to Mother") is a poignant reminder of immigrant times, when the children were in the New World far from their mothers in the Old.

△ △ △

One should note that the sound commonly used to indicate pleasure, contentment or satisfaction is the closed-lips particle, *mmh.*

"Did you have a good time at the party?"

"Mmh, *mmh!"* *

△ △ △

In an extraordinary paper, "About the Sound *Mmh* . . . ," the late Dr. Ralph Greenson remarks:

> The fact that the sound "mmh . . ." is made with the lips closed and continuously so throughout the utterance seems to indicate that this is the only sound one can make and still keep something safely with the mouth. Apparently it is the sound produced with the nipple in the mouth, or with the pleasant memory of expectation. . . . The word mama which consists of a repetition of this sound [doubles] the pleasurable labial sensations associated with the act of nursing. Piaget and Spielrein have come to similar conclusions . . . on the basis of their clinical material.
>
> *Explorations in Psychoanalysis* (International University Press) **

Mama-Tata

See TATA-MAMA. *Mama-Tata* for "parents" (instead of the reversed order) appears to be obvious; but it is inauthentic: Jews never say that, in Yiddish or Yinglish. (I agree with the hisses I hear from the ranks of Women's Lib.)

✡ Marrano

Rhymes with "Romano." Spanish: pig.

---

* Sounds of displeasure or disgust never take the labial closure; they tend to be explosive and air-expelling, as *Feh! Peeoo!* or *Yech!* Psycholinguists can go to town on this: I have no doubt that deep psychological gratifications are involved in, and expressed by, expletives that begin with a fricative *(f, s, v, z)* or an unvoiced stop consonant *(p, k, t).* I will go even further, if you realize I am showing off: the labiodental consonants *(f, v)* are used in many languages for scatological epithets.

** Are you aware of the number of languages in which the word for mother begins with an *m?* Swiftly: English, Yiddish, French, German, Russian, Polish, Spanish, Italian, Portuguese, Swedish, Danish, Norwegian, Polish, Dutch, Czech, Serbian, Croatian, Greek, Swahili . . . In Hebrew, mother is *em.*

The Jews who were forcibly converted to Catholicism some 500 years ago.

Many of the Jews who chose nominal apostasy to unspeakable tortures secretly continued, as "crypto-Jews," to practice their faith. "The tears of the Jews blended with the waters of the Baptism."

At least three popes (Clement VI, Boniface IX, Nicholas V) were scandalized by conversion-via-horror, threats of death, the expropriation of worldly possessions, and the seizing of Jewish children as hostages. But the ecclesiasts in Spain and Portugal persisted in their un-Holy Inquisition. Spain became a vast auto-da-fé for Jewish bodies, if not souls: through Torquemada's persuasion, all nonconverted Jews were formally expelled from Spain and Portugal. They went—those unmurdered, I mean—to Italy, Turkey, Amsterdam, London, Greece, Persia, North Africa.

Query: Did Iberia ever recover?

See Cecil Roth, *History of the Marranos* (Oxford); *The Jewish Encyclopedia;* Poul Borchsenius, *History of the Jews* (Simon and Schuster).

△ △ △

> Would you believe that as the flames were consuming the innocent victims, the Inquisitors . . . were chanting our prayers? These pitiless monsters invoked the God of mercy and kindness and pardon while committing the most atrocious, barbarous crime, acting in a way which demons in their rage would not use against brother demons.
> —VOLTAIRE, *Sermons du Rabbin Akib*

> The Jews hunted out of Spain in 1492 were cruelly expelled from Portugal. Some took refuge on the African coast. Eighty years later the descendants of the men who had committed or allowed these enormities were defeated in Africa, whither they had been led by their king, Dom Sebastian. Those who were not slain were offered as slaves at Fez to the descendants of the Jewish exiles from Portugal. "The humbled Portuguese nobles," the historian narrates, "were comforted when their purchasers proved to be Jews, for they knew that they had humane hearts."
> —MORRIS JOSEPH, "Judaism as Creed and Life," from *On the Making of Books*

matzo

matse (standard)

Pronounced MA-tsa. Hebrew: *matsa.*

Flat, unleavened (unrisen) bread. You know all about the flight from Egypt (thirteenth century B.C.E.), and the Hebrews who had to eat on the run, so could not pause for the dough to rise. Wherefore Exodus 12:15 tells us: "Seven days shall you eat unleavened bread"—those days being Passover.

△ △ △

A rabbi bought a parrot, which he trained so skillfully and so long that the bird was saying, "Polly wants a matzo . . . Polly wants a matzo . . ."

△ △ △

Mrs. Belovski stormed into the store and banged an opened box of matzos on the counter. "This you call matzos? They're so hard you need an ax to break them!"

"Just a minute!" retorted the owner. "If our ancestors, crossing that terrible desert in Egypt, had matzos like these they would be damn grateful!"

"Sure they would; when they were crossing that desert these matzos were fresh!"

△ △ △

An Englishman in New York for the first time ate at a world-famed Jewish restaurant. Observing a plate of soup at the next table, with two round yellow objects in it, he asked the waitress, "What sort of soup is that? I mean with those two—"

"Them's matzo balls."

"Ah. I shall try them."

The waitress brought him the dish.

The Englishman ate it with relish. "Excellent! Tell me, what other part of the matzo do you people cook?"

maven

meyvin (standard)

mavens (pl.)

meyvinim (pl.)

mavin

> Yinglish par excellence. Rhymes with "haven." The plural is pronounced m'-VEE-nim. Hebrew: understanding.
>
> 1. An expert.
> 2. A connoisseur.

American and English newspaper stories, editorials and advertisements use *maven* with such abandon that it has generally become accepted as proper English. It adorns page 410 of the *Oxford American Dictionary*. (Will *Webster, Random, Heritage* be far behind?)

△ △ △

The government of Israel, concerned over the growing division of support among American Jews, hired a hotshot public-relations firm in New York. For three months, the PR *mavens* conducted polls, interviewed Jewish leaders, discussed the political parameters (tsk, tsk!) in Washington.

The final report, 465 pages long, contained graphs, charts, tables, statistics. And the last chapter, entitled *Conclusions and Recommendations,* began:

1. Change "Israel" to "Irving."

maybe

1. Perhaps. ("You are maybe joking?")
2. I don't believe it. ("He said he'll endow a chair in his late wife's name . . . maybe.")
3. Wouldn't that be nice? ("They maybe won't show up!")

Older Jews never meant "perhaps" when they said "maybe." In fact, they rarely used the English "perhaps" at all. Since "maybe" is the English for *efsher,* its use as Yinglish takes on comparable innuendos, as seen above.

See COULD BE.

△ △ △

MAN: Doctor, I've come to see you about my wife.

DOCTOR: What's wrong with her?

MAN: A month ago she began to develop the most terrible inferiority complex—

DOCTOR: Um. And you want—?

MAN: I want you to tell me how maybe to keep her that way.

mazel

maz'l (standard)

Rhyme with "nozzle." Hebrew: luck. Since *Mazel tov* is now accepted as English *(The Oxford American Dictionary) mazel* should, perforce, be in the same ranks.

Luck.

△ △ △

When a man has *mazel,* even his rooster lays eggs.

Should luck come in—quick! Give him a seat.

Even the luckless need luck.

Coins are round: if you're lucky, they roll toward you: if you're not, they roll away.

From luck to misfortune is but an inch; from misfortune to luck is a hundred miles.

The lucky don't have to be smart.

Too good is bad.

Weep for the man who does not know how lucky he is.

—FOLK SAYINGS

△ △ △

In the powder room of the Ritz Hotel in London, bejeweled dowagers, attending a great charity ball, fluttered about the mirrors. Several noticed an enormous diamond on the pink and ample bosom of Lady Gwendolyn de Plotnick. "I may say," said Lady de Plotnick, "that this is the third-largest diamond ever known. The largest was the Cullinan diamond; the second largest, the Kohinoor; and third is—the Plotnick."

"Gracious!"

"My!"

"How fortunate you are!" cooed the ladies.

"We–ell, not all that meets the eye is fortunate," said the admired one. "As my ancestors often said, 'Nothing is all *mazel*.' So it is with this diamond. Alas, whoever wears the Plotnick diamond inherits the Plotnick Curse."

"Oh."

"What's the Plotnick Curse?"

Sigh. "Plotnick."

Mazel tov

Maz'l tov (standard)

> Rhyme with "nozzle cuff." Hebrew.

1. Good luck.
2. Good luck to you; I wish you luck.
3. Congratulations.
4. Thank God!
5. At last!
6. I'm surprised—and I admit it.

Ah, what an interesting, useful, versatile and subtle benediction. You would not expect *Mazel tov!* to contain a smidgeon of subtlety. But the occasions on which the exclamation is proper, and those on which it would be scandalous, require explication. Herewith, a Handy-Dandy Guide to *Mazel Tov:*

1. On any happy occasion, to celebrate any felicitous event (a birthday, engagement, wedding, birth, *bris*, graduation, promotion, merger, winning a prize, hitting the jackpot, opening a store, publishing a book) *Mazel tov!* is proper and pleasurable to both sayer and sayee.

2. Never say *Mazel tov* where it might be taken to mean "About time . . ."

> "I'm going to take a bath."
> *"Mazel tov!"*

or:

> "Don't get up: I'm leaving."
> *"Mazel tov!"*

—unless you *mean* "And it's about time, too." Otherwise, *Mazel tov!* is a no-no.

3. Never say *Mazel tov* where it might be taken to mean "I can't believe my eyes!" or "I never thought you'd do it!"—*e.g.*, to a prizefighter entering the ring.

4. Don't say *Mazel tov* to anyone about to have an operation: it plants the seed of doubt that the operatee may survive.

5. Don't say *Mazel tov* to a surgeon, dentist, plumber or general about to plunge into action: the one thing these *meyvinim* are presumed to have is expertise; only amateurs/bunglers need good luck.

6. Say *Mazel tov* to a surgeon, dentist, etc. *after* the successful completion of a difficult operation; this congratulates him on his skill in performing what you now admit you knew was a risky business.

7. Say *Mazel tov* to a pilot just before his first command. This displaces the sentiment from his first flight to his lofty status; here the expression of luck shows good manners, not doubt about his flymanship.

8. Don't say *Mazel tov* to a pilot who lands after a long and difficult flight: it suggests you're surprised he made it.

9. Say *Mazel tov* to a man who comes out of prison. It means "At last."

10. Don't say *Mazel tov* to a man about to go to prison. It means "So, at last, they caught you!"

11. Say *Mazel tov* in Yinglish where you would say "Congratulations" in English:

> "I passed the SATs."
> *"Mazel tov!"*

"We're going to have a baby."

"Mazel tov!" (Purists would say "May it be in a fortunate hour.")

12. Say *Mazel tov* where you would say "Thank God!" in English.

"They found the lost boy!"

"Mazel tov!"

13. Use *Mazel tov* ironically (or even pejoratively) to mean "Really? Hooray! I certainly am surprised to hear that."

"I just boiled an egg—"

"Mazel tov."

Profuse indeed are stories to illustrate the uses of *mazel,* to say nothing of *Mazel tov.* I shall try to restrain myself.

△ △ △

At a casino in Atlantic City, two recent divorcées went to the roulette table. "Elsie," said Miriam, "I never before played this game."

"All you need is *mazel,*" said Elsie.

"How should I choose a number?"

"With something lucky," said Elsie. "Like your age."

"Oh, good." Miriam placed a ten-dollar chip on number 33.

The wheel spun and spun: the little ball nestled in the cradle of 41.

Miriam fainted.

△ △ △

Sadly, slowly, Duved Krekman entered the headquarters of the Lantsmon's Philanthropic League. He trudged into the office of the Executive Secretary and sighed, "Glaser, I'm here." He sat down. "I have to make arrangements for the League to bury my wife."

"Krekman!" exclaimed Mr. Glaser. "Don't you *remember?* We buried your darling wife two years ago!"

Mr. Krekman nodded. "I remember, I remember. That was my first wife. I'm here about my second."

"Second? *Mazel tov!* I didn't know you remarried."

△ △ △

Larry Barvess asked a patriarch in the synagogue: "Maybe you can advise me. My wife just gave birth to a girl—"

"Mazel tov!"

"Thank you. Can we name her for a relative?"

"According to Jewish custom, you can name a baby after a *departed* father, mother, brother . . ."

"But they are all alive," said Barvess.

"Oh, I'm terribly sorry."

△ △ △

PLACE: *Crowded Bus in Tel Aviv*

Old man Gussov glanced about. Not a seat was vacant. Then he edged his way to a fat woman sprawled defiantly over two seats. "Well, well!" exclaimed Mr. Gussov. *"Mazel tov!"*

"Oh, thanks." The fat lady moved over, making room. "Excuse me; do you know me?"

"No."

"So what for was the *Mazel tov!?*"

"To celebrate I was going to get a seat."

McKenzie

> A pun on the Yiddish: *M'ken zi:* we know her.

> 1. One who shops and shops in a store, but does not buy a thing.
> 2. A shoplifter.

This cryptic designation was once popular among Jewish retail clerks who would call a signal to each other: *Mrs. McKenzie!* meaning "Keep an eye on her."

> 3. A girl who is known to allow physical intimacies.

In the days of jazz, flappers and drugstore cowboys, Jewish young men would describe a girl as "Miss McKenzie"—meaning *M'ken zi toppen* ("You can feel her" or "She'll let you . . .").

I was surprised to hear from a twenty-two-year-old in a *yarmulke* that "McKenzie" is being used in his circles today.

megilla

megile (standard)

> Pronounced: m'GILL-a. Hebrew: scroll. The plural is *megilloth.*

> 1. The Scroll (roll volume) of Esther.
> 2. The Song of Songs, the Book of Ruth, Lamentations, Ecclesiastes are the other *megilloth* in the Old Testament.*

---

* The Book of Esther is a beautifully written, colorful tale, with a miraculous denouement: the saving of the Jews of Persia by Queen Esther, who succeeded the petulant, if not rebellious, Queen Vashti. Why is this tale considered a bore? Because the book is read aloud in the synagogue after the fast and the evening prayer on Purim. This reading is

3. (In popular usage) Any very long, boring or verbose rigmarole.
4. The same old familiar story or excuses.

Megilla is used quite widely in theatrical circles ("Then he gave me the same old *megilla*") and in police departments ("Get a stenotypist; take down the whole *megilla*").

△ △ △

Channah Chorowski was a pious woman but given to garrulousness beyond endurance. One day she went to see a *tsadik.* "My health is so bad, *Rebbe,* I'm absolutely beside myself. My back is killing me—a back like that you wish on your worst enemy. And my stomach, you should excuse me, is like—like a blacksmith's anvil! Eyes? My eyes are so weak, I can barely hold them open. And I have to *see,* after all, because my ears are so bad that any day now I'll be deaf! . . ." On and on and on she yakked until, after fifteen uninterrupted minutes of this *megilla*, she paused to exclaim, "You know something, *Rebbe?* I came in with the most terrible headache of my whole life—and it just disappeared!"

The *tsadik* sighed, "No, no, lady. Your headache didn't disappear. *I* have it."

△ △ △

PLACE: *Airplane*
Adjoining seats
SEAT 1: My name's Aarons. What's yours?
SEAT 2: Mr. Aarons, my name is Goluber and I'm fifty-eight and I know I don't look it. I'm in real estate, I have a son at Cornell, my wife's maiden name was Shiffel, and she was from Philadelphia. I don't like bridge *or* golf. I spend my summers in California. I go to a Conservative synagogue. I don't have any relatives in wherever you are going. I don't think we'll have a depression. Yes, I love Chinese food. And if I've left anything out of this *megilla* ask me now, because I want to sleep until we reach San Diego.

---

interrupted and prolonged by the permitted racket made by youngsters every time the name of Haman (the would-be destroyer of the Hebrews) is uttered. Now, since no food may be consumed before hearing the *megilla,* and since by convention a special Purim feast has been prepared and waits at home, Jews are on *shpilkes (q.v.)* for the services to end. Moreover, the reading is in Hebrew—which is not understood by many in the congregation, and by no more than a handful in Reformed temples.

✡ mekheteneste

machetayneste

> Hebrew: mother-in-law.

melamed

> Pronounced m'-LOMM-ed. Hebrew: teacher.
>
> 1. Teacher of elementary Hebrew to children.
> 2. Anyone who works or thinks by rote and blind repetition.
> 3. An unworldly person. ("You can sell him the moon.")
> 4. An incompetent. ("As a plumber, he is a *melamed*.")
> 5. An unlucky man or woman.

Little prestige, oddly enough (considering the respect Jews accord to teaching), rubbed off upon the poor *melamed*. "The luck of a *melamed*" is a phrase applicable to the young man, shipwrecked on a desert island, who found one beautiful girl there: his sister.

Many Jewish names derive from *melamed:* Malamed, Malamud, Malumed, etc.

menorah

menoyre (standard)

> Pronounced m'-NAW-ra or m'-NOY-ra (Yiddish). Hebrew: candelabrum.
>
> The branched candelabrum lighted on the eight happy evenings of Chanuka.

The menorah in the great Temple had seven lamps or lights. But the Chanuka ("Feast of Lights") menorah has seven, eight or nine branches. The center candle is called the *shamus,* and from it the other candles are lighted.

Some Jewish mothers, lighting a candle for each child in the family, close their eyes as they utter a benediction and pass their hands quickly across the flame toward themselves, as if directing God's spirit ("the soul is the Lord's candle") toward themselves.*

---

* This poetic interpretation is scoffed at by those who point out that the ceremony involves a technicality of ritual importance: a *brokhe* (blessing) must precede, never follow, the

△ △ △

In Exodus 37 you will find a detailed description of the candelabrum made by Bezalel for the Tabernacle in the wilderness. The Arch of Titus, which commemorates the conquest of Judea by the Romans, shows a menorah.

mentsh

Rhymes with "bench." German: *Mensch:* person.

1. An upright, honorable, decent person ("Come on, act like a *mentsh!*")
2. Someone of consequence; someone to emulate; of noble character. ("Now, there is a *mentsh!*")
3. A personification of worth and dignity, requiring the highest respect and approbation; totally trustworthy.

Mentsh is being used more and more in English. An extremity of scorn or contempt is contained in the simple declaration: "He did not act like a *mentsh.*"

Neither wealth nor status nor success nor fame nor popularity qualify one to be called a *mentsh*. A king may be a *paskudnyak;* a doctor can be a *bulvon,* a scholar a *klutz.* The key to *mentshlichkayt* is character: rectitude, responsibility, decorum, generosity of spirit. Abraham Lincoln, say Jews, was the model-ideal of a *mentsh.*

meshugge (adjective)

meshuge (standard)

meshugas (noun)

meshugene (standard, noun, f.)

meshugener (standard, noun, m.)

Yinglish, *con brio.* Pronounced m'-SHU-geh. Hebrew. I spell it *meshugge* to emphasize the third syllable, thus circumventing the two-syllable monstrosity heard among Connecticut Jews: *me-shug.* (I am not inventing this.)

---

performance of the *mitzve.* Now this is difficult when the mother lights the Sabbath candles, because the very instant the blessing is enunciated, the Sabbath rest starts, which means no fire may be lighted. That is why the candles are lighted before any blessing, and the blessing is uttered with eyes closed: a *private* prayer is made by the mother, then she opens her eyes: the seeing of the light is counted as the *mitzve,* not the lighting.

1. Crazy.
2. Obsessed.
3. Maddened by a phobia.
4. Bizarre.

I suspect it is the seductive *sh* followed by the percussive *gg* which has made *meshugge* so popular in Yinglish. To call someone a *meshuggnitzkeh* is an indulgent way of characterizing a female wacko.

△ △ △

Poor old Mr. Zhitlov had not slept for weeks. Hot baths, hot milk, hot tea; syrups, sedatives, tranquilizers—none made so much as a dent on Itzchak Zhitlov's insomnia. In desperation, the old man's grandson, Jeffrey, called in Dr. Herman Karinsky, a noted hypnotist.

"Mr. Zhitlov," said the doctor in soothing timbre, "just relax, do what I ask, and you'll go to sleep like a blissful child." He held up a watch. "Focus on the watch . . . Good." He swung the timepiece back and forth slowly, intoning with marmalade croons, "Right . . . left . . . easy . . . nice . . . oh, that's lovely . . . eyelids heavy . . . heavy . . . *close* those eyelids . . . ah . . . yes . . . sleep . . . sleep. . . ."

Low hung the old man's head; his breathing was deep and rhythmic; a soft snore caressed the air.

Dr. Karinsky glanced at Jeffrey, put his finger to his lips, and tiptoed out.

Just as Jeffrey began to emit a sigh of relief, one of the old man's eyes opened. "Jeffeleh . . . is that *meshuggener* gone?"

△ △ △

Mr. Fralich returned from the hospital where he had visited an uncle in the psychiatric ward. "Poor Uncle," he sighed to his wife. "He raves nothing but *meshugas*."

"How terrible. Couldn't you even *talk* to him?"

"I tried. I talked about his children, his old business, the fifty dollars he owes us—"

"Aha! And did he remember?"

Fralich snorted, "That *meshugge* he's not."

△ △ △

An audacious pun adorns the story of a committee which was examining architects' renditions for a new temple. One, very impressive, was modeled on Notre Dame. The chairman of the committee said, "We *can't* have a temple with Gothic arches."

"Why not?"

"Because within ten minutes there will be fifty jokes about how this committee lost its sense and became *meshegothic*."

mezuze (standard)

mezuza

> Pronounced m'-zu-za. Hebrew: *mezuzah:* doorpost.

> The tiny tin oblong container that is affixed, in a slanting posi-
> tion, to the right of the front door jamb of his home by a Jew
> who believes in putting up a *mezuze.*

An Orthodox Jew touches his fingers to his lips, then to the *mezuze,*
every time he enters or leaves his home.

Inside the tin oblong is a rolled-up paper or parchment on which
are printed verses from Deuteronomy:

> Hear O Israel, the Lord our God is one . . . Love the Lord your God,
> and serve Him with all your heart and with all your soul. . . .

The *mezuze* consecrates the home, which is, in fact, a temple.

△ △ △

Herman Krauzaner hated Jews. He had always hated Jews. He especially hated the Mendel Waxmans, who moved next door to him in
Spring Valley, Long Island.

One night, when the Waxmans were away, Herman Krauzaner
pried the *mezuze* off the door frame of their door and hurried home.
There he broke open the tin oblong. Inside was a tiny rolled-up parchment. "At last," crowed Herman, "the secret that unites Jews around
the world!" With bated breath, Herman Krauzaner unrolled the magical
parchment. It read:

> *To whoever finds this:*
> Help! Help! I am a prisoner in Krauzaner's *mezuze* factory.

milliontshik

miliontshik (standard)

> 1. A millionaire of whom the speaker is fond.
> 2. A millionaire through luck rather than talent.
> 3. Just another millionaire.

For me to say "Julie Picharnek is a millionaire" conveys no affect; it
gives no clue as to how you should feel about Mr. Picharnek; it offers
no hints or innuendos about Julie's character.

But for me to say "Julie Picharnek is a *milliontshik,*" means:

   a. Julie is a nice fellow—maybe even a *shlemiel.*
   b. I am not resentful of Julie's million.
   c. I do not envy Julie's million.
   d. Julie should not be criticized or ostracized because of his boodle.
   e. It was not superior brains or ingenuity (which we would be justified in resenting) that accounts for Julie's *mazuma;* it was probably plain luck (or his wife's father's guiding hand).
   f. So what? Millionaires are a dime a dozen these days.

Which of these six meanings is intended is, of course, easily communicated via intonation, expression or accompanying sounds; a smile signifies meaning of *a, b* or *c;* a cluck of approval telegraphs interpretation; a sniff signifies *d;* a snort clearly designates *e;* and a sneer leaves no doubt that *f* is in the saddle of the referent's affect.

All in all, *milliontshik* is a prime example of the pleasure Jews take in embroidering language, to say nothing of the warming dimension rendered a word by tacking on the Slavic particle *-tshik,* which is the more mischievous twin of *-nik,* which is, God knows, mischievous enough.

minyen (standard)

minyon

> Pronounced MIN-yon. Hebrew: number.

> The ten male Jews required for religious services.

To have ten men is to have a "synagogue." (Children do not count: they are not mature enough to understand prayers.)

From ancient times down, rabbis have held that God's Presence *(Shechinah)* descends upon ten male Jews who congregate for worship or study. You remember, of course, that when God announced he would destroy Sodom and Gomorrah, father Abraham reminded the Almighty that there were righteous souls in Sodom, too; whereupon God said he would spare the cesspool if ten righteous men could be found there. Then the Lord sent angels to help Lot, Abraham's nephew, escape—and rained fire and brimstone upon the entire fertile plain in which the two vicious cities lay.

The book of Genesis does not tell us that God could not find ten virtuous souls in Sodom; but that must have been the case, else why would God have exterminated the place?

△ △ △

Nine saints cannot make up a *minyen*—unless a cobbler joins them.

—FOLK SAYING

mishling

>Pronounced MISH-ling. German: hybrid, crossbreed.

>Someone of mixed racial or ethnic parentage.

As used in my circles, *mishling* refers to someone with one Jewish and one non-Jewish parent. History bursts with the names of important *mishlings*.

Although anthropologists use *mishling*, I have not found it in a single dictionary of English, including the great *Oxford*. I strongly recommend the adoption of this word; it is much nicer than "half-Jewish" or "half-Gentile" or "half-breed" or half anything.

△ △ △

Groucho Marx, married to a *shikse*, asked a friend, "How do I go about joining that posh beach club in Santa Monica?"

"Don't try to get into that club," the friend said uneasily. "They're —anti-Semitic."

Groucho reflected. "Do you think they'd let my son go into the water up to his knees?"

mish-mash (standard)

mish-mosh

>Do not say "mish-mash." Rhyme this with "pish-posh." From German/Danish.

>A mess, a hodgepodge, a hopeless mix-up.

Mish-mash is a German word, defined in Cassell's *New German Dictionary* as "medley . . . hotchpotch."

Yes, I do know that the great *Oxford English Dictionary* traces *mish-mash* back to the Danish *misk-mask* and the sixteenth century. In the United States, where little Danish is spoken, it was East Side Jews who latched on to the vivid German word with the two *sh*'s, already so common in Yiddish mock appellations (*shlemiel, shlemazl, shmendrick, shmuck*), to enrich their Yinglish.

mishpokhe (standard)

meshpoche

mishpoche

> Pronounced mish-PAWKH-eh, with the palatal *kh* rattle. Hebrew: family.

> A family, including the most remote kin: cousins' cousins, third cousins once removed, nephews of nephews, *et alia*.

Anthropologists are careful to study the "extended family" *(mishpokhe)* of any tribe they examine.

For reasons I cannot fathom, Brockhaus' *Illustrated German-English English-German Dictionary* includes the word *mischpokhe*, but identifies it as "vulgar" and defines it as "rabble." To me this illustrates the fact that lexicographers need not have an ounce of sense.

△ △ △

When Chase Manhattan Bank started an advertising campaign slogan:

YOU HAVE A FRIEND AT CHASE MANHATTAN

an Israeli bank on Fifth Avenue is said to have put this sign in the window:

—BUT HERE YOU HAVE MISHPOKHE.

✡ mitzve (standard)

mitsva

mitzvah

mitzves (pl.)

mitzvoth (pl.)

> Pronounced MITZ-veh, to rhyme with "fits a." Hebrew: commandment.

> 1. Divine commandment.
> 2. A meritorious act, one that expresses God's will.
> 3. A kind, considerate, ethical deed.

Mitzves are regarded as an inescapable obligation, yet they must be performed not from a sense of duty but with "a joyous heart." There are 613 (!) separate *mitzves*. Maimonides remarked that a man who performed only one out of the 613 deserved salvation—if he did so entirely out of love. Said Eleazar ben Simeon: "Happy is he who performs a good deed: that may tip the scale for him and the world."

△ △ △

Mr. Feinschriber stood before the Recording Angel, who was scrutinizing his page in the Golden Book. "Fantastic!" exclaimed the Recording Angel. "Mr. Feinschriber, can it *be*? Your record shows nothing but *mitzves!* Tell me, in your whole life didn't you commit one *averah* (sin)?"

"Mr. Angel," quavered Mr. Feinschriber, "I tried to live like a God-fearing Jew."

"But in a whole lifetime, not one—single—sin?"

"I'm s—sorry."

"I can't let you into heaven, Feinschriber! You already are an angel! . . . I am going to send you back to earth for twenty-four hours. And if you want to get into heaven, you'll appear back here with at least one sin on your record! Goodbye!"

Poor Feinschriber was scooped back to earth. He wandered about, desolate, seeking to stray from virtue, not knowing how. . . . The hours passed. Feinschriber grew uneasy. Only twelve hours left! "Oh, God, blessed be Your name, help me. Help me to sin. Just *once!*"

And then a woman signaled to him from a doorway. . . . How swiftly Feinschriber responded! The voluptuous woman led him to her room . . . and to her bed. . . .

Hours later, Feinschriber awakened. "What time is it?"

"Half past six."

Mr. Feinschriber smiled. "Seven o'clock someone is picking me up. . . ." He started to dress, chuckling.

But the chuckles froze when, from the bed, he heard the woman sigh, "I'm over forty years old, and I was a virgin—Oh, Mr. Feinschriber, what a *mitzve* you performed last night!"

△ △ △

A man was about to jump into the Sea of Galilee when an Israeli policeman ran up to him. "No! No! How can you, a Jew in the prime of life, think of killing yourself?"

"Because I don't want to live!"

"But if you jump I'll have to go in after you. I can't swim. I have a wife and two children. I would drown! Would you want such a thing on your conscience? So don't be so selfish. Perform a real *mitzve*. Go home, and in the peace and comfort of your own home, hang yourself."

mnyeh

m'nye (standard)

> Pronounced m'n-YEH. Onomatopoeia.

1. N—no.
2. So?
3. Maybe (but I think not).
4. Who knows?
5. What difference does it make?

6. I should live so long.
7. You should live so long.
8. Tell it to Sweeney!
9. Nonsense!
10. That's what *you* say!
11. That's what *he* (she) says!
12. Oh, well . . .

The range, subtleties and dialectical force of *mnyeh* are rivaled only by such Yinglish All-American winners as *oy, nu, feh* and *ay-yay-yay!* A master of intonation can make *mnyeh* jump through hoops of deft sarcasm, polite dubeity, heartless deflation, ironic dismissal or icy derision.

Just match the definitions above to the illustrations below:

1. "Don't you *love* my wife's chopped liver?"
   "Mnyeh."
2. "I expect to double my money!"
   "Mnyeh."
3. "Are you going to Florida this year?"
   "Mnyeh."
4. "He'll make the best President since Roosevelt."
   "Mnyeh."
5. "Should we take Broadway or Riverside Drive?"
   "Mnyeh."
6. "I hear you bought a Rolls-Royce."
   "Mnyeh."
7. "Are you going to give me a birthday present?"
   "Mnyeh."
8. "The Russians will cooperate."
   "Mnyeh."
9. "Do you think inflation is ended?"
   "Mnyeh."
10. "You should be ashamed of yourself!"
    "Mnyeh."
11. "He's giving the Temple five thousand dollars!"
    "Mnyeh."
12. "It's going to *pour.*"
    "Mnyeh."

Mnyeh may be thought of as the opposite of *pssssh!* (*q.v.*)

If *oy* is the quintessential Yiddishism, and *nu* its mirror image, *mnyeh* is a star of only slightly less illuminatability.

△ △ △

Said Mr. Gans to Mr. Plisker, a lawyer: "I'll hire you—if you're positive I'll win the case."

Said Mr. Plisker, "Let's hear the facts."

Mr. Gans launched upon a detailed account of a ruptured partnership, ending, "Now: can I sue and get back my money?"

"Absolutely!" said Mr. Plisker. "I've rarely heard such an open-and-shut case!"

Gans made a sour face. *"Mnyeh."*

"What's the matter?"

"I told you *his* side of the story."

mockie

mockey

> Vulgarism. Origin unknown.

> A vulgar synonym for "Jew."

Don't confuse *mockie* with *moxie*, which you will meet soon. No one seems to know where *mockie* comes from. Maurice Samuel thought the word was descended from "Makalairy," children's slang he heard in Manchester, England, as a contemptuous form of "Jew." This is both news and Greek to me.

I never heard *mockie* until I came to New York. In my innocence, I thought it meant courage or guts. (*I* was confusing *mockie* with *moxie*.)

The list of derogatory appellations for a descendant of Abraham is long: *Abie, Arab (sic!), Ikey, Izzy, Jake, motzer, sheeny, shonacker, smouch, shnozzle, shnozzola, Yid, Yiddisher.* But before you conclude that the Chosen People are chosen for special opprobrium, consult commodious section #385 in Berrey and van den Bark's monumental *American Thesaurus of Slang* (Crowell). The list of offensive names for everyone from an Australian to a Zionist would fill five of these pages.

Mogen David

Mogen Dovid (standard)

> Pronounced MAW-ghen DU-vid. Hebrew: Shield of David.

> 1. The six-pointed Star of David.
> 2. The symbol of the nation of Israel.
> 3. The shield of King David.*

---

* On the other hand, maintain some, the double triangle, making a six-pointed star, seems to have been first used in amulets, on a shield, to protect the wearer from evil forces from all six directions. *Six* directions, you grin? Certainly: north, south, east, west, up, down. In

No one is sure when the Star of David came into use as a symbol of Jewry. No reference to the *Mogen David* is found in rabbinical writings until the thirteenth century. The first Jewish association did not occur until the seventeenth. Sorry.

Moishe Kapoyr

> In Yiddish, literally: "Moses backwards." Recommended for Yinglish.
>
> 1. Someone who always does things backwards.
> 2. A contrary type, compelled to act as most sensible people do not.

A *Moishe Kapoyr*, in any language, describes a contumacious, stubborn misfit. The name won popularity among Jews because the *Jewish Daily Forward* ran a single-frame cartoon feature so named.

momzer

mamz'r (standard)

> Pronounced MOM-zer. Hebrew: bastard.
>
> 1. A bastard. ("Leonardo da Vinci was a *momzer*.")
> 2. A mischievous, amusing person. ("At a party, she's a *momzer*.")
> 3. Someone very clever, quick, skillful. ("That Edison—some *momzer!*")
> 4. A resourceful, ingenious person.
> 5. An impudent or irreverent type. ("What nerve! What a *momzer!*")
> 6. An untrustworthy, bad character. ("Watch out. He's a real *momzer*.")

A Jewish grandparent will chortle, "My grandchild? What a clever *momzer!*" (This is in the tradition, observed in many cultures, that believes bastards to be especially intelligent.)

△ △ △

A policeman saw a man hurrying across Red Square with a bulging briefcase under his arm. "Stop!"

---

time the symbol was used to decorate sacred objects: a *talis*, the *tefillen* cover, the wrapping used around the scrolls of the Torah. During the Middle Ages, the *Mogen David* won popularity as a talisman for warriors, and as a family escutcheon.

The man froze.

"What's your name?" asked the policeman.

"Isaac Chavitski."

"A Jew! Open that briefcase."

The Jew opened the case. It was packed with rubles.

Exclaimed the policeman, "Where did you get all that money?"

"Gambling."

"You must take me for a fool!"

"I'll prove it. I—I'll bet you five rubles that you can't take off your pants inside of five minutes!"

"Five *minutes* to take off my pants?"

"That's right." Chavitski displayed a five-ruble bill.

"Done!" The policeman swiftly unlaced his boots and tore off his pants. "Finished! Less than *two* minutes!"

"You win." Chavitski gave him the five-ruble note. "Officer, how many people do you figure are in that crowd over there, watching us?"

"Oh—sixty, seventy."

"Seventy-three," said Chavitski. "And every one of them laid down ten rubles I couldn't talk you into taking off your pants in the middle of Red Square."

(Will anyone deny that Chavitski was a *momzer?*)

△ △ △

A handsome scalawag was trying to persuade a pretty girl to go to bed with him, but all his smooching and blandishments failed: the girl kept turning him down.

"Give me one good reason," he said. "*One* reason why you won't."

The girl said, "I'll hate myself in the morning!"

"Oh, well," said the *momzer,* "so sleep late."

M.O.T.

1. Code for "Member of Our Tribe."
2. A Jew (when identified as such *by* a Jew).

Like "F.H.B." (Family Hold Back—on the food), *M.O.T.* is not meant to be understood by the person in whose presence it is used. "Is he *M.O.T.?*" means "Is he Jewish?"

I never heard these initials used in Chicago. When I first heard them, in New York, I was totally at sea.

moxie

moxy

moxey

English slang. Rhymes with "Coxey." Derivation unknown. (Do not confuse with *mockie*.) A staple of Lower East Side Yinglish.

1. Courage, nerve.
2. Initiative: get-up-and-go-ness.
3. Shrewdness, know-how in street matters.
4. A soft drink (no longer).

Moxie is used a good deal in sports circles. I *think* it was first used by Dashiell Hammett to describe the bravery or brashness of a young prize-fighter. I do not think he coined the word.

It is rare for a writer to invent a colloquialism he has not already heard. Gelett Burgess did with "blurb," but failed with "huzzlecoo" (see SHMOOS). I thought I could make history when I proposed "Nokay!" as a retort to the interrogative "Okay?" I failed.

△ △ △

Billy Shnier was a compulsive gambler, and a constant loser. His wife told him that if he gambled once more she would leave him forever.

Business took Billy to Detroit for three days. And for three nights he participated in poker games. He lost everything but his return ticket. On the plane back to New York, he pondered how to keep his wife from knowing the truth. . . .

When he got off the plane, he went to a men's shop, bought a red handkerchief and took a taxi home. At the door, he tied the handkerchief around his face, then rang.

His wife opened the door. "Billy! Oh, my God! What happened to you?"

"Detroit," gasped Billy. "I was mugged. By three men. They put a knife to my throat. Said unless I gave them every penny, they would cut off my nose!"

She fainted.

Billy got some ice. The red handkerchief he kept on. When his wife came to, she gasped, "Oh, God. Without a nose! . . . Billy, Billy—why didn't you give them all your money?!"

Said Billy as he removed the kerchief, "I did."

(You wanted an example of moxie? That's an example of moxie.)

moyl (standard)

mohel

Rhymes with "Boyle" (and if you ever hear of a *moyl* named Boyle, telephone the *Forvitz*). Hebrew: circumciser.

> The professional who circumcises a male baby born of a Jewish mother on the eighth day after his birth. (The ritual is called *Brith Milah:* "the circumcision covenant" of Genesis 17:7–12.)

Oriental Jews perform the ceremony in a synagogue. In the West, the *brith* (or *bris, q.v.*) takes place at home, or at the hospital.

△ △ △

No story I ever heard struck me as so triumphant as the classic about the Englishman in New York who stopped at a window in the middle of which stood one lone clock. The Englishman went inside. "He-llo!" he sang out.

From behind a curtain stepped a bearded man in a skullcap.

"Would you please inspect this watch?" The Englishman worked at the strap. "Tell me whether it needs—"

"Why are you asking me?" asked the bearded one.

"Aren't you a jeweler?"

"No. I'm a *moyl.*"

"A what?"

"A *moyl.* I make circumcisions."

"Good Lord!" exclaimed the Englishman. "But why do you have a *clock* in your window?!"

"Mister," sighed the *moyl*, "what would *you* put in the window?"

N

narr

nar (standard)

> Rhymes with "car." German: fool.

> 1. Fool.
> 2. Buffoon, clown.

The generic name for a fool is *Shmerl Narr (q.v.).*

Delightful irony graces the Yiddish saying *Er iz nisht (nit) kayn groyser khokhem, und nit kayn klayner narr.* (He is no big brain, and no small fool.)

△ △ △

Police Headquarters in Tel Aviv sent a "Wanted for Bank Robbery" poster, with six different mug shots of the robber, to every police station in Israel.

A week later the phone in Headquarters rang: "Hello, here is Flensky from Station 32, the Negev. Good news! I already arrested five of those crooks, and I think I'll grab the last one before nightfall."

△ △ △

Two Jews from Brooklyn emigrated to Israel. They bought a house and began to put up a wooden fence. Each nailed a board to a stake from his side. After several minutes, Shimon said, "Zvi, why do you keep throwing away all those new nails?"

"The ones I throw away are *made* wrong. They have the points on the wrong end! Look."

"*Oy*, Zvi, are you a *narr!* . . . Those are for my side of the fence!"

nayfish

nefish (standard)

> Possibly (experts disagree) from Hebrew: *nefish:* a being; soul.

1. A weak, ineffectual, complacent person.
2. An innocent.
3. A *shlemiel*—in spades.

△ △ △

The *nayfish* demanded: "Mr. Schlaum, either you give me a twenty-dollar raise or else!"

"Or else what?"

"Or else—I'll work at the same salary."

△ △ △

Three Jews stood before the firing squad, whose captain said, "Do you have a last wish?"

"A cigarette," said the first.

"Here . . . And you?"

The second man spit in the captain's face.

"Oh, God!" cried the third. "Please, Joe, don't make trouble!"

(There can be no doubt that he was a *nayfish*.)

nebech

nebekh (standard)

neb (diminutive)

nebbish

nebechel (diminutive)

nebochem (pl.)

> Yinglish, and well established. Noun and interpolation. Accent the *neb;* the *ch* is as in German *Ach!,* not as in English "choo-choo." The pronunciation *nebish,* with *sh* replacing *kh,* is an Americanism for those who know no Yiddish but need the word. From Czech: *neboky:* unfortunate.
>
> *As a noun:*
> 1. A weak sister.
> 2. A born loser; a very unlucky person.
> 3. A small, thin, unimpressive sort *(nebechel).*
> 4. A nonentity.
> 5. A namby-pamby *shlemiel.*

Nebech is a pointed, expressive name for a character type found in almost any culture.

"Don't ask that *nebech* to come to the rescue."

"Whom did she (he) marry? A *neb.*"

Better ten enemies than one friend who is a *nebech*.

—FOLK SAYING

Note: *Nebech* contains a large ingredient of pity on the part of those who use it: we feel sorry for a *nebech*. The difference between a *nebech* and a *shlemiel* may be this: you can dislike, or get angry with, a *shlemiel* —but not a poor *nebech*.

Woody Allen (or, at least, the character he plays in his films) may be crowned our current King of *Nebechs*, successor to such classic archetypes of ineffectuality as Harry Langdon and Stan Laurel. It was Mr. Allen (né Konigsberg) who cried, "If there is a God, why is there poverty and baldness?" He was no less querulous about life after death: "I don't believe in it, but I'm taking along a change of underwear."

> *As an interjection* (a marvelous, versatile epithet):
> 6. Too bad; alas. ("The poor chap had to go to the hospital, *nebech*.")
> 7. Unfortunately. ("He, *nebech*, lost his shirt.")
> 8. Dismay. ("She looked, *nebech*, like a lunatic.")
> 9. Sympathy. ("Lost his wife, *nebech*.")

As an interjection, *nebech* is "mal-recognitive" (says James Matisoff), the supreme Yiddishism for lamenting one's plight or expressing sympathy for the misfortune of another:

> "So I, *nebech* (alas), lost the key."

> "The widow fainted, *nebech* (poor thing)."

> "He was terribly embarrassed, *nebech*." (I feel sorry for him.)

Nebech is never used to express satisfaction or pleasure; hence the exquisite irony in the statement of the 1940s: "You know what would make me the happiest man in the world? To be sitting in the sun, on a beautiful summer's day, saying to my girl: 'Look, darling. There, *nebech*, goes Adolf Hitler.'"

Nebech has an old provenance, back to the fifteenth century, meticulously traced by Max Weinreich (*History of the Yiddish Language*, pages 542–43).

See SHLEMIEL, YOLD.

△ △ △

A *nebech* is the person in a group you always forget to introduce.

A *nebech* is the dope who always picks up what a *shlemiel* knocks over.

The *nebech* is the customer on whom the *shlemazl* of a waiter always spills soup.

Once a *nebech* always a *nebech.*

A man is, *nebech,* only a man.

△ △ △

△ △ △

A *nebech* began to park on a busy street in the garment district. Along came a cop.

"Officer," asked the *nebech*, "is it okay to park here?"

"Absolutely not!"

"B–but, how about all those cars that are already parked?"

"They," sneered the cop, "didn't ask."

Neturey Karta

Pronounced ne-TU (as in "put")-rie KAR-ta. Aramaic: guardians of the city.

A sect of Jews who refuse to recognize Israel as an independent state, and who periodically protest against "the enemy of the Jews": Zionism.

Does this puzzle you? The ultra-Orthodox claim that a true Israel, a holy sovereignty, could only be established by the Messiah—and the Messiah has surely not yet come.

In Israel, these pious Jews stone automobiles that move about on the Sabbath, and curse male Jewish tourists who do not wear a hat or *yarmulke.* The mass demonstrations against Israel by the American *Neturey Karta* are familiar to New Yorkers. An advertisement of the group in *The New York Times* (May 15, 1981) attacked

> . . . the Zionist state [Israel] . . . because Zionism seeks to change the essence of Judaism and substitute chauvinism and militarism. . . . The Jewish nation was not founded by Zionist politicians . . . but was determined on Mount Sinai. . . . The Jewish redemption will come with the coming of the Meshiach. The establishment of the Zionist state before that time is heretic and indeed blasphemous.

nexdoorekeh (f.)

nexdooreker (m.)

The next-door neighbor.

△ △ △

I once had a *nexdooreker* who told me this yarn:

The owner of the Sporting Goods Arcade watched Klinger, his new salesman, declaim to a customer, "Now, why not buy some new fishing line?"

"All right."

"And with a new line, why not a spinning reel?"

"Uh—sure."

"And a fishing vest? Here's a special."

"Good."

"And boots? Look at these hip-high beauties."

"Okay, okay."

Klinger wrapped the purchases, made out a sales ticket and pumped the customer's hand. "'Bye."

The owner came over. "Klinger, in all my years in this business, I never saw a salesman to compare to you! A man comes in for one lousy fishhook and you talk him into—"

"He didn't come in for a hook," said Klinger.

"What did he come in for?"

"Aspirin," said Klinger. "He thought this was a drugstore. He said, 'Aspirin. For my wife. She—she's having her period.' So I said, 'Well, since she'll be out of action for a few days, why not go fishing?' "

next

> Used as a noun: Yinglish, lock, stock and barrel (which is a great deal to be if you are a one-syllable word).
>
> 1. Next.
> 2. Turn.

It still amuses me to hear a clerk or barber sing out, "It's your next!" That does not happen on Piccadilly or Fifth Avenue, but you can hear it on Delancey Street or Fairfax Avenue or all over the Upper West Side.

△ △ △

Jeremy Krim, an impossible bore, finally came to Dr. Tish, psychiatrist. "Doc, what's *wrong* with me? My wife don't talk to me, also my son, my friends, my partner. A waitress, a cabdriver, even a barber don't talk to me. I ask you: Why?"

Dr. Tish thought for a minute, then called, "Next!"

nifter-pifter

> From the Talmudic euphemism: *nifter:* departed, died.

Dead.

Nifter-pifter, abi gezunt! (Dead-shmead, just so he's healthy.) This is the crown of absurdity, and itself sufficient reason to draft *nifter-pifter* into the ranks of Yinglish.

Talmudists, when asked, "And how is So-and-so?" would reply "He is, alas, *nifter.*" A Jew unfamiliar with Hebrew would beam, "*Nifter-pifter,* as long as he's in good health."

-nik

-nick

A suffix, from Slavic languages, well-ensconced in Yinglish.

This syllable can convert a verb, noun or adjective into a colorful pejorative for an ardent lover, cultist or devotee of something: *jognik, peacenik, richnik. Alrightnik* is, of course, the prime example.

-Nik lends itself to exhilarating inventions. A *sicknik* is one who fancies black humor. A *Freudnik* is an uncritical acolyte of the Master. Homosexuals refer to heterosexuals as *straightniks.* Diligent cruise-takers are, obviously, *cruiseniks.* A hypochondriacal nut about medication is a *pillnik.* And I surely need not explain what a *pornonik* is.

△ △ △

PEACENIK: Why don't the leaders of the world realize that nations can solve all their problems if they just decide to live together like one big family?
CYNIC: God forbid.

no-good (as noun)

no-goodnik

"No good" elevated to a compound noun; and "no-good" suffixed into a universal character type.

1. A person, male or female (or both), who is not worth a plugged nickel.
2. A low-life.
3. A wastrel.
4. A never-get-mixed-up-with-him type.
5. A you'd-be-a-damned-fool-to-trust-him type.

△ △ △

Mendel and Yitzchok were on the subway when a gang of hoodlums came into their car. "This is a stickup! Hand over all valuables!"

Mendel and Yitzchok removed their wallets fast. But just before the *no-goodniks* reached them, Mendel handed a bill to Yitzchok: "Here's that twenty I owe you."

△ △ △

HARTZ: You are a no-good! You went back on your word!

TARSHER: I resent that! In my whole life, did you ever heard my honesty questioned?

HARTZ: Questioned? I never even heard it mentioned!

nokh (standard)

noch

Pronounced NAWKH, with the Scottish *kh.* German: another.

1. Another.
2. Else, more. (Give him *nokh* time.)
3. Yet (of surprise). See below.

The last is characteristically Yiddish:

"From him you expected honesty, *nokh?*"

"For such disgusting behavior he was praised, *nokh?*"

See YET.

△ △ △

The best usage I know of *nokh* occurs in the story of old Mr. Weinstock, who takes a seat in the subway next to a black man. To Mr. Weinstock's astonishment, the black man has his nose buried in the *Forvitz (Jewish Daily Forward).*

Mr. Weinstock watches. His neighbor reads and reads, absolutely riveted to the page, turns it (from right to left, not left to right) and reads on.

Mr. Weinstock can hardly contain himself and finally blurts, "Excuse me, mister. Can you read Yiddish?"

The black man nods. "Uh huh."

"My! Tell me—are you Jewish?"

The black man lowers the paper and slaps his knee in disgust. *"Dos felt mir nokh!"*

nosh

nash (standard)

nosher

noshen (verb)

Rhyme *nosh* with "gosh." German: *naschen:* to eat on the sly.

1. A snack.
2. Anything eaten between meals and, presumably, in small quantity: fruit, "a piece cake," a candy.

nosher

1. One who eats between meals.
2. One who has a sweet tooth.

noshen

Noshen (to *nosh*) is to "have a little bite before dinner" or to "have a little something between meals."

Standard Yiddish spells the word *nash;* but I have yet to run across a single instance where the word, quite common in English today, is spelled that way. Let pedants gnash their dentals over my *nosh.*

nova

This does not refer to a phenomenon in the galaxies, nor to the wholly admirable television series that bears this name. In Yinglish, *nova* is the instantly recognized abbreviation for Nova Scotia, and by "Nova Scotia" the deli counterman, waiter or customer does not intend to refer to a portion of the North American continent. *Nova* means the unsurpassed salmon, less salty and more expensive than lox *(q.v.).*

△ △ △

SCENE: *A Deli on Lexington Avenue*

CUSTOMER: This salmon—is from a can?
WAITER: What *can?* This salmon comes from Nova Scotia!
CUSTOMER: Uh, was it imported or deported?

Now he (she) tells us!

"We offered him twice the value of his stock, and finally, after he turned us down nine times, we went elsewhere and got the stock for one-third less. *Now* he says he'll accept our offer!"

"I wanted to take her to Palm Beach in January, when it was ten below in New York and eighty-five in Florida. Today, it's a beautiful day in New York and ninety-eight in Palm Beach. *Now* she wants to go!"

△ △ △

The nuclear complaint packed into that simple, one-syllabled "now" is an example of Yinglish at its most acidulous.

Perhaps the most famous (and justified) deployment of the adverb followed the revelation that a soldier of the American army had undergone a change-of-sex operation in Denmark, to become Miss Christine Jorgenson. In Jorgenson's old barracks, above the cot Jorgenson had recently occupied, appeared this sign:

NOW HE TELLS US!

nu

nu(?!)

nu-nu

Rhymes with "do." From Russian: well; so; and German *nu* and *nun*. Cognates of *nu* are common in Indo-European tongues, but in which is *nu* put through such prodigious psychological acrobatics as glorify it in Yiddish?

A huffy/whimsical emphasizer, qualifier, interjection, sigh, aside, lament, expletive or comment.

Nu and *oy* are quintessential Yiddish and sturdy Yinglish. These versatile utterances are the sonic equivalents of a moan, a groan, a nod, a sob, a grin, a grunt, a sneer, a complaint. . . . Consider the nuances of this two-lettered arsenal:

1. "*Nu?*" (How are things? What's new?)
2. "Should we go? *Nu?*" (What do *you* say?)
3. "*Nu,* what could I do?" (Well . . .)
4. "I saw her leave your apartment at three A.M. *Nu* . . . ?" (So–o–o? Explain.)
5. "—he ran out! *Nu?*" (Can you beat that?)
6. "Listen, I want the money. *Nu?*" (Will you or won't you pay?)
7. A.: "I'm going to a funeral."
   B.: "*Nu?*" (So what's the hurry?)
8. "They raised the rent again! *Nu.*" (Nothing can be done.)
9. "They liked the book. I—*nu?*" (I did not, but I leave it to you to guess why.)
10. "—so buy the damn thing. *Nu?*" (Put an end to the shilly-shallying.)

When used in tandem, *nu* becomes a sentence:

"Can you imagine how I felt? *Nu-nu.*" (I know you can, so I'll skip an elaborate description.)
"They argued, they fought—*nu-nu.*" (Why go on?)

"She says you're an animal! *Nu-nu?*" (You've got to respond to that.)

I should warn the unwary that to ask a Jew *"Nu?"* invites the frustrating, even infuriating, reply: *"Nu-nu?"*

Other uses:

1.

"Would you like a Danish?"

"Nu-nu?" (Of *course* I want a Danish.)

2.

"Listen, Jerry. The whole building knows . . ."

"Nu?" (So what?)

"Don't give me with the *'Nu?'* Jerry! *Nu-nu?*" (Open up. Talk.)

3.

"Hector, are you Jewish?"

"Nu? (What else?) Are you, Claude?"

"Nu-nu?" (Of course I am.)

△ △ △

Not until 11 A.M. did Hyman Movitz come to work—hobbling on a cane, a bandage on his head, one arm in a sling.

"Movitz!" called the boss. "You're two—hours—late!"

"Mr. Lessman, I was trying to fix my screen—and I fell down three stories!"

"Nu? That takes *two hours?!"*

△ △ △

Sign over an ice machine in Tel Aviv Hotel

NOTICE

If everything else you try doesn't work, *nu*—
try reading the directions.

△ △ △

Marovitz owed Ziegler 150 dollars. Ziegler decided to send him a telegram. In the Western Union office, he wrote:

YOU OWE ME 150 DOLLARS ALREADY 2 YEARS. NU? WHEN WILL YOU PAY ME BACK?

Ziegler reread this thoughtfully. It was expensive to send so many words. He struck out "You owe me 150 dollars already 2 years." (Marovitz had a memory like an elephant.) Then Ziegler struck out "back." (How else can you return money to one from whom you borrowed it?) Then he struck out "me." (Who else should Marovitz send the money to?) Then he struck out "When will you pay?" (Why give Marovitz the impression that he could pay at his pleasure?) The telegram now read:

NU?
—Ziegler

He received the following answer:

NU-NU?
—Marovitz

nudnik

Rhymes with "good Dick." From Russian: *nudna*.

1. A persistent nag or pest.
2. Someone who bores others—monumentally.

See NUDZH.

A *nudnik* is never pleasant, however otherwise good, intelligent or generous.

A *phudnik* is a *nudnik* with a Ph.D. And the groves of Academe burst with both.

△ △ △

PATIENT: All day, all night, I talk to myself!
DOCTOR: Oh, many people do that.
PATIENT: But they're not such *nudniks!*

nudzh (noun)

nudzheh (verb)

Beginning to appear as Yinglish. Use the *u* of "put," not "nut." From Polish, Ukrainian, Russian, via Yiddish.

As a noun:
One who pesters, nags, annoys. ("He may be good-hearted, but what a *nudzh!*")
As a verb:
To act the boring *nudnik*. ("Stop *nudzhing* me!")

American films and television talk shows are using *nudzh* (no less than *nudnik*) as staples of Yinglish.

nyotting

Pronounced ny-OTT-ing. Fashioned by Jews from Eastern Europe to accentuate meaning.

Nothing.

In Yiddish, the word for "nothing" is *gurnisht* (or *gurnit)*, which is both an adjective and a noun. "He is *gurnisht*" takes on added pungency as "He is a *gurnisht*." There is a saying *"Gurnisht mit gurnisht"* ("Nothing plus nothing," or "It all adds up to zero").

And what is *nyotting*? Nothing but a palatalized embellishment of "nothing": a jocular bit of verbal embroidery, prolonging the time of both utterance and enjoyment.

△ △ △

ACT ONE: *June*

"Listen, Morrie: are you having an affair with our new telephone operator?"

"You bet I am, Al. I took her to a hotel last night—and I tell you, compared to her, my wife is *nyotting!*"

ACT TWO: *July*

"Listen, Al. Are *you* having an affair with our telephone operator?"

"*Am* I! And you were right, Morrie: Compared to her, your wife is *nyotting.*"

O

olav ha-sholem

olev ha-sholem

    See ALAV HA-SHOLEM.

omeyn (standard)

awmayn

    Pronounced aw-MAIN. From Hebrew: So be it.

    Amen.

Used by Jews, Christians and Muslims, "amen" is surely the most universal symbol uttered to signify:

    1. Affirmation, at the end of a prayer.

The Talmud declares that "Amen" should be announced not softly nor mechanically, but "with the full power of the voice." This decree was taken so seriously by the ultra-pious that they came to believe that a thunderous rendition of "Amen!" helped open the gates of Heaven. In ancient Alexandria, the Great Synagogue was so vast and so packed during prayer that worshippers spilled onto the stone steps of the entrance outside and could not hear the cantor—hence could not know when a prayer was completed. So an attendant would wave a big flag to effect a mighty "Amen!" from the throng.

    2. A recognition of wrongdoing.

The forceful reiteration of "Amen" became attached to the voicing of repentance, a feeling of great power in Judaism.

    3. Agreement and reinforcement of a wish.

It was inevitable that the interjection used in religious services would carry over into life outside. "Amen," pronounced "Awmain" by Ash-kenazim, came to decorate ordinary discourse:

> "She should only get well and come home in one piece!"
> *"Omeyn."*

> "Oh, if only my wish comes true—to meet the right man and get married—"
> *"Omeyn."*

4. An expletive of malediction, joining someone who has invited disaster upon an accursed enemy, or milder misfortunes upon someone merely disliked.

> "I hope he loses every dime he ever made."
> *"Omeyn!"*

> "May he live in a house with a hundred rooms, and in each room there should be a bed, and let him toss from bed to bed for the rest of his life and *never* get one night's good sleep."
> *"Omeyn!"*

For a flamboyant arsenal of abusive wishes, see James A. Matisoff's mind-boggling collection, *Blessings, Curses, Hopes and Fears* (Institute for the Study of Human Issues).

See CURSES.

Omission of preposition "of"

> Yinglish. Ungrammatical (and unaesthetic).

Americans ask for "a cup of coffee" or "a glass of milk." Even in haste, they do not drop the preposition; they may resort to a slurred fusion: "cuppa" or "glassa." But Yinglish speakers do not use the preposition at all, because in Yiddish it is ungrammatical—nay, impossible!—to say "a bowl *of* soup" or "a glass *of* milk." (Many languages have gotten rid of the partitive genitive, you should excuse the expression, *q.v.*)

In American fiction and theater, the omission of "of" brands the speaker as 1) Jewish; 2) from New York; 3) not a college graduate. But American journalism, to say nothing of oratory, is opening its arms wide to such barbarisms as "He is the type person. . ." This type usage should positively be avoided.

△ △ △

Mr. Fechter met his cousin, who had arrived in America only six months ago. "So how goes it?"

"Terrible. I was sick last month; and the doctor bills—! I had to pay forty-seven dollars!"

"Forty-seven dollars isn't so terrible."

"No? In the old country, for that kind money, I could be sick two years!"

△ △ △

Mrs. Rimess was on the witness stand. The lawyer for the defense asked: "You are Hilda Rimess?"

"Absolutely."

"Wife Alexander Rimess?"

"Naturally."

"And what does your husband do?"

"He's a well-known manufacturer."

"Children?"

Mrs. Rimess blanched. "Mi*god,* no. Underwear."

△ △ △

Edwin Wittengrad went into the bank and to the desk of the president, R. Franklin Peurifoy.

"Mr. President, my name is Ed Wittengrad. I own Home Hardware Haven on Second Avenue. My business is booming. So I want to expand. So I'm here to ask a loan one hundred thousand dollars."

Mr. Peurifoy nodded. "For a sum that substantial, we need a statement."

"Certainly." Wittengrad cleared his throat. "I am absolutely, positively optimistic!"

ongepatshket

Pronounce it un-g'-potch-kat. From Russian: *pochkat:* to soil, to dirty, or German: *patschen:* to slap, to splash through.

1. Overdecorated; gussied up; so ornate as to be in bad taste. ("Her gown was *ongepatshket;* she looked ridiculous.")
2. Created carelessly. ("That painting looks like something my grandchild smeared with fingerpaints: *ongepatshket!*")
3. Too crowded, confused or improvised to be readily understood. ("Our foreign policy is so *ongepatshket* no one believes in it.")

△ △ △

Solly Berman bought an "ultra-reductionist" piece of sculpture called "Destiny" by one Stanislaus Kropotski: the sculpture consisted of a black plank with a white nail at one end. Proudly, Berman asked his friend Si Altoff, "Isn't that magnificent?"

Altoff forced himself to nod.

A year later, Berman bought a second Kropotski. This *trompe d'chutzpa* consisted of a black plank with *two* white nails at one end. "A masterpiece!" cried Berman. "Right?"

Altoff closed one eye, cocked his head, and murmured, "Isn't it a wee bit—*ongepatshket?*"

Only in America . . .

> . . . is this possible.

Not a week passed during my boyhood (or two weeks, since then) without my hearing this exclamation. It is the immigrants' testament, an affirmation of the opportunities imbedded in that Promised Land, that haven of minorities, that proven land of the free that is America. Scarcely a new shop, a new product, a new journal or school or fad could appear without ecstatic *Only in America!*s.

Henry Ford announced an automobile for $600? *Only in America.*

Benny Leonard, a Jew, was lightweight boxing champion? *Only in America.*

The Rockefellers were setting up a philanthropic foundation? *Only in America.*

You can buy a radio and hear the opera in New *York? Only in America.*

Malted milk sodas?! *Only in America.*

The zipper? *Only in America.*

Galoshes? Airplanes? Ballpoint pens? Disposable anythings? *Only, only, only in America!* The author of "God Bless America," words and music, was a Jew from the East Side, Irving Baline (Berlin).

△ △ △

Little Arthur and Melvin got into such a heated argument that little Arthur cried: "And my father can beat the pants off your father!"

"What?" frowned little Melvin. "My father *is* your father."

(Only in Hollywood.)

. . . on you (him, her, them), it's becoming

> Born of English: transposed phrase for emphasis.

This phrase can be used straight ("That's not a color I wear, but on you, it's fine"), or with a barb ("That fur came from a baboon, but on *her*, it's attractive").

△ △ △

The classic use of the phrase occurs in the story about the two women on the porch of a hotel in the Adirondacks.

A young man approached from the lake.

"Mein Gott!" exclaimed the first woman. "Look at that ugly! Did you ever see such big ears? Such a potato nose? Such fat lips—"

"That," iced the second woman, "happens to be—my—son."

The first woman gulped—for but an instant. "You know, on *him,* it's becoming!"

△ △ △

Placing the phrase at the beginning of a sentence adds the power of delayed effect to a statement: *e.g.,* the climax of the following story:

Into an office of NASA came an old man in a *yarmulke,* hunched over a cane. To the receptionist, he handed a newspaper clipping: "Who should I see about this ad?" The clipping read:

WANTED

For training as Astronaut. Age: 21–26. Should have degree in science or engineering. Must be in perfect health. Write National Aeronautics and Space Agency.

The receptionist said, "Our Mr. Fleming is in charge of recruiting. . . ."

"Tell him I'm here. The name is Gittelman. Sol Gittelman."

"Excuse me, sir, but—for whom are you here?"

"For mineself."

"Your*self?!* Mr. Gittelman, do you—have a degree in science—"

"No. Also no for engineer. Plus, I am over seventy-four years old."

"Then why do you want to see Mr. Fleming?"

"I want to tell him," said Mr. Gittelman, "that on *me,* he shouldn't depend!"

opgeflikt

Pronounced UP-ge-flikt. From the German: *abpflücken:* plucked, plucked clean.

This melodious word is used less often to describe the de-featherment of a fowl than the mulcting of a pigeon. . . . The sucker in a shell game has been *opgeflikt* not if he has merely been tricked (in which case he would be *opgenart*) but only if he has been *oysgeleydikt—i.e.,* cleaned out.

△ △ △

MR. ESTRIN: Aren't you the salesman who gave such a wonderful description of the car I bought last month?
SALESMAN: I'm the one.
MR. ESTRIN: Please tell me again. I'm getting discouraged.

opstairsikeh (f.)

opstairsiker (m.)

> Pronounced with accent on the "stairs."

> The upstairs neighbor.

△ △ △

In Herzlia, our hotel *opstairsikeh* told us that there was a judge in Israel, famed for his tact, who told women witnesses on the stand: "The witness will state her age—after which the clerk will swear her in."

. . . out of this world

> From Yiddish; perhaps from the common Yiddish *an oysnam fun der velt* (a taking-out—or exception—from the world). A comparable Hebrew idiom states that something exceptionally pleasurable (sleep, sex) is a whiff of the "world to come"—*i.e.,* something "not of this world," hence "out of" it.

This etymology, attractive and persuasive to me, is by no means persuasive to the scholar who suggested it with a wince.

1. Beyond comparison.
   "What sort of harpist is she?"
   "She's out of this world."
2. Utterly unique.
   "How would you describe sex?"
   "Simple: It's out of this world."
3. Remarkable.
   "As a poet, he's just out of this world."

△ △ △

Here's a joke that is surely out of this world:

Quietly, expectantly, the great throng waited at the foot of the mountain. Moses had been gone for *hours*.

Suddenly his white robe was seen fluttering in the breeze. Breathlessly, the Lawgiver stood before his flock: "People of Israel! I have been four hours with—*baruch ha-Shem*—the Lord! And I now come to you with—good news, and bad news. . . ."

"Speak, O Moses, our Teacher!"

"The good news," said Moses, "is that I have managed to bring His 'don't' list down to—ten!"

A great cheer swept across the land. "And O Moses, our Teacher," cried a patriarch, "what is the bad news?"

Moses cleared his throat. "Adultery is still in."

oy

Quintessential, 150 proof, 24-karat Yinglish.

1. Oh, woe.
2. Oh, mi*god!*
3. Don't tell me!
4. Great Scott!
5. You don't mean it!
   Etc. (see below).

I think the best way to describe this all-purpose, heartfelt, shmaltz-smeared ejaculation is this: *Oy* is not a word; *oy* is a vocabulary.

Once that is understood I may tell you that *oy* is a cry of dismay, a howl of pain, an exclamation of fear, an obeisance to horror, a flag of protest, a reflex of relief, a—well, perhaps it would be better simply to illustrate the many, many uses of this phoneme:

1. Contentment: "How we enjoyed that lunch—*oy* . . ."
2. Relief: "*Oy*, she's home safe."
3. Uncertainty: "What should I wear? *Oy*."
4. Startledness: "*Oy!* Who's there?"
5. Surprise with a note of apprehension: "*Oy!* What was that noise?"
6. Minor dismay: "*Oy*, he's come early."
7. Joy: "*Oy!* What a lucky break!"
8. Revulsion: "You expect me to eat *that? Oy!*"
9. Awe: "He actually scored 99 on the test?! *Oy*."
10. Irony: "*Oy*, are you clever."
11. Irritation: "Take that mess away. *Oy!*"
12. Large astonishment: "*Oy gevalt!* He wants to be a pilot!"
13. Pain (moderate): "*Oy!* That hurt."
14. Pain (considerable): "O–o–*oy*."
15. Pain (extreme): "O–o–*oy, Gotenyu!*"
16. Anguish: "Please, I beg you, o–o–*oy* . . ."
17. Horror: "You swallowed an open safety pin? *Oy!*"
18. Despair: "What's the use? O–*oy*."
19. Shock: "What? Her? Here?! *Oy!*"

20. Flabbergastication: "What in God's name can we do now? O–*oy!*"
21. Lamentation: "*Oy* . . . what a man to lose . . . what a mind . . . what a heart . . . O–*oy.*"
22. Outrage: "Never bring that swine into this house! *Oy!*"
23. Numbed disbelief: "My own child . . . a thing like that . . . *Oy.*"
24. Utterly at-the-end-of-your-wittedness: "I can't stand another minute! Go! Go! O–o–o–*oy!*"

You will of course have noted certain similarities between *oy* and *Gevalt!* The differences are greater. *Gevalt!* is rarely used for declamations of relief or pleasure; it is associated with "Help!" or "Oh, God!"

Oy vey: A common Yiddish reflex; it literally means "Oh, pain," but in effect signifies: "Oh, woe is me." It is the truncated form of *"Oy vey iz mir."* ("Oh, what a sadness/misfortune for me.")

Oy-oy: A duet of surprise.

Oy-oy-oy: The triad of lamentation. If you wonder how to distinguish *oy* from *ai* or even *ah!,* or *oy-oy* from *ay-yay-yay,* permit me to shed light:

When you plunge into a very cold lake, you cry *"Oy!"*—but then you like it and say *"Ay . . ."*

When you commit a sin, you love it and go *"Ah . . ."* but then, realizing what you've done, you wail *"O-o-oy!"* . . .

When you find a purse with $10,000 in bills, you shout *"Ay-yay-yay-yay-yay!"* and when you find out they're counterfeit, you moan *"Oy-oy-oy-oy-o-o-o-oy!"*

△ △ △

"Hollo," Elzer Rafkin answered the phone.

A fruity Mayfair female voice asked, "May I speak to Mr. Roland Witherspoon?"

"Who?"

"Mr. Roland Witherspoon the Third."

"Oy, lady, did you get a wrong number!"

△ △ △

Mrs. Sersky dialed her daughter's number and sang out, "Hel*lo,* dolling! So how are you?"

*"Ter*rible, Mama. My back is killing me, the children are acting like wild Indians, the house is a mess—and to top it off, I have six guests for dinner!"

"Stop, dolling! I'm coming right over! I'll feed the children, I'll clean up your place, and I'll cook a dinner your guests will never forget!"

"Oh, Mama! You angel! . . . How's Papa?"

"Papa? . . . Dolling, are you crazy? Your papa died nine years ago."
Pause. "What number are you calling?"

"Alton 6-4491."

"This is Alton 6-4494."

"*O–O–oy!* I dialed the wrong number!"

"Wait! Please!" the voice wailed. "Does that mean you're not coming over?"

△ △ △

SCENE: *A restaurant in Hitler's Vienna*

Four Jews are in a coffee house, seated glumly before their *schlag.*

FIRST MAN: *Oy . . .*

SECOND MAN: *Oy vey . . .*

THIRD MAN: *Vey iz mir . . .*

FOURTH MAN: If you three don't stop talking politics, I'll get out of here.

oys-

Proposed for Yinglish. Exquisite prefix. Rhymes with "voice." From German: *aus.*

1. Out of.
2. Finished.
3. No longer.

The prefix *oys-* is an expressive syllable with a declamatory impact; its purpose is the cancellation of whatever follows:

"A top violinist, and in one second, losing that finger—*oys*-fiddler."

"The minute I saw it was registered mail, I knew I was *oys*-Vice President in Charge of Production."

"He tried out for the team, but in two minutes he knew he was *oys*-athlete."

English uses "ex" to indicate a condition ("once" or "whilom"); but "ex" does not convey the idea of an abrupt and undesired termination, which *oys-* certainly does.

△ △ △

Siggy Tobias approached the desk of the vice president of the bank. "Mr. Dalloway, I've come about that loan you made me. . . ."

"Yes, Mr. Tobias. A hundred and eighty thousand dollars, if I recall."

"You recall right."

"Well?"

"Mr. Dalloway, what do you know about the hook-and-eye business?"

"I? Nothing, Mr. Tobias. Absolutely nothing."

"Maybe you should learn it fast," said Tobias, "because I'm *oys*-business, and you're in it."

P

pareve

> Pronounced PAR-eh-va. From Russian: *parovoy:* a field not seeded for a particular crop, hence neutral. (This derivation came as a surprise to me.)*
>
> Kosher because neutral: *i.e.,* neither meat nor dairy.

The dietary laws for observing Jews do not permit them to eat meat and dairy products at the same meal (see KOSHER).

Modern chemistry has passed on its wonders to pious palates: margarine can be made without butterfat or milk; ice cream is made of soybean oil; even cream has a *pareve* substitute.

paskudnak

paskudnyak

> This colorful word waits, with confidence, in the anteroom of Yinglish; no English word approaches it in psycholinguistic effect. Rhymes with "poss good lock." From several Slavic tongues.
>
> 1. A disgusting, odious character.
> 2. An ungrateful, selfish, treacherous person.
> 3. A hypocrite.
> 4. A greedy trickster.

---

* Says Professor Susskind: "The derivation seems farfetched, but that is how needed words are coined by simple folk."

Adding the *y* to make *paskudnak,* more greasily, *paskudnyak,* is to endow contempt with cadence. All in all, the three syllables convey more disgust than any English synonym I can think of.

The best way of describing a *paskudnyak* is through case studies, like those below.

△ △ △

Mr. Elfenbein said to Rabbi Hyman: "It's too sad to believe! Imagine, Rabbi: a widow, three little children, owes four hundred dollars in rent, and unless she pays before Saturday she'll be evicted!"

"How terrible," said the rabbi. "I'll make an appeal. And here is fifty dollars of my own."

"Thank you, Rabbi."

"You are a good man, Mr. Elfenbein. Are you related to the widow?"

"Oh, no."

"What got you interested in this case?"

"I'm the landlord."

(He certainly was a *paskudnyak.*)

△ △ △

In Vienna, an old Jew, crossing the Ringstrasse, bumped into an anti-Semite.

"*Schweinhund!*" roared the *paskudnyak.*

The Jew bowed: "Ginsberg."

△ △ △

The shabby man stood before the rich man and asked for help. The rich man called his butler. "*Look* at this wretch! His trousers are patched. His shoes are worn out. He looks as if he hasn't been able to bathe for a week. It breaks my heart to see such misery—throw him out."

(*That* is a *paskudnyak.*)

✡ Passover

> In Yiddish: *Peysekh,* with a Caledonian *kh.* Often printed in English as *Pesach.*
>
> The eight- or seven-day holiday that is the most cherished of all Jewish commemorations. It is also called "The Festival of Freedom."

Passover is celebrated for eight days by Orthodox Jews, and for seven in Israel and among Reform Jews.

Pesach celebrates the freeing of Israel from enslavement in Egypt some 3,200 years ago. (The whole story is, of course, in Exodus.)

patshke (standard)

potchke

potchkee

> Pronounce it POTCH-ka and, for playful effect, POTCH-kee. From German, via Yiddish.

> To fuss around or mess around. (I spent the weekend *patshkee-ing* around the garden.)

It is the echoic attraction of *patshke* that recommends itself to Yinglish. Linguists may note how vivid are the unvoiced stopped consonants *p* and *k*. "Unvoiced" does not mean silent, but without vibration of the vocal cords.

△ △ △

"Mr. Dorfman," said the mechanic, "your car needs a complete overhaul. Three hundred dollars. But when I'm done, this baby will purr like a cat!"

Mr. Dorfman swallowed a Tum. "Tell me, how much will it cost if you don't *patshke* around and just make it meow like a pussy?"

a person

> Yinglish.

> The genteelism used instead of "I," "one," or "someone."

> This is a transposition into English of the Yiddish *emetzer* (someone) or *mentsh:* a person.

> "A person could think you're having an affair!"

> "Listen, don't you share your happiness with a person?"

How H. W. Fowler excoriated such fustian, foolishly thought to be "less vulgar, less improper, less apt to come unhandsomely betwixt the wind and our nobility."

The most famous deployment of the euphuism is, of course, "Adelaide's Lament" in *Guys and Dolls:* "A per-son could develop a cold."

△ △ △

The woman on the couch said, "My family doctor insisted that I come to see you. God only knows what gave him such a silly idea! A person happily married, loves her home, hasn't been sick a day in her life—"

"Stop," said the psychoanalyst. *"How long has this been going on?"*

peyes (standard)

payess

> Rhymes with "say less." From Hebrew.

> The long unshorn ear ringlets and sideburns worn by ultra-Orthodox male Jews. (See Leviticus 19:27.)

In the Middle Ages, church powers often forbade Jews to trim their beards (to be certain that Jews could be identified); but for a time *peyes* were forbidden by law in Czarist Russia.

To wear or to cut the *peyes* became an important question among Jews in the United States during the great immigrations from Europe.

△ △ △

West Forty-seventh Street in New York, where hordes of Hasidim carry on trade in gems, is known as the *Rue de la Peyes*.

pfui!

phooey!

> From German via Yiddish.

> Phooey!

I would hesitate to offer Yiddish as the provenance for this emphatic expletive, which has come into wide English usage since the 1920s, were it not for the attribution by Stuart Berg Flexner (*I Hear America Talking*, Van Nostrand).

Phooey is a clone of *feh!*—than which no phoneme is more expressive. Jews are not the only people, of course, who enlist the labiodental fricative (*f* or *v*) for the utterance of sounds of disgust. Rex Stout loved to put *pfui!* into the conversation of the masterful Nero Wolfe.

See FEH!

△ △ △

"What great news, Grampa! Our men have reached the moon!"
"Pfui!"
"How can you *say* that?"
"Look, *boychik:* if you have money, you travel."

Ph.G.

> Yinglish, and only Yinglish.

> Acronym, popular among the young and the cynical, for *Papa hot gelt* ("Her/his father is loaded").

In-group phrases such as Ph.G. are, of course, meant not to be understood by outsiders—*i.e.,* those who do not understand Yiddish.

Other examples, which you will find in this chrestomathy, are J.A.P., M.O.T., A.K., A.M.—but not D.U.T. (Don't use them).

pilpul

> A splendid word for Yinglish. Rhymes with "sill full." Hebrew: analytic debate . . . intense dialectics.
>
> 1. Extremely intensive argumentation used in discussions of passages in the Talmud.
> 2. Hair-splitting that is meant to show off reasoning instead of increasing clarity.
> 3. Logic-chopping carried to absurd lengths.
> 4. Farfetched correlations; too-elaborate justifications.

The casuistic properties of *pilpul* are neatly illustrated (and mocked) in this story:

Rabbi Tarshover was a great logician. He could answer any question —even on the most difficult points in the Talmud. His powers of reason seemed so great that one of his disciples said: "Our rabbi can think his way through *any* dilemma!"

"It is true that our rabbi has a mind of unparalleled power," said another acolyte, "but what if he were tired, drowsy . . . would his reason still prevail?"

The students decided to test their beloved genius. At the feast of Succoth they gave the rabbi enough wine to make him tipsy. Then, when he dozed off, they carried him to the cemetery, where they tenderly laid him—and hid behind the tombstone.

After a while, the great reasoner stirred, sat up, looked about and, in the traditional singsong of *pilpul*, chanted, "*Nu-u,* i–if I am alive, what am I doing here? . . . Bu–ut if I am dead, why do I have to go to the bathroom?"*

△ △ △

Two kitchenware stores, directly across the street from each other, one named Metski's, the other named Boretz, sprouted huge banners:

GOING OUT OF BUSINESS!!

EVERYTHING MUST GO!!

---

* In Yiddish: *Farum darf ikh geyn pishn?*

A passerby asked Mr. Boretz, "How do you feel about that fellow across the street?"

"Metski? That no-good? He'll be out of business in a week! *I'll* be here twenty years from now. You know why? Because my reputation for going-out-of-business is A Number One! People know they can rely on me. Metski—they know is a faker!"

△ △ △

If you say "I'm right!" long enough, you're wrong.

"For example" is not proof.

—FOLK SAYINGS

△ △ △

In the annals of *pilpul* there must be a special spot for Samuel Goldwyn's imperishable observation: "It's an absolutely impossible situation—but it has possibilities."

△ △ △

A *shnorer* came to Mrs. Zhitlov's back door. "Lady, I haven't seen food in four days. I'm starving!"

"Oh, you poor man! I don't have much food—"

"I'll eat anything!"

"Would you—uh—like some *kugel,* left over from last night?"

"I'd *love* it!"

"Good," said Mrs. Zhitlov. "Come back tomorrow."

✡ Pishe Peyshe

Pronounced PISH-a PAY-sha.

A simple card game for two—one of whom is usually a child.

The game is an English game, called "Pitch and Patience," which was transmogrified by Cockney Jews as "Pisha Pasha." Amazing.

Many Jewish children were taught to count by playing Pishe Peyshe. Without such educational intentions, card games were frowned upon by Jews. (Times have changed.)

platke-macher

plyotke-makher (standard)

Pronounced PLOT-keh-ma-kher (with a Caledonian *kh*). Slavic: *platke:* gossip; and German: *Macher:* maker.

1. A gossip—malicious.
2. A troublemaker.
3. An unpleasant *yente (q.v.)* or *yachne.*

A *platke-macher* is a specialist who can make a mountain of disrepute out of a handful of innuendo.

△ △ △

The Hasidim tell a telling tale about gossip-makers: A *platke-macher* had told so many malicious untruths about the local rabbi that, overcome by remorse, he begged the rabbi to forgive him. "And, *Rebbe,* tell me how I can make amends."

The rabbi sighed. "Take two pillows, go to the public square, and there cut the pillows open. Then wave them in the air. Then come back."

The rumormonger quickly went home, got two pillows and a knife, hastened to the square, cut the pillows open, waved them in the air, then hastened back to the rabbi's chambers. "I did just what you said, *Rebbe!*"

"Good." The rabbi smiled. "Now, to realize how much harm is done by gossip, go back to the square . . ."

"And?"

"And collect all your feathers."

△ △ △

What's easy to say may be hard to bear.

It's easier to hear a secret than to keep it.

A tongue can be a dangerous weapon.

Run from gossip as you would run from ghosts.

—FOLK SAYINGS

People pierce each other with the sword of their tongues.

—TALMUD: *Yomah,* 9b

Your friend has a friend, and your friend's friend has a friend (so be discreet).

—adapted from TALMUD: *Kethuboth,* 109b

Gossipers start with praise and end with derogation.

—MIDRASH: *Tanhuma,* 9

Even if all of a slander is not believed, half is.

—MIDRASH: *Genesis Rabbah,* 56:4

pletsl

A thin, flat roll garnished with poppy seeds or onion. A staple in Jewish bakeries.

Try one. Unique taste.

△ △ △

SCENE: *Lipsky's Bakery*

"Twenty cents for a *pletsl?*" protested Mrs. Schar. "Why, Tunkel the Baker is charging only ten!"

"So buy them from Tunkel," said Mr. Lipsky.

"Well, Tunkel happens not to have any *pletsls* left today."

"Lady," said Mr. Lipsky, "when I don't have any I charge only five cents."

plosher

Rhymes with "kosher." German dialect: *plauschen:* chat.

1. An overly talkative person.
2. A constant boaster.
3. A gossip.
4. An unreliable, because exaggerating, person.

A stalwart archer in the phalanx of derogation, *plosher* is a synonym, in one or another subtle aspect, for *bluffer, fonfer, fifer, hoo-ha-nik, k'naker, platke-macher, smarkatch, tumler, trombenik.*

I think the plosive *plo* and rushing *sh* combine to make the aural image as admirable as it is accurate.

△ △ △

I assume you have heard of the Texan *plosher* who declared he did not need his glasses when driving his Rolls-Royce: "I had the windshield ground to my prescription."

△ △ △

Mrs. Verna De Kofsky, an *alrightnikeh* of yore (and a *plosher* before), was boasting about the trip she and her husband had taken to Europe. "Rome is falling to pieces! The Colosseum has no roof! All the statues have broken arms and noses!"

"But we had an audience with the Pope," said her husband.

Their friends oohed and aahed.

"*Nu,*" asked one, "how did he impress you?"

"Him, I adored!" said Mrs. De Kofsky. "Her, I found boring."

△ △ △

PROUD MOTHER (to guests): My Sammy, only six weeks in school, and you should see how much he knows already! I'll show you. Sammy, tell us: if you take three apples and add three apples, how many apples do you have?

SAMMY (knitting brow): Five.

MOTHER (beaming): See! Only missed by one!

△ △ △

SCENE: *Airliner to Phoenix*

MACTOLIVER: I can't wait to get out into that sun and onto the course. . . . Are you by any chance a golfer?

SLOTSKY (a *plosher*): Am *I* a golfer? Golf is my life!

MACTOLIVER: Well, well. I manage to play in the seventies.

SLOTSKY: Exactly what I do! But if it gets one degree colder, I head right back to the hotel.

△ △ △

What is the sign of a fool? He talks too much.

—*Zohar*

As long as words are in your mouth, you are their Lord; the moment you utter them, you are their slave.

—IBN GABIROL, *Choice of Pearls,* 33

How can you say, "It was only words. No harm was done." Were this true, your prayers—and consolations—would be a waste of breath.

—NACHMAN OF BRATSLAV

plotz

plats (standard)

> Yinglish, with juice. Rhymes with "dots." German: *platzen:* to burst.

1. Bust, burst, explode. ("I laughed so hard I thought I would *plotz!*")
2. To be aggravated, frustrated or infuriated to an extremity. ("He was so furious he almost *plotzed!*")

Yes, I know, there is another meaning for *plotz:* a place, a seat: ("You are in my *plotz.*"). But English does not need a Yiddish word for *that* simple meaning; whereas *plotz*—the percussive punch of the *pl,* plus the dentalized, explosive *otz*—is a vivid sonic image.

△ △ △

"Front desk?" Mr. Bristik shouted into the hotel phone at 2:30 A.M. "I'm ready to *plotz!* Nothing less! You ever heard of the straw that broke the camel's back?"

"Yes, sir."

"Well, I'm sleeping on it!"

pogrom

> From Russian: *pogrom:* destruction.

> Massacre—of Jews.

I wish I did not have to include this entry. What other word covers so much horror, and such a horrifying history?

It would be foolhardy for me to try to describe the gory multitude of beatings, lootings, rapes, torture, slaughter of Jewish babies, kidnappings of Jewish boys, burnings of synagogues with the Jews locked inside—for which God's "chosen people" were chosen.

> The central feature of this year's report [1906, American Jewish Year Book] is the table of massacres of Jews in Russia, during the period whose entrance and exit are guarded by Kishineff and Bialystok as bloodstained sentinels. The figures frightfully arrayed are so heart-rending that one is impelled to apologize for perpetuating them. It would be a wanton harassment of the feelings, were it not a document to stimulate Israel to self-help, and gentiles to self-introspection.
> —*Of Making Many Books*, edited by Joshua Block
> (Jewish Publication Society)

I have never forgotten the account, by Disraeli's father, of one extraordinary incident:

> The castle [at York, in 1190] had sufficient strength for defence . . . but the cruel [English] multitude felt such a desire of slaughtering those they intended to despoil, that . . . the attacks continued, till at length the Jews perceived they could hold out no longer. . . .
> When the Jewish council was assembled, the *Haham* (rabbi) rose and addressed them . . . "Men of Israel! . . . If we fall into the hands of our enemies, which we cannot escape, our death will be ignominious and cruel. It is therefore my advice that we elude their tortures; that we ourselves should be our own executioners; that we voluntarily surrender our lives to our Creator. God seems to call for us; let us not be unworthy of that call." Having said this, the old man sat down and wept. Some departed, but every man [remaining] . . . fearful of trusting to the timid and irresolute hand of the women, first destroyed his wife and children, and then himself. . . .
> In the morning the walls of [York] castle were seen wrapt in

flames, and only a few . . . beings, unworthy of the sword, were viewed on the battlements, pointing to their extinct brethren. When they opened the gates of the castle, these men verified the prediction of their late Rabbin; for the multitude, bursting through the solitary courts, found themselves defrauded of their hopes, and in a moment avenged themselves on the feeble wretches who knew not how to die with honor.

—Isaac d'Israeli, *Curiosities of Literature*, vol. 2

pssssh!

Expletive, depending for its meaning on sound, not substance:

1. Remarkable!
2. How astonishing!
3. Can you imagine that?!

Sholom Aleichem, the most irresistible of Jewish writers, decreed that the principal parts of "much" (in Yiddish) are "much . . . more . . . *pssssh!*"

This all-purpose expression is one of the fondest recollections of my boyhood, perhaps because my father (who never lost his keenness of appreciation or surprise) cried *"Pssssh!"* so often. He greatly enjoyed sharing his astonishments. In the course of a day he might exclaim:

"You saw in the paper what the President said? *Psssh!*"

"Look at this picture. *Psssh!*"

"If I had that much money . . . *psssh,* what I would do!"

"You actually *did?* . . . *Psssh!*"

△ △ △

"Ah," crooned Mr. Mitzmacher, "New York, New York . . . it's not the same. *Psssh!* . . . In the good old days—"

"When New York was New York?"

"N–no; when Mitzmacher was Mitzmacher."

pupik

Pronounce the *u* of "put," not the *u* of "pupil." From Slavic.

1. Navel (belly-button).
2. Gizzard (of chicken).

Why should one ever use *pupik* for "navel"? Because it *sounds* funnier. *Pupik* is a sonic tonic: one bilabial *p* percusses sarcasm; two are a duet of derogation.

Who could forget this description of a pedant: "He's the kind of man who worries whether a flea has a *pupik*."

Pupik has a variety of idiomatic uses:

"Stick it in your *pupik!*"

"May onions grow in her *pupik*."

"Oh, gee, thanks—to your *pupik!*" ("Thanks for nothing.")

"If he had as much brains in his head as my boy has in his *pupik*, he'd be better off."

"That just goes into my *pupik*." ("It doesn't make a dent on me.")

"I've had it up to my *pupik!*" is a heartfelt way of saying: "I can't *take* any more!" or "I'm fed to the teeth!" (even though teeth scarcely belong in the same metaphor with navel).

Moishe Pupik (or Pipik) is a generic name for dumbbells, dolts and oafs.

✡ Purim

> Do not use the *u* of "pure"; pronounce it POOR-im. Hebrew: *pur:* lot.

> The Feast of Lots; it commemorates the rescue of the Jews in Persia from Haman's plot to exterminate them.

Lots had been cast by Haman, Minister to King Ahasuerus (Xerxes) to decide on the date on which the Jews would be slaughtered. A miraculous deliverance was effected by Queen Esther (who was Jewish), and Mordecai, her uncle. Haman ended up on the gallows he had erected to dispatch Mordecai. The legend is told in the Book of Esther.

I say "legend" because centuries of scholarship have failed to authenticate the tale. Two thousand years ago, Jews had already challenged the validity of the Book of Esther, which was first set down in Persian, and rejected its right to be included among the canonical works of the Bible.

As for the feast of Purim, "little or nothing is known" about its origin (John Dyneley Prince, *Jewish Encyclopedia*, vol. 5, page 237).

The celebration of Purim has been strictly forbidden to Jews in different times and places by hostile governments.

Purim may well be the most Jewish of holidays, in the sense that it is the most beloved and ever contemporary: *i.e.,* thousands of celebrations, called "little Purims," are held in Jewish families to commemorate a miraculous personal deliverance, escape or rescue. A scholar tells me he considers Purim *the* holiday *par excellence*, "more Jewish than Yom Kippur and Rosh Hashanah."

pushke

pishka

> Used in Yinglish by any who know it in Yiddish. This word is pronounced PUSH-keh by Polish Jews and PISH-keh by Litvaks. From Polish: *puszke*.
>
> 1. The small container (usually a tin can) kept in the home (usually the kitchen), in which donations to one or another charity were dropped.
> 2. The money a wife "keeps out" (saves) of the household money. Such subtractions are inviolately hers, to be spent for presents, delicacies, a holiday, an emergency. . . .
> 3. The money a girl has before she marries, which remains hers.

There was a time where every Jewish home had an array of tin cans lined up on the kitchen windowsill; each can carried the label of a worthy cause.

For a mind-boggling list of organizations named on *pushkes,* see *The Joys of Yiddish;* here, I cannot resist naming (in addition to orphans, widows, the lame, the halt, the blind, the ailing, the aged):

> For the Immigration of Romanians to Palestine.
>
> For Adding a Social Hall to the Local Synagogue.
>
> For the Families of Victims of Pogroms in Bessarabia.
>
> For Bringing a Famous Cantor from Warsaw (Odessa, Kiev) to Officiate at Rosh Hashanah Services.
>
> For Training Immigrants to be Farmers in the Mid/Far West.
>
> For Sending a Rabbi-Saint to the Holy Land Before He Dies.

△ △ △

Mr. Bielenson called a repairman to come and fix the venetian blind in his living room.

The following Tuesday the repairman came to the Bielenson flat. Mr. Bielenson was not in.

"What do you want?" asked Mrs. Bielenson.

"I've come for the venetian blind."

She gave him a dollar.

putz

Rhymes with "cuts." German: *Putz:* ornament.

(Vulgar)
As a noun:
1. Penis.

But *putz* is often used, with condescension, for

2. A dolt, a fool.
3. A *shmegegge,* a pigeon, a yokel.

As a verb:
4. To waste time (as the English "futz").
5. To sleep around, to be promiscuous.

Some arbiters of language hold that *putz* is slightly (but only slightly) less vulgar than *shmuck* (*q.v.*); others consider *putz* slightly more offensive because it aims to be euphemistic. Avoid both words. (But to those who love the punch of the colloquial: use *putz* only after you see who's present.)

See SHMUCK (taboo).

△ △ △

DR. FROLICH: You're going to have to make a real change in your way of life, Mr. Cooperman.
COOPERMAN: Like what?
DR. FROLICH: Like you have to give up *shnaps* and cigarettes. And you can't *putz* around at your age. This will be the best thing in the world for you!
COOPERMAN: Doc . . . What's the second best?

R

✡ rabbi

In Yiddish, *rebbe* (REB-beh). From Hebrew: *rabi:* my teacher.

1. The ordained Jewish cleric, spiritual leader of a congregation.
2. The revered leader, not necessarily ordained, of a Hasidic sect, always called *rebbe*.

Unlike "minister" or "priest," the title *rabbi* does not indicate the role of an intermediary between the congregation (or a pray-er) and the Lord. A rabbi's authority is built only upon his knowledge and his character. The rabbi is freely engaged—and disengaged—by the members of the community. There is no hierarchy in Judaism. (Originally, *rabbi* was the honorific accorded teachers at a yeshiva. The title was not used until the Christian era began.) Let me here quote the great scholar Louis Ginzberg:

> The rabbi of centuries gone by was neither an official of the synagogue nor its minister. He was master over none but himself; he was servant to none but his God. In the good old times every Jew . . . was an eager participant in the worship service. There was no need of an orator, nor of a specialist who recites the prayers for the rest of the worshipers. In short, the rabbinate as a profession is of comparatively recent growth.
>
> —in *A Treasury of Judaism*,
> edited by Philip Birnbaum (Hebrew Publishing Co.)

The relation of a Hasid to his followers is another matter. The Hasidic *rebbe* is considered a saint, a paragon of wisdom, so venerated that he is credited with supernatural powers.

△ △ △

A goat has a beard, but that doesn't make him a rabbi.

A rabbi whose congregation does not want to drive him out of town isn't a rabbi; and a rabbi they do drive out isn't a man.

—based on a saying in the TALMUD

It was hard for Satan alone to mislead the whole world, so he appointed rabbis.

—attributed to Nachman of Bratslav

△ △ △

"Rebbe," asked the immigrant, "how can I live the life of a good Jew on what I make?"

"How much do you make?"

"Twenty-six dollars a week."

"On twenty-six dollars a week," said the rabbi, "that's *all* you can do."

real-estatenik

1. One who is obsessed by real estate.
2. One who does (or has done) well in selling/buying properties.

△ △ △

"Hello, Rabbi Korkuff?"

"Yes."

"This is John Reilly, deputy director of the Manhattan branch of the Internal Revenue Service. I'm calling about a member of your congregation, Samuel J. Prischoff, who is in the real-estate business."

"Y–yes?"

"Mr. Prischoff has claimed a five-thousand-dollar deduction on his tax return. He says he contributed that amount, in cash, to your temple. Did he?"

"Mr. Reilly," said the rabbi, "if you call back tomorrow, the answer, I assure you—will be 'Yes.' "

△ △ △

A visitor to Houston asked Mr. Glickman, "I'll bet you own many oil wells."

"Not one."

"Cattle?"

"Who knows from cattle?"

"You must own land, then; a ranch."

"Well, maybe three acres."

"That's very little for a ranch. What do you call it?"

"Downtown."

Reb

Hebrew: *rabi:* master.

Mister.

But *Reb* (unlike *rebbe* or rabbi) is never used by itself; it must be followed by a first name: Reb Norman, Reb Yankel, Reb Timothy. (*"Timothy?"* Yep. I know several Timothys whose parents are—or were born—Jews.) Many Jews think *Reb* is an affectionate abbreviation of *rebbe* (rabbi), but this is incorrect. *Rebbe* means "my spiritual master," "my teacher," whereas *Reb* is simply a term of address, like "mister" or "sir."

Reb Yankel

A foolish Jew.

△ △ △

One recent census form contained the following crucial information:

Name: Yankel Kleinberg
Address: 2406 Harper St., St. Louis
Length of residence: 52 feet

refusenik

Someone behind the Iron Curtain who is refused an exit visa, no matter how often he/she applies for one.

Refusenik is used by the Committee of Concerned Scientists, which sponsors meetings of Soviet scientists who have been denied exit visas to Israel from the glorious Fatherland, and who lose their jobs or research posts as well.

△ △ △

It is probably apocryphal, but good to believe, that a Jewish pharmacist in Moscow placed this sign in his window:

LAXATIVE
Soft . . . Painless . . . Proven . . .
to
LET MY PEOPLE GO

△ △ △
scene: *Office of the Commissar of Visas, Kremlin, Moscow*

"So I've come to you, Comrade Commissar," said Lev Brodsky earnestly, "after three years of applications, petitions, interviews—"

"Da, da."

"—to ask why, *why* can't I leave the Soviet Union?"

The Commissar said, "Becouse in brain you hold vary importont scientific secret! You will give tham to copitolistic contries!"

"That's absurd!" cried Brodsky. "I've been barred from my physics laboratory for ten years; I haven't been allowed to attend scientific meetings; and even when I was working on missiles, ten years ago, the Americans were so far ahead of us that our weapons were laughable—"

"Dot," thundered the Commissar, "is de secret!"

△ △ △
A KGB agent saw a Jew on a park bench reading a book. "What are you reading?"

"A Hebrew grammar."

"Why bother, Jew? We'll never let you go to Israel."

"Well, in Heaven they speak Hebrew."

"Ha! Suppose you go to Hell?"

Sighed the Jew, "I already know Russian."

regular

> Yinglish for:
> 1. Actually, really.
> 2. Virtually, practically—though not actually.
> 3. Authentic.

Examples, in same numerical order:

1. "That Nat: a regular expert on Blue Cross."

2. "Sonya? She's a regular pharmacist." (But not a certified one.)

3. "What do you mean you don't believe Marvin? He's a regular lawyer!" (Marvin is not an amateur; nor does he *pretend* to be a lawyer. He is a *bona fide* counselor-at-law, with a diploma and a J.D.)

△ △ △
Years ago a bearded Jew from Boston, visiting a relative in Alabama, was followed everywhere by a group of goggle-eyed Southern children. Finally the old man addressed the magpies: "What's a mare, kiddies? You never before saw a regular Yenkee?"

Repetition—to escape the obvious and maximize persuasiveness

> "I'm going, I'm going."
> "I know, I know." (Usually "I know, I *know*.")
> "You'll like it, you'll *like* it."

The latter has, of course, won international attention as an advertising slogan.

This kind of repetition is a staple of Jewish communication and illustrates the propensity of Yiddish to employ irony for the banishment of the banal. The difference between "You'll like it" and "You'll like it, you'll *like* it" is as monumental as the difference between "I don't know," which is bloodlessly phatic, and "I don't know, I don't *know!*" which is a defiant confession of ignorance.

Ridicule through repetition

No sarcasm is more devastating than that which answers a question simply by repeating it to the questioner:

> Q. Do you like cheesecake?
> A. Do I like cheesecake?

The meaning is: "What sort of idiot goes around asking people if they like cheesecake?" Or, if you prefer: "What kind of dummy does *not* like cheesecake?"

The question-repeated is a double-edged sword, for it also cuts in reverse, namely, "What kind of person do you think I am? Some creep who *doesn't* like cheesecake?"

I do not doubt that at this point many a reader will cavil, as about certain other entries, "But surely this is English? Why classify it as Yinglish?"

Well, the words are English; the syntax is English; but the force and function are Yinglish. The intonation, inflection, expressions accompanying the seemingly straightforward echo surround the question with an irony that answers the question asked by repeating it in a manner which means, "Surely you can't mean what you've just asked: just listen to the words. . . ." And that brand of fraudulent literalness is a feature of Jewish parlance.

Another way of making my point: Was it not the persistent usage by Jews of this conversational ploy (Jewish writers/comedians) that rooted and nourished it in the soil of English?

✡ Rosh Hashanah

Rosh Hashone (standard)

Rosh Hashonah

Rosh Hashona

> Pronounced rawsh ha-SHAW-neh (rhyme with "cautious fauna").
> Hebrew: beginning (of the) year.

> The holiday that celebrates the birthday of—the world.

So ruled the rabbis of old. *Rosh Hashanah* begins the Ten Days of Penitence which end with the solemn Yom Kippur. During these days, mankind presumably passes before the Heavenly Throne, and God looks into their hearts. Orthodox and Conservative Jews celebrate two days of Rosh Hashanah; Reform Jews celebrate only one.

S

salesslady

salessmon

> Yinglish to the core.

> A salesperson.

Can anyone deny that the consonant clusters *-sl* and *-sm* (in "saleslady" and "salesman") are tricky to articulate? Immigrant Jews solved the difficulty with aplomb: they simply inserted a helpful and delaying syllable.

If you bridle at the idea of foreigners running around adding phonemes to perfectly respectable English words, let me know how you feel about the 3,745,904 Americans who say "a-tha-let-ic."

Sarcasm via the use of innocent adjectives/adverbs in malefic contexts

> "She wasn't depressed: she merely tried to hang herself."

> "He knocked out only four of my teeth."

> "I doubt that he ate more than fifteen sandwiches."

> "Was that much to ask: a measly million dollars?"

Scorn (achieved by placing the grammatical object before the grammatical subject)

> "The race? Sure he won. Last place, he won."
> "*Thanks* she expects for losing my credit cards?"
> "*Two* arms he broke."

△ △ △

The Judge said, "Mr. Edelstein, you are a key witness. You must tell us only what you actually saw. You must not give hearsay evidence. Is that perfectly clear?"

"Yes, sir."

The prosecuting attorney asked: "What is your name?"

"Emanuel F. Edelstein."

"How old are you?"

"That depends on when I was born. And that I can't tell you, even though I was there. Hearsay evidence, that's all I have."

"Second Avenue"

The generic allusion to the Yiddish Theater in America.

The theaters in which Yiddish plays appeared in New York were not confined to Second Avenue; they also clustered around the Bowery, Houston Street, and lower Broadway: Jacob Adler's Grand Theater, Maurice Schwartz's Yiddish Art Theater, Boris Thomashevsky's famous playhouse, the much-loved Mayfair.

One could fill an encyclopedia with tales of the Yiddish theater. In New York, remarkable companies offered Yiddish-language productions of Shakespeare, Chekhov, Gogol, Schiller, Strindberg, Ibsen, O'Neill. Jewish playwrights created a treasury of dramas and comedies, in Yiddish, on themes dear to the hearts of immigrant audiences. Jewish "art theaters" from Moscow, Warsaw, Vilna, including the great Habima Theater, often came to Manhattan, then toured the United States and South America.

The passion of Jews for the theater was of an intensity that can scarcely be described without hyperbole. Sweatshop workers earning ten dollars a week would pay five dollars for a ticket. The theater was not only the main amusement for its audiences, who patronized no sporting events (and very rarely visited a saloon): the *teater* (tee-AH-ter) was the meeting-ground in which to find old friends, make new acquaintances—and gossip. The lobbies were jammed (before the performance, during the intermission, afterwards) with impassioned acolytes of Culture.

The actors enjoyed a popularity that bordered on adulation, which I observed for myself in the Café Royale *(alavasholem)* on Second Avenue, the Sardi's-*cum*-"21" of the Yiddish stage. You may go deeper into the surprises in my "Valhalla on Second Avenue," in *The 3:10 to Anywhere* (McGraw-Hill).

As for the audiences: they were altogether remarkable. A contemporary's description has come down to us from Hutchins Hapgood's classic, written in 1901:

> ... the theatre presents a peculiarly picturesque sight. Poor working-men and women with babies of all ages fill the theatre. Great enthusiasm is manifested, sincere laughter and tears accompany the sincere acting on the stage. Pedlars of soda-water, candy or fantastic gewgaws of many kinds, mix freely with the audience between the acts. Conversation during the play is received with strenuous hisses, but the falling of the curtain is the signal for groups of friends to get together. . . .
> The supremacy of the Yiddish actor has its humorous limitations. The orthodox Jews who go to the theatre on Friday night, the beginning of Sabbath, are commonly somewhat ashamed of themselves and try to quiet their consciences by a vociferous condemnation of the actions on the stage. The actor who . . . is compelled to appear on Friday night with a cigar in his mouth, is frequently greeted with hisses and strenuous cries of "Shame, shame, smoke on the Sabbath!" from the proletarian hypocrites in the gallery.
> —*The Spirit of the Ghetto,* reprinted 1965 (Schocken)

Most of the plays I saw in Chicago and New York were admirable: the acting, lighting, sets, costumes were altogether superb. Many a Gentile actor or director frequented the Yiddish theater.

Excellent recent books about "Second Avenue" are Nahma Sandrow's *Vagabond Stars: A World History of the Yiddish Theater* (Harper and Row, 1977), and Lulla Rosenfeld's *Bright Star of Exile: Jacob Adler and the Yiddish Theater* (Crowell, 1977).

Seltzer water

The effervescent beverage made by charging water with carbon dioxide.

This drink, a great favorite with Eastern European immigrants, was also known as "for two cents plain"—that being the price, in happier times, for a glass of soda water without syrup (chocolate, strawberry, etc.).

The "Seltzer" comes from the name of the town in Germany, Niederselters (near Wiesbaden), where a natural spring provided bubbly water believed to possess salubrious chemicals. The word "soda" derives from the fact that bicarbonate of soda was added for an effervescent and supposedly restorative effect.

"Seltzer" has been replaced by "club," since "Seltzer" became identified as a remedy for headaches, indigestion and hangovers.

The Dictionary of Word and Phrase Origins, by William and Mary Morris, points out that in parts of the Midwest (and, say I, in the South) ordering "soda" would get you a sweet, orange- or lemon-flavored children's drink. To mix this confection with hard liquor produced a rather loathsome beverage. Adding the posh "club" to "soda" ended the confusion.

△ △ △

The big Motsner Seltzer Water delivery truck, fully loaded, ran into a fire hydrant and turned over on its side with a terrific crash. Bottles and siphons flew out in all directions, and they smashed, and bubbling waters poured into the street. A crowd swiftly assembled.

"Oy, oy," the driver was crying. "My boss will expect me to pay for all this!"

An elderly man stepped forth and turned to the crowd. "This is terrible! A nice, hard-working Jew—ruined. . . ." He took off his hat. "Let's take up a collection. Ladies, open your purses! Gentlemen, dig into your pockets! This is a real *mitzve* we can perform."

Dollar bills and coins soon filled the hat.

The old man dumped the contents of the hat into the driver's spread apron and went off.

"My, my!" sang one onlooker.

"There is a real Jewish heart!"

The driver shrugged. "That was Mr. Motsner."

Sephardi

Sephardim (pl.)

> Pronounced seh-FAR-dee, to rhyme with "Bacardi." Hebrew: Spanish. (Spain, in Hebrew, is Sepharad.)
>
> 1. Spanish and Portuguese Jews, or their descendants. (In Israel, the name *Sephardim* includes Jews of the Middle East and North Africa.)
> 2. Those Ashkenazic Hasidim who follow part of the Sephardic liturgy.

Sephardic thinking, an amalgam of Talmud and Greek philosophy (especially Aristotle), dominated Judaism from around 1000 C.E. until the end of the fifteenth century, when Spain and Portugal, to their everlasting misfortune, expelled the Jews from Iberia. Those who survived forcible conversion, drownings and assorted disasters settled in Holland, England and along the Mediterranean, especially in the Ottoman Empire.

Sephardic Jews, familiar with Latin, Greek, French, Spanish, brought mathematics, medicine, astronomy and physics into Judaic thought. Sephardic Jews held important posts in Spain, Portugal, North

Africa: physicians, financiers, philosophers, poets—advisers to kings and courts. (Sephardic writers wrote in Judeo-Arabic, even when writing about Torah and Talmud.) They were aristocrats: their religious services, their style of living, were invested with a splendor such as poor Eastern European Jews did not know.

Today, Sephardic Jews are found throughout South America, Asia Minor, England, Holland, Latin America and, of course, the United States.

See ASHKENAZI. See also Solomon Grayzel's *A History of the Jews* (Jewish Publication Society, Philadelphia), Cecil Roth's *The Jewish Contribution to Civilisation* (Macmillan, London), and Chaim Potok's magnificently illustrated *Wanderings* (Knopf, 1978).

sh—

shm—

> Yinglish. As in Yiddish, these prefatory particles mock or negate the word they prefix.
>
> 1. *Sh*— designates scorn or dismissal when used to prefix a word:
>   "Sick-shtick, he should be in the office!"
>   "Low-shlow, it can't go higher."

In addition to such snickery, the *sh*— sound introduces an astonishing number of Yiddish/Yinglish words to describe character, and freights them with disdain:

shlemazl	shmeer	shnorer
shlemiel	shmegegge	shnuk
shlepper	shmendrick	shreck
shlock	shmo	shtunk
shlump	shmontses	shtus
shmatte	shmuck	shvantz

At this point some linguists are no doubt declaiming, "But it's the German word, from which the Yiddish was taken, that contains the negative aroma!"

To this I reply:

- Some of the words come from Hebrew, not German *(shtus)*.
- Some of the words are neologisms, unknown in German *(shmo)*.
- Some of the words come from Polish *(shmatte)*.
- Some of the words are Ameridish—coined by American (not English) Jews *(shmegegge)*.

• Some of the words were invented by Jewish writers *(Shmendrick,* a character in an Abraham Goldfaden operetta).

I would also point out the aural effect of the *sh—* or *shm—.* The linkage of *sh* to anal symbols is impressive: consider the profane words, in English and German, that refer to feces, defecation, sweating. (I hope this does not *sh*ock you.)

> 2. *Shm—* extends the scorn (as seen in the list above) by adding the nasal phoneme *m* to the soothing but ironic sibilants.

"Clone-shmone, how will they keep their identity?"

"Rich? Rich-shmich, he doesn't know how to live!"

The fusion of the derisive *shm—* to a word in order to deflate it has been called "mock-language" (by Noah Prylucki). Max Weinreich remarks that the *shm—* prefix "became universalized only toward the end of the nineteenth century; earlier, forms with *shp—, shm—,* or simply with *p-* or *m-* would do" *(History of the Yiddish Language,* page 623).

Examples of the *shm—* gambit have been found by Ernest Henri Levi in German dialects as far back as the thirteenth century. The oldest written evidence (so far) of a *shm—* usage is a manuscript of 1600, written near Augsburg.

Some of the mock-words Jews used were part of "secret" language —the disguising of certain words about whose usage Jews harbored anxiety (*e.g.,* the Trinity).

> . . . in German the use of this mock-mechanism (*sh—, shm—*) was never extensive, and has progressively declined since the Middle Ages; the cases recorded from modern German dialects seem to be loans from Yiddish. This, of course, does not preclude the beginning of the phenomenon from having been German, but we have no complete certainty. . . .
>
> — MAX WEINREICH, *op. cit.,* pages 623–24

△ △ △

MRS. PITKIN: Is it true her son is seeing a psychoanalyst?

MRS. NAGLER: That's right.

MRS. PITKIN: So what's his problem?

MRS. NAGLER: The doctor says he has a terrible Oedipus complex.

MRS. PITKIN: Oedipus-shmoedipus, just so he loves his mother.

△ △ △

SHERRY: Stop! I never kiss on a first date!

JOEL: First-shmirst . . . how about a last?

✡ Shabbes

Shabes (standard)

> Pronounced SHAH-biss in Yiddish and Yinglish. Hebrew: *Shabbat:* cessation of labor.

> Sabbath.

To "make *Shabbes*" is also to celebrate something, or to plunge into festivity, revelry, song, dance.

Shabbes is "the Bride of the Week," a transfigured time when, with the setting sun of *Erev Shabbes* (Sabbath Eve), the holy *Shechinah,* the Divine Presence itself, descends upon the homes and temples of the pious.

In the *shtetl, Shabbes* brought the hint of angels, visions of heaven and golden thrones and miracles. (Jews are grateful for, but not astounded by, miracles: only through them could the Jews have survived.)

And in the New World? Hear Harry Golden:

> The Irish and Italian boys had Christmas once a year; we had exaltation every Friday. In the most populous neighborhood of the world, rent by the shouts of peddlers and the myriad noises of the city, there was every Friday evening a wondrous stillness, an eloquent silence. Two blocks from the synagogue you could hear the muffled chant of the cantor and the murmured prayers of the congregation. Once the service was over, you came home to find your mother dressed in her wedding dress with a white silk scarf around her head. And your father told you all the sufferings throughout the centuries were dedicated for this moment, the celebration of the Sabbath.
> —Introduction to 1965 reprint of Hutchins Hapgood,
> *The Spirit of the Ghetto,* page 26

For a detailed description of *Shabbes* rules and rituals, prayers, doings, food, see Rabbi Hayim Donin's excellent *To Be a Jew* (Basic Books), with the Hebrew prayers and their translation. Chapter Five is beautifully titled "The Sabbath: An Island in Time."

△ △ △

Rabbi Stephen O. Magnus, the new rabbi, loved sports. One Saturday, after the morning prayer, the rabbi donned big sunglasses and drove to a golf course miles and miles from his synagogue. He briefly prayed to the Lord to forgive him for breaking the Sabbath and teed off.

Moses, happening to look down from heaven, cried, "Lord! Is that Rabbi Stephen O. Magnus? Playing golf on Your Holy Day?"

The Lord glanced down. "Dear Me . . . yesss . . ."

"Lord, You must punish him!"

The Lord cupped his hands, and just as Rabbi Magnus hit the ball off the second tee, let out a long, cosmic *"whooosh"*. . . . The Lord's wind caught the rabbi's ball, lifted it a hundred yards, swerved it between two trees, where it struck a big rock, bounced and—*mirabile dictu!*—dropped into the cup.

Moses gulped. "A hole in one?!" He stared at his Maker. "A hole in one? God, what kind of punishment is that?"

Sighed our Lord, "Tell me, Moishe: whom can he *tell?*"

✡ shadchen

shadkh'n (standard)

> Pronounce the *ch* as a hearty Glaswegian *kh.* Rhymes with "cod pen." Plural: *shadchonim,* pronounced shod- KHUN-im. From Hebrew: *shidukh:* marital match.
>
> 1. A marital matchmaker (professional).
> 2. Anyone who maneuvers a meeting that results in a wedding.

In Eastern Europe, the *shadchen* performed a very important social function. Not only did he scour communities for eligible boys and nubile girls; he was the prime source of news/gossip as well to *shtetlach* bereft of newspapers, radios, travelers. He became an expert on affinity (family background, personality factors) in an undertaking that is now assigned to computers.

The fate of the *shadchen* was sealed when Jews broke away from the *shtetl;* when economic and social progress made dowries no longer imperative; with the decline in orthodoxy; with the rise of proletarian consciousness; in the rebellion of the young against parental authority and tradition; and with the dramatic change in the feelings of Jews who wanted to marry for love, not by parental fiat.

△ △ △

SHADCHEN: Mr. Mintik, your daughter looks like she soon will be forty!

MR. MINTIK: Looks, looks. Don't go by looks!

SHADCHEN: You told me she's only twenty-eight years old! Is that *true?*

MR. MINTIK: Uh—partly.

△ △ △

"Seymour," beamed the *shadchen,* "I've got for you a girl—one in a million! Libby Spornish!"

"The redhead?" frowned Seymour. "She must be forty years old."

"Older women make grateful wives."

"But she's so short—"

"She'll buy her clothes in the Junior Department."

"—and skinny—"

"So your food bills will be nothing!"

"—and she stammers—"

"So she won't talk much, she'll be ashamed—"

"And her complexion—"

"Stop!" cried the *shadchen*. "I am very disappointed in you, Seymour. I bring you a girl, one in a million, and you find one little fault and that's all you can think of?!"

△ △ △

Blanche Gurfein, a pillar of the suburban community, was proud of her abilities as a matchmaker. One day, Mr. Greenthal, a divorced man, telephoned her: "Blanche! You know that widow you talked me into dating?"

"A *wonderful* woman—"

"Wonderful-shmonderful, she has a terrible *limp!*"

"Only when she walks!" snapped the *shadchenteh*.

Shah!

Sha (standard)

> Rhyme it with "Pa" and be emphatic. Onomatopoetic.

> "Quiet!" ("*Be* quiet.")

This word has no relation to the late monarch of Iran. (Iran is not the modern name for Persia: "Persia" was a modern replacement of the ancient "Iran" —before the country went back to being called "Iran.")

Until recently no Anglo-Saxon or American exclaimed "*Shah!*" but "Sh!" or "Hush!" or "Quiet!" or "Shut up!" The use of "*Shah!*" is nearly always jocular.

Among Jews, "*Shah!*" may be used as a cryptonym signaling other Jews (say, in a community meeting) to take their tongues off the oral gas.

△ △ △

When Julius Flaxman and Manny Kitzer sold their hardware business, they celebrated by taking a trip to Africa.

One twilight, separated from guide and gunbearers, stalking through the jungle, they were frozen in their tracks by a low roar. "Manny . . ." quaked Julius.

"I heard . . ."

"*Shah!* . . . For God's sake, *whis*per. . . . Look behind me . . . is it a tiger? A leopard? A lion?"

"How should I know?" moaned Manny. "Am I a furrier?"

Shalom (Hebrew)

Sholem (Yiddish)

> Pronounced in Hebrew sha-LOAM, and in Yiddish SHOW-lem. The Hebrew root means "entire," "peace."
>
> 1. Peace.
>
> *As a greeting:*
> 2. Hello.
> 3. Goodbye.
> 4. *Au revoir.*

The traditional greeting of Jews upon meeting, or when entering or leaving a group. The full phrase is "*Shalom (Sholem) aleichem.*" (This is a salutation Muslims use, too, with an *s* for the *sh* and a *k* for the *ch/kh.*)

△ △ △

On its maiden voyage, the *S.S. Shalom,* the first ocean liner of Israel, steamed into the harbor of New York to a truly tumultuous greeting. Even those who were not tumultuous said, "It doesn't *look* Jewish!"

△ △ △

In a Jerusalem courtroom, the prosecuting attorney was firing questions at old Mr. Markovitch—who answered by leaning forward and replying in a low tone.

The Judge said, "The witness must speak louder—and to the jury."

Mr. Markovitch turned to the jury. "*Shalom.*"

△ △ △

The lieutenant, accompanied by two soldiers, banged on the door. "Open up! KGB! Security!"

The door creaked open. A man in frayed pajamas quaked, "*Shalom.*"

The lieutenant pushed him to one side. Six other persons lay on mattresses, crammed into the cold room. "Does Yussel Polonsky live here?" barked the lieutenant.

"No," said the man in pajamas.

"*No?* . . . What's your name?"

"Yussel Polonsky."

The lieutenant glared, "Didn't you just say you don't live here?"

Polonsky sighed, "*This* you call living?"

shamus

shames (standard)

> Rhyme with "promise." Hebrew: *shamash:* servant.

> 1. The sexton, caretaker of the synagogue; hence, the "servant" of the congregation.

The *shamus* keeps the synagogue clean, sees that prayer books and ceremonial objects are safely preserved, etc. In the *shtetl*, he would make the morning rounds, waking up Jews, calling them to prayer: "to the service of the Lord." He announced the beginning of holidays and the Sabbath (often by trumpet). He acted as a bailiff in the religious court, collected synagogue dues, made funeral arrangements, rounded up a *minyen*. He could even fill in for the rabbi or the cantor (never mind the musical quality of the cantillation).

> 2. (American slang) A detective.

Shamus enjoys wide popularity in detective fiction and movies. It pains me to hear it pronounced "shay-mus," which is how to vocalize the name Seamus, but Irishmen are on safe ground in calling a detective or private eye a "shay-mus," because so many Celts became cops in America.

> 3. A private eye.
> 4. An unimportant menial, "chief cook and bottle washer." ("A *shamus* in a pickle factory" is about as condescending a putdown as you can contrive.)
> 5. Sycophant; hanger-on.
> 6. A stool pigeon; an informer.
> 7. The center-raised candle of the Menorah, which is used to light the others.

There are many colorful uses in Berrey and Van den Bark's *American Thesaurus of Slang*.

△ △ △

The Jewish *shamus*, as a breed, is known to be officious, independent, and airily presumptuous.

Rabbi Teichler stopped in the middle of his sermon and beckoned the *shamus* to the *bema*. "Look. Fourth row," whispered the rabbi. "That heavyset man. Absolutely asleep!"

"So?" the *shamus* grunted.

"*So?!* Wake him up."

"I don't think that's fair."

"Not *fair?* What does that mean?"

"*Rebbe,* it was you who put him sleep. In my opinion, it should be you who wakes him up."

See SIDONDER.

sharopnik

sharopnikel

> The latter rhymes with "jar topical." Becoming obsolete, alas.
>
> 1. One who annoys others by constantly snapping *"Sharop!"* ("Shut up!").
> 2. Baby's pacifier, teething ring, or security blanket.

How sad that this bold fusion of English and Yiddish (adding *-nik* to create a character type, and *-nikel* to confer affection upon a device) has slipped into limbo. It was the bright invention of immigrants; their sons and daughters spurned so déclassé a loan-word.

But I think *sharopnik* deserves a respected place in suburban discourse. How much blunter is *sharopnik* than "pacifier," which could mean a Valium, or a Swedish arbitrator; *sharopnik* excludes images of either diplomacy or drugs. And the sheer euphony of *sharopnikel,* which might well open an aria in Ukrainian opera, lingers in my hopefulness.

sheygets (standard)

shaygets

> Pronounce it SHAY-gits (or -gets). Hebrew. Plural: *shkotzim.* Feminine: *shikse.*
>
> 1. A Gentile boy or young man. "She married a *sheygets.*"
> 2. A clever lad (Jewish or Gentile): handsome, mischievous, charming. "He's a real *sheygets!*"
> 3. An uneducated boy; one who has no intellectual ambitions. "You won't study? Do you want to grow into a *sheygets?*"
> 4. An irreligious or peccant youngster.

Lest you think meaning 3 condescending: when the overwhelming majority of Europeans were illiterate, Jewish males could read Hebrew, Yiddish (or Ladino), and the tongue of the nation in which they lived.

△ △ △

Mrs. Tarshis was dreaming ecstatically, for into her dream had wandered a handsome *sheygets,* who began making love to her. She sighed, moaned, then cried, "Oh, God! Footsteps! It's my husband!"

Mr. Tarshis jumped out of the window.

shihi-pihi

> Proposed for Yinglish. Pronounced sHE-he PE-he. Origin: Hebrew acronyms (see below).

> 1. Something not to be taken seriously; trifles.
> 2. Empty words. ("His speech? A flood of *shihi-pihi.*")

This charming rhyme-word comes from the Hebrew phrases for "Today is *Shabbes*" and "Today is *Peysekh,*" i.e., *sh . . . pe. . . .* Haman denounced the Jews to his king as malingerers with these constant excuses for not working: "Today is the Sabbath," or "Today is Passover." The Talmudists described these accusations as trifling, and the acronym came to mean a trifle, too. Few words have a more beguiling provenance.

△ △ △

To the top of Mount Katamogu, a pilgrim plodded. And when at last he beheld the old man sitting under a great umbrella, the pilgrim babbled, "Oh Holy One, I have journeyed across deserts of fire and fields of ice, to ask you: What is the meaning of life?"

"Ah, my son," murmured the holy man, "the All-Knowing has guided you to me. You must ponder my answer for two years and a day; then what seems strange will become simple. Life? Life is like a golden lute with invisible strings . . ."

So the pilgrim went down Mount Katamogu, crossed the fields of ice and the deserts of fire to his humble hut. And there for two years and a day, he pondered and pondered . . .

He set forth for Katamogu again. He plodded across the deserts of fire and fields of ice until he stood before the Holy Man again. "O Holy One, I could not decipher your meaning. Please, in the name of the All-Knowing . . . *why is life like a golden lute with invisible strings?*"

The holy man stared at Jake Paunitz (which was the pilgrim's name) and shrugged: "So—*shihi-pihi*—life *isn't* like a golden lute with invisible strings. . ."

shikker

shiker (standard)

> Yinglish (for at least a hundred years). Rhyme it with "ticker."
> Hebrew: *shikor:* drunk.

> *As a noun:*
> A drunken man or woman. ("Is he a *shikker?*")
> *As an adjective:*
> Intoxicated. ("She is a wee bit *shikker.*")

The souse is rarely encountered in Jewish folklore or literature. There are plenty of stories about getting tipsy, but the alcoholic as a type was alien to Jewish experience. (As for today and tomorrow, see below.)

The rabbis believed that wine possesses curative properties; "Where wine is lacking, drugs are necessary," Rabbi Huna said. But the sages stressed moderation in drinking as in all else—except study.

> . . . Drunkards were rarely seen among Jews. When night came and a man wanted to pass away time, he did not hasten to a tavern to take a drink, but went to pore over a book or joined a group which—either with or without a teacher—revered books. . . . Physically worn out by their day's toil, they sat over open volumes, playing the austere music of the Talmud . . . or the sweet melodies of . . . piety of the ancient sages.
>
> —A. J. HESCHEL, *The Earth Is the Lord's* (Farrar, Straus)

Drinking has sharply increased among American Jews; one even hears of what was at one time unthinkable: Jewish alcoholics.

△ △ △

> A saloon can't corrupt a good man, any more than a synagogue can reform a bad one.

> A man betrays himself by three things: his tumbler, his tipping, and his temper.
>
> —TALMUD

> When a man tells you you're *shikker,* hesitate; when two men tell you, slow up; when three men tell you—lie down!
>
> —FOLK SAYING

> The drunkard smells of *shnaps,* but so does the saloonkeeper.

> Better dead drunk than dead hungry.

△ △ △

Traditional Jewish pride in sobriety is eloquently expressed by Israel Zangwill in his classic *Children of the Ghetto* (1892):

> The Ghetto welcomed the Sabbath Bride with proud sound and humble feast. . . . All around, their neighbors sought distraction in the public-houses, and their tipsy bellowings resounded through the streets. . . . Here and there the voice of a beaten woman rose on the air. But no Son of the Covenant was among the [drunken] revellers or the wife-beaters. The Jews remained a chosen race, a peculiar people, faulty enough, but redeemed at least from the grosser vices—a little human islet won from the waters of animalism by the genius of ancient engineers.

△ △ △

SCENE: *A Cocktail Party*

WIFE: Arthur! Don't you think you ought to stop drinking? Your face is already beginning to look blurred!

△ △ △

"Milly," he whispered, "drinking brings out all your beauty!"

"But I haven't been drinking!"

"I know . . . *I* have."

△ △ △

BOY: And everything in the South changed, Papa, when Eli Whitney invented the cotton gin.

FATHER: The what?

BOY: The cotton gin.

FATHER: *Gevalt!* In the South they drink cotton?

shikse (standard)
shiksa

> Pronounce it SHIK-sa, to rhyme with "picks a." Yiddish from Hebrew: *sheygetz.*

1. A girl or woman who is not Jewish.
2. (To orthodox Jews) A Jewish housewife who does not keep a kosher kitchen.
3. A Jewess who does not respect the Jewish faith.

Yiddish has borrowed so many words from German that it is nice to report that German has borrowed from Yiddish, too—but incorrectly: *e.g., shicksel:* Jewish girl(!). See Heath's *New German-English Dictionary.* For another Teutonic boo-boo see *Meshpoche.*

△ △ △

An old story with a lovely moral:

In Warsaw, a famous rabbi and five of his disciples sat down to table. The servant girl poured water from the well in the courtyard into six small basins. The men washed their hands, as is mandatory before eating.

One acolyte said, "*Rebbe*, why are you so sparse with the water?"

"I do not want to be pious," said the old man, "at the expense of a servant—even a *shikse*."

shlemazl (standard)

shlimazel

> Rhymes with "rim nozzle." From German: *shlimm:* bad; and Hebrew: *mazel:* luck, fortune.

> Someone for whom nothing goes right or turns out well; a born loser.

Let me illustrate by combining four folk sayings: "When a *shlemazl* winds a clock, it stops; when he kills a chicken, it walks; when he sells umbrellas, the sun comes out; when he makes coffins, people stop dying."

△ △ △

> He is such a *shlemazl* that his junk mail arrives "Postage due."

> They say the poor have no *mazel*, which is true; for if the poor did have *mazel* would they be poor?

> Only a *shlemazl* believes in *mazel*.

△ △ △

A twelfth-century poet, Abraham ibn Ezra (Browning's Rabbi ben Ezra, may his tribe increase), described the *shlemazl*'s fate when he wrote:

> If I sold lamps,
> The sun,
> In spite,
> Would shine
> At night.

△ △ △

"Oh, what terrible, terrible times!" moaned Saul. "Inflation, unemployment, housing—I tell you I can't remember when I last had a good night's sleep."

"Really?" replied Lemmy, a *shlemazl*. "Me, I sleep like a baby!"

"*What?* Do you mean that?"

"Absolutely. I get up every two hours and cry."

shlemiel

shlemil (standard)

> Rhymes with "reveal." Note: *shlemiel* is often spelled *schlemiel:* I
> shudder. In Hebrew and Yiddish, the single letter *shin* repre-
> sents the *sh* sound; to begin an English word with *sch* is to call
> for the *sk* sound, as in "school" or "scheme." A *shlemiel* is plagued
> by enough disrespect without our adding orthographic sores.
> Origin (probably): see 7, below.
>
> 1. A simpleton. "He has the brains of a *shlemiel.*"
> 2. An unlucky person; a born loser. "The *shlemiel* falls on his
>   back and breaks his nose."
> 3. A clumsy type. "Why does a *shlemiel* like that ever try to fix
>   anything?"
> 4. A social misfit. "Don't invite that *shlemiel* to the party."
> 5. A pipsqueak, a Casper Milquetoast.
> 6. A trusting, gullible customer. (This usage is common among
>   furniture dealers, especially those who sell the gaudy gim-
>   crack stuff called "borax.")
> 7. Anyone who makes a foolish bargain or a foolish bet. (This
>   usage is wide in Europe; it probably comes from Chamisso's
>   tale, *Peter Schlemihl's Wunderbare Geschichte*, in which the hero
>   lost his shadow and sold his soul to Satan.)

A *shlemiel*, like a *nebech*, deserves our pity. The classic definition goes:
"A *shlemiel* is always knocking things off a table; the *nebech* always picks
them up." Or, "A *shlemiel* is always spilling hot soup—down the neck of
a *shlemazl.*"

Shlemiels may be *shlemazls*—but that need not be: A *shlemiel* can make
a fortune through sheer luck; a *shlemazl* can't.

A popular but erroneous interpretation (I made it in *The Joys of
Yiddish*) is that Shlumiel was a general (Numbers, 2) who always lost his
battles.*

---

* The reason for the misconstruction is complicated. The Talmud identifies Shlumiel as
the Zimri in Numbers 25:14. Zimri and his paramour were pierced with a spear whilst
fornicating. So far, so good (or, so bad). Among Talmudists, Shlumiel became a generic
name for anyone caught in an unfortunate yet amusing(!) predicament. Among the Ashkenazim, Shlemiel became the archetypical fall guy.

See CHAIM YANKEL, NEBECH, SHLUMP, SHLEPPER, SHLEMAZL, SHMO, SHNOOK.

△ △ △

My favorite definition of a *shlemiel:* A *shlemiel* will throw a drowning man a rope—both ends.

△ △ △

When a *shlemiel* takes a bath, he forgets to wash his face.

△ △ △

A *shlemiel* ran to his rabbi, distraught. "Rabbi, advise me! Every year my wife brings forth a baby. I have ten children already! Rabbi, what can I do?"

The sage thought scarcely a moment. "Do nothing."

△ △ △

When a *shlemiel* wants to hang himself, he grabs a knife.

A *shlemiel* measures water with a sieve.

A *shlemiel* doesn't know how to find a notch in a saw.

shlep

shlepper

shleper (standard)

> From German: *schleppen:* to drag.
>
> *shlep* (verb)
> 1. To drag, pull, lag behind. ("Don't *shlep* those packages; the store can deliver them." "Pick up your feet; don't *shlep*.")
> 2. To delay; to drag out; to move or perform slowly, lazily.
>
> *shlep* (noun)
> *shlepper* (noun)
> 1. A drag; a jerk. ("What a *shlep* he is!")
> 2. Someone unkempt, run-down-at-the-heels. ("Hike up your slip; you look like a *shlepper*.")
> 3. A beggar or petty thief. ("How does he earn a living? He's a *shlepper*.")
> 4. A hobo, a bum.

Shlepper has become an established part of movie and theater argot, just as have *shtik, cockamamy, bubeleh.*

△ △ △

At the food department of London's famous Fortnum and Mason, a New York woman bought jar after jar of marmalade, package after package of biscuits, cookies, candies.

"And where," asked the wing-collared salesman, "shall we deliver these, madam?"

"I'll carry them."

"But we'll be *happy* to deliver."

"I don't mind, I'm from the Bronx."

"I understand, madam; but still—why *shlep?*"

shlock

shlak (standard)

> From German: *Schlag:* a blow.
>
> 1. A shoddy, cheap article. ("It's *shlock.*")
> 2. A fake article; an object you were cheated over. ("That watch will never keep time; it's *shlock.*")
> 3. A slob. ("There's a *shlock* of a girl.")
> 4. The gaudy items sold at circuses.
> 5. Dope, narcotics. (Since *shlock* means "junk" and "junk" has come to mean narcotics, *shlock* has leapfrogged "junk" to mean "dope.")

In television argot, a *shlock-meister* ("*shlock*-master") is the agent who provides free gifts (for free plugs) on television game programs. Manufacturers employ a *shlock-meister* to get their products displayed on TV. Never was such huge publicity gained at such low cost.

△ △ △

On a street packed with pushcarts, a bustling *baleboste* rummages through the *shlock* of one peddler. She holds up a broken fork. "How much for this old, broken *gupel?*"

"A penny."

"A panny? That's too much!"

"*Nu,* lady: make me an offer."

shlock-house

> 1. A store that sells very cheap, defective, "fire sale" articles.
> 2. A store that sells furniture that has been knocked around.
> 3. A gyp joint.

In the furniture business, *shlock-house* merchandise was called "borax." No one knows why. I think there may be a connection to 20-Mule Team Borax, the cleaning compound widely used in immigrant neighborhoods.

△ △ △

For years, Mordecai Schmelkin's friends had been begging him to get a hearing aid. "I hear fine!" the old man objected. "People just don't talk loud enough."

One day, he passed a discount store on whose window a large sign announced:

SELLING OUT!
FANTASTIC BARGAINS! EVERYTHING MUST GO!
Pocket radios——Sun glasses
Hearing Aids

Mordecai Schmelkin hurried in. Within five minutes he had been fitted for a hearing aid that had been reduced to ten dollars. (What it had been reduced from, I do not know.)

The old man went into the street with a smile on his lips, prepared to savor the pleasures of an amplified world. Soon he saw Moey Glickstein. "Say, Moey—come here! Look!" He pointed to his ear. "I bought one—a hearing aid. You were all absolutely right. What a difference! I can hear like a twelve-year-old! What an instrument!"

"That's wonderful," said Moey. "What kind is it?"

Mordecai glanced at his wrist. "Half-past three."

shlump

> Pronounce the *u* as in "put." German: *Schlumpe:* a slovenly female.

> *As a noun:*
> 1. A drip, a wet blanket. ("That *shlump* depresses everyone.")
> 2. A slovenly man; a slattern of a woman.

A *shlump* is a *shlep* with droopy shoulders. The Yiddish name for Cinderella, by the way, is *Shlumperel*.

> *As a verb:*
> 1. To drag about.
> 2. To do anything with a minimum of skill, effort or enthusiasm. "She *shlumps* through a role," said *Time*.

Shlumpik or *shlumpedik* means sloppily, in a careless manner.
   See SHNOOK, KALYIKE, NEBECH, CHAIM YANKEL, KUNYE LEML.

△ △ △

A lady buyer from Topeka, in New York on her first trip, filled out the registration card at the hotel:

> *Name:* Rachel Yalkin
> *Address:* 665 Lark St., Topeka
> *Firm:* Not very.

shmaltz

shmalts (standard)

> From German/Yiddish: *Schmaltz:* fat drippings. *Shmaltz* is in many English dictionaries (at long last).
>
> *As a noun:*
> 1. Cooking fat (usually chicken), rendered, used in frying or as a spread on bread. Among poor Jews, *shmaltz* on a piece of bread was equivalent to caviar. Lovers of chopped liver are connoisseurs of *shmaltz,* which obliterates dryness with a heavenly dollop of fat.
> 2. Excessive sentimentality; bathos. "He delivers a line with enough *shmaltz* to fill a shovel."
>
> *As a verb:*
> 3. Showing inappropriate emotion. "She *shmaltzed* up her speech like it was the Fourth of July."

Shmaltz is a staple in the technical vocabulary of show business. I once heard John Barrymore, who could be a superb actor no less than a *shmaltzy* ham (excuse the oxymoron), say, "George Arliss? A veritable master of *shmaltz.*"

   "If he used less *shmaltz,* he would get more tears."

   "His summation to the jury was ten percent fact and ninety percent *shmaltz.*"

> 4. Wealth. "He lives in silk and *shmaltz.*" To marry rich is to fall into a *shmaltz-grub,* a pit filled with riches.
>
> *As an adjective:*
> *shmaltzy*
> *shmaltzed up*
> 1. Corny, mawkish.
> 2. Hackneyed.
> 3. Greatly exaggerated.

Thus: "The play was too *shmaltzy*"; "*Love Story* was a hit because it was so *shmaltzed* up."

△ △ △

The following story has no hint of *shmaltz* in it:

SCENE: *Cramer's Frame Store*

"I want a frame," said Mrs. Korngold, "for a twenty-thousand-dollar picture."

Mr. Cramer gasped. "Twenty thousand—lady, I never before had an order like that! Where is this picture?"

"Here." She handed Cramer her son's college diploma.

shmatte

shmate (standard)

> Pronounced SHMOT-ta. From Polish: *szmata:* a rag.

1. A rag.
2. Cheap; junk. ("I wouldn't wear a *shmatte* like that." "The movie? A *shmatte!*")
3. A softy, a pushover, unworthy of respect. ("They treated him like a *shmatte*." "Stand up for your rights; don't be a *shmatte!*")
4. A woman of weak character, weak will, or wicked ways; a slattern. ("She has the self-respect of a *shmatte*.")
5. A fawner; a sycophant; a toady. ("That *shmatte* sucks up to everyone.")

△ △ △

"My husband treats me like a *shmatte!*" moaned Mrs. Gerstein. "Every night he stays out until two–three o'clock!"

"*My* husband used to do that, but he hasn't come home late in ten years!" beamed Mrs. Krasner.

"So what changed him?"

"What changed him," said Mrs. Krasner, "is every time he opened the door I called out 'Is that you, Ronald?' "

"*That* stopped him?"

"Sure. His name is Al."

△ △ △

PARIS: *A Boutique*

MRS. SLOVKOVITZ: How much is *cette chemise?*

PROPRIETRESS: *Cette chemise?* Four hundred francs.

MRS. SLOVKOVITZ: Four hundred francs?! *Mais* it is *un shmatte*.

PROPRIETRESS: *Un shmatte*, Madam? *Quelle chutzpa!*

shmeer

shmir (standard)

> German: *Schmiere:* grease.
>
> 1. To smear—paint, mud, polish.
> 2. To spread. ("*Shmeer* it on the bagel.")
> 3. To bribe; a bribe. This usage has long been part of American slang. ("They *shmeered* the cop to look the other way.")
> 4. The whole deal. ("How much do you want for the whole *shmeer?*")

This familiar slang verb/noun thrives wherever Yinglish has penetrated or seduced English: in Hollywood, on Broadway, in Washington or London's West End. I have heard it used in the most matter-of-fact manner from San Francisco to Park Lane, and in between.

△ △ △

"I think it will help, Miss Brotfisch, if you took this simple test." The psychiatrist drew a large circle on the blackboard. "What does that bring to your mind?"

"A handsome, naked man—ready for you-know-what."

The psychiatrist drew a large square. "And this?"

Miss Brotfisch narrowed her eyes. "A virile, naked boy—doing it."

The psychiatrist now *shmeered* a meaningless blob on the board. "And this?"

"That's a big, naked brute advancing right toward me!"

The psychiatrist hesitated. "Miss Brotfisch . . . your responses show an unusual obsession—about sex."

"My responses?" cried the girl. "*You* draw all those dirty pictures!"

shmegegge

> Rhymes with "the Peggy." Derivation: unknown (alas).
>
> 1. A drip, a *shlepper*, a jerk.
> 2. A clumsy *klutz*.
> 3. A sycophant.

This admirable, disdainful neologism, an epithet for a class of human nerds, is a gem in the coronet of Yinglish. It won my heart when I first heard it in New York. I had never heard *shmegegge* in the Jewish enclaves of Chicago, Washington or Los Angeles. I have never been able to find so much as a hint of a spoor of its origins.

I think of a *shmegegge* as the fruit of a *nebech* and a *shlemiel.*

The word owes much of its vitality to the sneering sibilant *shm-* followed by double-voiced aspirate *gs*—a combination any French phoneticist would hail as *formidable!*

See NARR, KLUTZ, SHMENDRICK, SHMO.

△ △ △

Yosha Haimovitch stood on the weighing scale in Penn Station and dropped a penny in the slot. A voice from inside the machine intoned: "You weigh 168 pounds . . . and . . . you . . . are . . . Jewish."

Yosha was thunderstruck. He quickly dropped another penny in the slot. The needle hit 168 again. Now the monotone said: "You weigh 168 pounds . . . You're Jewish . . . and you are waiting for the 4:03 train to Ellenville in the Catskills."

Yosha could not believe his ears. He pondered, went into the men's room, put on a pair of sunglasses, altered the shape of his hat, removed his tie, draped his jacket over his arm—and again dropped a penny in the scale. And now that maddening voice droned: "You still weigh 168 pounds . . . You're still Jewish . . . and you just missed the 4:03 to Ellenville, you *shmegegge!*"

shmei

shmay (standard)

shmy

> Rhymes with "spry." From Yiddish *shmayen:* to amble about, which comes from the Polish *shmiewacz:* to promenade, which two words were fused to make the Yiddish *shmeyeven.*
>
> 1. Amble around pleasantly, with no destination or purpose.
> 2. To browse or shop aimlessly.
> 3. To busy oneself (says M. Weinreich).

This word has become popular in Los Angeles and in movie circles: "I'll *shmei* around Rodeo Drive." "Do you want to go into town? We'll *shmei* around."

△ △ △

The Gittelbergs moved to the suburbs. One day Alvin Gittelberg, age seven, was playing under the sprinklers with a neighbor, Mary Clanahan, age six. Soon they took off their bathing suits. . . . All this Mrs. Gittelberg observed from her kitchen window.

When little Alvin came back into the house, Mrs. Gittelberg said, "What were you doing with—that little girl?"

"Oh, we just *shmeied* around."

"Uh . . . is there anything you'd—like to ask me, Alvin?"

"Well, I didn't know there was *that* much difference between Gentiles and Jews."

shmeikel

shmeyk'l (standard)

> Slang. Possibly from the Yiddish *shmeykh'l:* to smile, to flatter.
>
> *As a verb:*
> 1. To deceive, to fool, to swindle.
> 2. To flatter.
> 3. To fast-talk someone.
>
> *As a noun:*
> 1. A con game, a scam.
> 2. A piece of deception.

It is widely assumed that this term from underworld slang comes from Yiddish (Budd Schulberg used it in *What Makes Sammy Run?* back in 1941). I have no way of proving that it does. *If,* in fact, the word did grow out of Yiddish, it would have been through an indirect route: the connection between a swindler and his smiling personality.

△ △ △

"Mr. Kleinberg, I *have* to get a raise!"

   "Why?"

"I can't get married on the wages you pay me!"

"I know, *boychik.* And someday you will thank me."

shmeker (standard)

shmecker

> Pronounced as written. From German: *schmecken:* to taste.
>
> 1. Someone who smells (I do not mean *he/she* smells to others but someone who performs the act of smelling); hence:
> 2. A sniffer of drugs—notably cocaine.

△ △ △

Miss Shpier, the new secretary, was pleasant and *very* low-key. Mr. Elkos said, "Miss, get the phone number of Hal Yittelman, on Twenty-third Street. I want to call him the minute I get back from lunch."

   He went out to lunch. When he returned, he said, "Miss Shpier, what's Yittelman's number?"

   "I'm still working on it."

"You're still *what?*"

"Don't worry." She smiled dreamily. "I'm already up to *H*."

shmendrick

The word first appeared as the name of a character in an operetta written by Abraham Goldfaden.

1. A *shlemiel,* especially if thin or weak.
2. A meek, ineffectual Milquetoast; a child of a *nebech* out of a *nudnik.*
3. A little boy or young man.
4. A child, affectionately.
5. (Vulgar) The penis. (This usage is rarely used by men; vulgar women may deploy it to deride the diminutive.)
6. A nobody.

△ △ △

The classic illustrative anecdote describes how a *shmendrick* was being knocked around by his harridan of a mate. In desperation he crawled under the double bed.

"Come out of there!" snarled his wife.

"Not me," the *shmendrick* muttered. "I'll show you who wears the pants in this family!"

Shmerl Narr

Shmerl Nar (standard)

Shmerl: a man's name; *Narr:* German: fool.

Fictitious (and generic) name for a fool.

In Yiddish folk tales, certain types bear names that recur again and again, regardless of the tale or its chronicler, because the names identify human types. Thus, *Chaim Yankel, Moishe Kapoyr* (a modern archetype), *Shmerl Narr.*

△ △ △

Shmerl Narr saw his friend Toploff rushing down Cherry Street, mopping his brow and gasping.

"Hey, Toploff," called Shmerl. "What's going on?"

"Wh—what's going on is that all morning long I've been running around like a w—wild man, trying to get something for my wife!"

"Tchk, tchk, Toploff," Shmerl sympathized. "Couldn't you get even one offer?"

△ △ △

"That poor Shmerl! He has a memory like a blotter."

"Is that bad? A blotter soaks up everything!"

"Yeah—backwards."

△ △ △

"How thoughtful, how just is the Holy One, blessed be His Name," said Shmerl Narr. "To the rich, He gives food, and to the poor He gives appetite."

The luck of a *narr* is that he doesn't know that he doesn't know.

—FOLK SAYING

△ △ △

The doctor's phone rings.
DOCTOR: Hello.
SHMERL: Doctor, my wife! She's started having labor pains!
DOCTOR: How far apart?
SHMERL: All in the same place!

shmo

Rhyme it with "throw."

1. Euphemism for the absolutely vulgar word *shmuck*.
2. A fall guy, a victim, a helpless *shlemiel*.
3. A foolish, unresourceful type.

Shmo had been around for years, but its phenomenal spread throughout the non-Jewish world may be credited to Al Capp, the cartoonist, a fertile fabricator of Americana ("L'il Abner") who deserves a high place in the pantheon of humor. Capp (born Caplan) created the *shmoo*, a beguiling creature who gives milk and adores being kicked. Capp softened *shmo* to make the creature likable.

Fred Allen said on the radio, back in 1947, "I have been standing here like a *shmo* for twenty minutes."

△ △ △

MARVIN: Did you hear about Charley Wolstein?
MIKE: What about Charley Wolstein?
MARVIN: He won $10,000 in one night at Las Vegas! Jerry, ain't that true?
JERRY: It wasn't Charley; it was his brother Eddy. It wasn't in Vegas; it was in Atlantic City. It wasn't in one night, but in one week. He didn't win it; he lost it. Otherwise, you're absolutely right, you *shmo!*

See NARR, NEBECH, SHLEMIEL, SHMEGEGGE, SHNOOK, KUNYE LEML.

△ △ △

"Fishbach? I'll tell you what a *shmo* he is! He voted for Dwight D. Eisenhower!"

"Wait a minute! Millions of people voted for Eisenhower!"

"In yesterday's election?"

shmontses

Pronounced (usually with force and disgust) *Shmontses!* Used by German Jews: trifles.

1. Nonsense!
2. Foolish talk!
3. Trivia.

As an expletive:
4. Damn!
5. Baloney!

Shmontses! is an all-purpose equivalent of *shpilkes!* or *bobkes!* and is a sibilant synonym for the English "Nuts!"

△ △ △

I was riding with a friend down Wilshire Boulevard. He was driving. When the Cadillac in front of us turned sharply left, and the driver failed to put out an arm in the required signal, my friend shouted, "*Shmontses!*"

And when we saw that the errant driver was a woman, my friend leaned out and yelled, "Who do you think you are: Venus de Milo?"

shmoos

shmus (standard)

shmooz

Urgently needed in English. Rhymes respectively with "loose" and "lose." (I prefer the latter.) Hebrew: *shmuos:* things heard.

As a noun:
Friendly, aimless talk; chitchat. ("We had a nice little *shmoos*.")
As a verb:
1. To have a warm, gossipy conversation.
2. To engage in, and enjoy, a heart-to-heart talk. ("I love to *shmoos* with him.")

This unique Yiddish word oozes warmth and intimacy. I know of no word in any other language to substitute for it.

shmuck

Obscene as all get-out, but effective. From German: *Schmuck:* ornament . . . jewel . . . gewgaw.

A handful of readers of *The Joys of Yiddish* wrote to protest my including so "dirty" a word as *shmuck* in that lexicon. I cannot sympathize with their prudery. A dictionary is not a hymn book. Those who find *shmuck* too lewd for their sensibilities are hereby warned:

Danger: Vulgarity
SKIP THIS ENTRY!

For those still with me:

1. (Taboo) Penis.

Because *shmuck* is considered so improper, the truncated *shmo* was invented.

Never use *shmuck* before women, children or strangers. I may add that, on the whole, Jews are puritanical in public about the pubic.

2. (Still taboo) A fool, a jerk. ("What a *shmuck* to fall for that trick!")
3. (Still obscene) A traitor, trickster, hypocrite or hype artist. ("He's just a low-down, lying *shmuck!*")

As in any language, the word for the male member is extended to characterize boobs, dolts or detestable types.

Sex and its lieutenants are drafted into the service of vituperation in almost every language, I suppose; and in scatology, sex is the *sine qua non*.

Please note that *shmuck* began as the German word for an ornament or jewel. The word was not lewd in German nor obscene in Yiddish. How did the connotational leap take place from "jewel" to "penis"? By mothers bathing or drying their baby sons. They would croon over them. What better word for the "member" than "little jewel . . . ornament . . . cute pendant." In English, men josh about "the family jewels," and they do not mean rubies. German or Hungarian nurses and governesses, I am reliably informed, used the euphemistic *shmuck.** Jewish

---

* A vigorous literature has grown up about the etymology of *shmuck*, *putz* and *shlemiel*, through the efforts of Dr. Gerald Cohen of the University of Missouri. I cannot presume to judge among the embattled experts. Interested persons may acquire *Comments on Etymology*, vols. IX and X, from the amiable Dr. Cohen.

mothers and sisters were puritanical enough to refer to "that place" or "that (his, her) thing."

Shmekel is the affectionate diminutive of *shmuck;* and *shmekeleh* is even more diminutizing—and fond. (The fact that *shmek* means "to smell" is coincidental. I say that to discourage agitated correspondence from philologists, to say nothing of psychoanalysts.)

△ △ △

Samuel Johnson, upon being congratulated by a lady for omitting obscene words from his dictionary, *utzed* her: "So you have been looking for them, eh, madam?"

I have no doubt that amongst my readers are proper souls who would not disapprove of the custom in France, in the fifteenth century, of slitting the lips of those who used profane language. For their edification I offer an immortal verse by some great, unfortunately unknown intelligence:

> O banish the use of those four-letter words
> Whose meaning is never obscure;
> The Romans and Britons, those bawdy old birds,
> Were vulgar, obscene and impure.
> You stubbornly use any weaseling phrase
> That never says just what you mean,
> You prefer to be known for your hypocrite ways
> Than be vulgar, impure or obscene.
> Let your morals be loose as a libertine's vest,
> But your language keep always obscure;
> It's the word, not the act, that's the absolute test
> Of what's vulgar, obscene or impure.

△ △ △

PRUDES: DO NOT READ THE STORY THAT FOLLOWS:

Mr. Bintelman, a widower, addressed a neighbor at his hotel in Miami Beach: "Mr. Wilks, you are so popular. Every day, every night you're with people. I—don't know a single soul. How can I make friends?"

Mr. Wilks, a mean *momzer*, said, "Get a camel."

"Hanh?"

"Get a camel. And every day ride it up and down Collins Ave. Everyone will notice you. In no time, you'll get more invitations than you can handle."

Mr. Bintelman quickly called the zoo. He found out that a circus was wintering nearby. There he arranged to rent a camel. He kept it in the parking lot of the hotel.

Every morning, for the next week, Mr. Bintelman rode his camel up and down Collins Avenue. Everywhere people stopped short when they saw him, and talked and gesticulated in astonishment.

One morning, the parking-lot attendant telephoned: "Mr. Bintelman! Your camel! It's gone!"

Mr. Bintelman went to the police station. "My camel is missing, officer!"

The desk sergeant gaped. "Your *camel* is missing?"

"Yes, officer. I rented him."

"Well . . . I'll fill out a Missing Property form. What was the camel's name?"

"Who knows?"

"I mean, what did you call him?"

"I called him 'Hey, camel. Giddyap, camel. Stop, camel.' "

The sergeant cleared his throat. "What color was it?"

"*Camel* color," said Mr. Bintelman.

"Was it a male or a female?"

Mr. Bintelman blinked. *"Hanh?"*

"Was the animal a male or a female?"

"How should I know? What do I know from camels? . . . Wait! Yeah! That camel was a male."

"But you just said you didn't know—"

"I just remembered: every time I rode that camel up and down Collins Avenue, people would holler, 'Hey, look! Look at the *shmuck* on that camel!' "

shmulky (adj. or noun)

Origin unknown.

1. An ineffectual type; a name for such.
2. A pitiful person.
3. A sad sack.
4. A dopy, unbright specimen.

△ △ △

Shmulky gave the pharmacist a prescription. The pharmacist gave him three plastic tubes. "The white pills," said the druggist, "will help your headaches. The blue ones are for your asthma. And the red ones should calm your nerves."

"My, my!" said Shmulky. "Such little things—and already each one knows where to go!"

shnaps

German: brandy; whiskey.

Liquor.

There must be 1,249 Jewish sayings—sweet, dry, mellow, dazed—about *shnaps*. Most, to be sure, are about wine: Jews drank wine, usually, or *bromfen:* brandy.

△ △ △

Wine helps open the heart to reason.

When *shnaps* goes in, secrets come out.

Wine is the greatest medicine.

—FOLK SAYINGS

The Talmud decrees that judges may not drink any spirits for 24 hours before deciding a case that involves a capital crime.
—*Sanhedrin:* V, 1–5

Wine is an unreliable messenger! I sent it down to my stomach, and it went up to my head!

—AL-HARIZI, *Tahkemoni*

shnook

shnuk (standard)

Born in Manhattan. Rhymes with "brook," not "duke." This American-Yiddish coinage was unknown in Europe. Derivation unknown.

1. A *shlemiel.*
2. A certain kind or clone of a *nebech, shmo* or *lemish.*
3. A timid, unassertive sap—pathetic, but not despicable.

Enter *shnook* in that brigade that contains such well-known fools of fortune as Chaim Yankel, Moishe Pupik, Joe Nebech, Rinaldo Shmo, Shmerl Narr, Moishe Kapoyr, Shimmel Shlemiel, Peregrine Shlepper, Lester Lemish, Shimon Shmegegge, *et alia.* Like these, the *shnook* is the member of a group one always forgets to introduce.

Shnooks are often sweet. They are more to be pitied than scorned; they are more pathetic than detestable. Were they aggressive, they would be *shmucks.*

On October 9, 1951, Jack Benny, then the most popular star in radio, in the midst of a dramatic-comic embroglio, said, "All the other *shnooks* in the business thought—" When I was in high school, *shnook* was bandied about with gusto, even in square circles. The word often appeared, after Benny's radio usage, in movies, in comic strips, and (emphatically) in night-club routines.

Every foreign-born speaker of Yiddish I know first heard *shnook* in the United States—not abroad. No informant heard it in Eastern Europe. Max Weinreich's *History of the Yiddish Language* does not have a single mention of *shnook, shnuk, schnook* or *schnuk*. Nor does his son Uriel's *English-Yiddish Dictionary*.

I know that there is a German word, *Schnuck* ("a small sheep") and that *Schnucki* is used in German vernacular for "darling . . . pet . . . wife." But experts assure me there is no demonstrable connection between those two words and the Yinglish pejorative noun.

Still, if *shnook* is an American-Jewish coinage: what did it come from?

△ △ △

For thirty-six years, Krasnitz had been a salesman—and a *shnook*. One day, a young salesman asked him, "How do you handle insults?"

"Insults-shminsults," replied Krasnitz. "I have been selling in stores, on the road, door-to-door. I have been kicked out of places. Had my samples thrown on the floor. Had doors slammed in my face. But insulted? Never."

shnorer (noun)
shnor (verb)

> Rhymes with "horror." German: *schnorren:* to beg; in German cant: *Schnorrer:* a cadger; *Schnarre:* a noisemaker or tinkler used by beggars.
>
> *As a noun:*
> 1. A professional panhandler, moocher, beggar.
> 2. A chiseler, compulsive bargainer.
> 3. An impudent indigent.
> *As a verb:*
> To *schnor:* to beg.

Every Jewish community had at least one *shnorer*. He was no more an ordinary moocher than a *nudnik* is an ordinary bore. The Jewish *shnorer* did not fawn or whine. He did not ask for alms, he claimed them. He was a professional man, accepted as such by the community.

Shnorers were expert in needling and quick in repartee. Their *chutzpa* was umbrageous. They often baited their benefactors, haggled over the alms, denounced those who underpaid. For *shnorers* had a license from the Lord (or so they acted): to help good Jews discharge their sacred obligation. Surely a man who serves as the agent for the performance and acquisition of *mitzves* is part of God's noble, albeit mysterious (and even contradictory) scheme. Any *shnorer* worth his salt could quote you a dozen hortatory passages from the Talmud.

Israel Zangwill's 1894 *The King of Schnorrers (sic)* (Thomas Yoseloff, 1956 reprint) contains these memorable observations: "... None exposed sores like the lazars of Italy, or contortions like the cripples of Constantinople. Such crude methods are eschewed in the fine art of *shnorring*.... He was no anonymous atom, such as drifts blindly through Christendom, vagrant and apologetic. Rarest of all sights, in this pageantry of Jewish pauperdom, was the hollow trouser-leg or the empty sleeve."

As a child, when walking with my parents on a Sunday, "our *shnorer*" (as my parents called him) would extend his palm without a word of comment. One day, he was nowhere to be seen. My mother said, "I hope he's not sick."

"Sick? He has the constitution of an ox," said my father.

"Then why isn't he on the street?"

"He's probably on vacation."

I have explored the psyche, mores, ethical assumptions and psychological rewards of both *shnorer* and *shnoree* in "The Shnorrer: A study in Piety and Paradox," in *Next Year in Jerusalem*, edited by Douglas Villiers (Viking Press). A noteworthy sociological analysis is Samuel Heilman's "The Gift of Alms," in the journal *Urban Life and Culture*, January 1975.

△ △ △

Whenever genius is discussed, I think of the *shnorer* who became the talk (and marvel) of his profession when he stood on a busy street in Berlin during Hitler's reign, with dark glasses, a tin cup, and this sign, which made coins from the *Herrenvolk* drop in a veritable shower:

I DO NOT ACCEPT

MONEY FROM JEWS

△ △ △

Every day, the Wall Street broker gave a dime to the *shnorer* stationed in front of his building with a box of pencils—without ever taking a pencil.

One day the broker dropped his usual dime and started into the building, when he felt a tap on his shoulder. It was the *shnorer*. "Mister, I've had to raise my prices. A pencil now costs a quarter."

△ △ △

The fur-coated magnate gave a *shnorer* two pennies and asked, "How did a strong, able-bodied man like you become a bum?"

"Because I was just like you," said the *shnorer,* "always giving enormous handouts."

△ △ △

A *shnorer* stopped an *alrightnik.*

"I," said the *alrightnik,* "never hand out money on the street!"

"So what should I do," asked the *shnorer,* "open an office?"

△ △ △

SHNORER: Lady, I'm *weak* from lack of nourishment. I haven't eaten in four days!

EARNEST WOMAN: You have to *force* yourself!

shnoz

shnozzle

shnozzola

> Yinglish. To pronounce, put a *sh–* before "nozzle." From German: *Schnauze:* snout.

> A large or unattractive nose.

Shnozzola is best known, of course, as the fond nickname of the late, much-beloved Jimmy Durante. (He was Italian and Catholic, not Jewish.)

It grieves me to report that in certain odious subcultures, *shnozzle* or *shnozzola* means a cocaine user (because the powder is ingested by sniffing).

shochet

shoykhet (standard)

> Pronounce it SHOY-khet (à la Scotland). Hebrew.

> An official slaughterer of animals, sanctioned by rabbis, according to kosher laws.

△ △ △

On Maxwell Street in Chicago, there was a butcher of such spotless reputation that his sign read:

STRICTLY KOSHER!
THE SHOCHET KILLS HIMSELF
EVERY MORNING!

shofar

shoyf'r (standard)

> Pronounced SHOW-fer. Hebrew: horn, trumpet.
>
> A ram's horn.

The ram's horn is sounded in synagogues some hundred times on Rosh Hashanah and Yom Kippur. In Israel it is blown on important occasions: as part of the inauguration of a new president, when the Western Wall was liberated, etc. The ram's horn was heard at Mount Sinai, says Exodus (13–15), when the Lord revealed the Commandments to Moses.

The curious crook in the horn symbolizes the human heart that bends before the Lord if repentance is true.

Abraham offered Isaac in sacrifice but was reprieved from this most dreadful deed by the Lord, who decreed that Abraham could sacrifice a ram instead. Hence, the horn reminds Jews of the ancient tale. The *shofar* was used as a musical instrument in the Temple, in processionals, and as a trumpet of war.

Sholem aleichem

Sholem aleykhem (standard)

> Pronounced SHO-lem (or SHAW-lem) a-LAY-khem; the *kh* should rattle the roof of your mouth. Hebrew: *shalom:* peace unto you.
>
> 1. The traditional salutation of Jews, used for "Hello," "How do you do?" etc. The response reverses the words, thus:
> 2. *Aleichem sholem* ("And unto you, peace").

This stylized exchange *("Sholem aleichem," "Aleichem sholem")* takes place both upon meeting and parting.

> 3. At last! Hurrah!
>   "Okay, I admit I owe you three dinners."
>   *"Sholem aleichem!"*
> 4. The pen name (he spelled it Sholom Aleichem) of Solomon Rabinowitz (1859–1916), the great Jewish writer and humorist, a master of the short story, a brilliant aphorist, a chronicler and illuminator of the life of the *shtetl,* author of the "Tevye" stories on which *Fiddler on the Roof* was based. He was often called "the Jewish Mark Twain."

It is said that when Mark Twain met Rabinowitz in New York, he said, "I am the American *Sholom Aleichem*."

Underlying all of this great artist's work is a running sense of the sad plight of his characters—and Jews in general. Chill irony often ends a funny tale. When asked why he wrote about poverty, illness, stupidity, tragedy, with such humor, Rabinowitz said, "If I didn't laugh, I would weep." It was from Sholom Aleichem that I learned:

"To a marriage, walk; to a divorce, run."

"Gossip is nature's telephone."

"April Fool: a joke repeated 365 times a year."

"A bachelor is a man who comes to work each morning from a different direction."

"The girl who can't dance says the band can't keep time."

"When a poor Jew eats a chicken, one of them is sick."

△ △ △

Eric Pellinton, the movie actor (né Aaron Pekarsky), sent his father in Minneapolis a fur-lined overcoat. The coat cost $650. His father promptly called Eric: "Oh, Aaronel, what a good son you are!"

"Papa, do you like the coat?"

"Like it? I *love* it! But you shouldn't spend so much—why, that coat must cost a fortune!"

"No, Papa," laughed Eric. "Don't worry. I bought it wholesale. It only cost me—uh, ninety-two dollars."

A week later, Eric received a letter:

> DARLING AARON:
>   Send 6 more coats. I sold mine for $325.
>   *Sholem aleichem!*
>   PAPA

should (for "may")

1. May you (I, he, she) . . .
2. If only . . .
3. I hope that . . .

Yiddish abounds with invocational phrases such as "You should (may you) live to a hundred and twenty!" In English, such supplications are phrased "If only that were so," or "I wish that . . ." and (in earlier centuries) "Would that we (I, they) . . ."

"It shouldn't happen to a dog!" is an eloquent example of Yinglish petitions to fate.

△ △ △

Adolf Hitler, plagued by nightmares, called in a faith healer. Stomping back and forth, he enumerated his afflictions, blaming each upon the damned Jews.

The healer made passes over a crystal ball, uttering phrases of impressive abracadabra. "O mighty Führer, the mist is clearing . . . I see —yes—you should die . . . on a Jewish holiday."

"Which one?"

"O mighty Führer, *any* day you die will be a Jewish holiday."

shpilkes

> Pronounced to rhyme with "milk us."

> Pins. (The singular is *shpilkeh.*)

This plain word is put to colorful usage:

1. Anything of little value. "It's not worth a mouthful of *shpilkes.*"
2. Anything foolish or absurd. "You know what the whole deal comes down to? *Shpilkes!*"
3. As an expletive of scorn or contempt, like "Nuts!" or "Baloney!"—which have become exhausted by overuse.
4. "To sit on *shpilkes*" means to sit on tenterhooks. (Not "tender hooks." Tenterhooks are nails on a frame across which cloth is stretched; "tender hooks" is an oxymoron.)
5. *"Goldeneh shpilkes"* means "fools' gold."

△ △ △

On Rivington Street, sixty years ago, Mr. Schonet carefully carried a milk bottle filled with yellowish fluid to the local clinic. To the nurse, he said, "My urine specimen."

"Come back in a week."

A week later, Mr. Schonet hurried to the clinic. The nurse said, "The laboratory has given you a complete bill of health. No diseases of any kind."

Schonet hurried to a telephone. And when his wife's voice came over the wire he shouted, "Tess?"

"It's me, Berel, I'm on *shpilkes!*"

"Tessie, the news is wonderful! I'm healthy, you're healthy, the children are fine, your brother is fine, my sister, your mother . . ."

See BOBKES, SHMONTSES.

shtarker

shtarkeh (f.)

> Pronounced SHTARK-air. From German: *stark:* strong.
>
> 1. Strong man.
> 2. Someone brave, even fearless.
> 3. A big shot.
> 4. (Derisively) No hero.

That last usage is prized by connoisseurs of irony: "Don't rely on that *shtarker*." "Listen, *shtarker*, if you have no choice, at least be brave."

△ △ △

Mrs. Janovich was on the beach with her son. The tot wandered into the water. A big wave came up.

"My boy, my boy!" screamed Mrs. Janovich.

On every side, people leaped to their feet—but stood transfixed as the wave sucked the lad out to sea.

And then a *shtarker* plunged into the surf and with powerful strokes swam out—and he finally grabbed the lad and brought him proudly ashore.

Mrs. Janovich cried, "He was wearing a *hat!*"

△ △ △

Walter Holzwasser was given to posing as a *shtarker*. One day, in a crowded bar, he declaimed, "Tough guys, shmuff guys. Show me a so-called tough guy and I'll show you a coward!"

A huge bruiser with a pug nose pushed his face next to Walter's: "I'm a tough guy."

"Oh . . . well, I'm a coward."

shtetl

shtetlekh (pl.)

> *Shtetl* rhymes with "kettle" or "fatal." German: *Städtlein:* a little town.
>
> The *shtetlekh* were the poor villages of Eastern Europe where, before World War Two, the remarkable culture of the Ashkenazim blossomed.

Maurice Samuel comments upon the ambivalence of American Jews toward the *shtetl:*

On the one hand [the *shtetl*] is remembered sentimentally . . . it sends up a nostalgic glow for those who have received the tradition from parents and grandparents. It is pictured as one of the rare and happy breathing-spells of the Exile, the nearest thing to a home from home that the Jews have ever known. On the other hand, it is recalled with a grimace of distaste. The *Shtetlach!* Those forlorn little settlements in a vast and hostile wilderness, isolated alike from Jewish and non-Jewish centers of civilization, their tenure precarious, their structure ramshackle, their spirit squalid. Who would want to live in one of them? . . . [The *shtetl* offers] a pattern of the exalted and the ignominious.

—*Little Did I Know* (Knopf)

Fiddler on the Roof, that supercolossal hit throughout the world, painted a highly romanticized picture of *shtetl* life. Let me be plain: life in those medieval enclaves was dreadful. Hunger was endemic, sanitation disgusting, housing unspeakable. The muddy streets, open latrines and ubiquitous garbage offended the nostrils. Neither water nor light blessed the huts and hovels. (Simply look at the old photographs in the archives of Yivo: 2 East 86th Street, New York.)

Safety was nowhere. Jews were spat upon, beaten, tormented. Their synagogues were frequently vandalized, their women raped, their children kidnapped—to be forcibly converted or sent into the Czar's army. Russian or Polish officials shrugged off the hooliganism of drunken thugs, the bloodbaths of murderous Cossacks, the pogroms instigated by fanatical priests.

Every morning of the year, in a *shtetl,* was heard the same loud summons: *Yiden, Yiden! Shtayt of l'avodat habora!* "Jews, Jews! Rise—and serve the Lord!" For in those impoverished, desolate backwaters the only raft of hope was—faith. Faith—intense, impassioned, invulnerable —in a merciful God and His promise of the Messiah soon to come. Torah was the miracle of deliverance, the inner light that healed pain, that sanctified poverty and despair and fear. *Shtetl* Jews were earthy, superstitious, and they stubbornly resisted secularism—or reality itself.

The Jews in Western Europe lived wholly different lives. "City Jews," in Eastern as well as Western Europe, were often wealthy: they were entrepreneurs, importers, exporters, bankers; they managed many a Gentile business. Invited and welcomed to Eastern Europe, they became the managers of huge estates of Russian and Polish aristocrats. (See the masterful opus of Bernard Weinryb, *The Jews of Poland: A Social and Economic History of the Jewish Community in Poland from 1100–1800,* Jewish Publication Society.)

The Jewish workers and tradesmen who lived in cities slipped away from orthodoxy. They were caught up in political and radical movements; they became socialists, trade unionists, reformers, revolutionaries. Their culture was as different from that of the *shtetl* as the culture of Scarsdale is from that of Biloxi.

But it was in the *shtetl* that the Ashkenazim produced their astonishing culture, a civilization unlike anything seen, I think, in human history. The children of these village ghettos produced a golden literature: songs, hymns, tales, memoirs, mysticism, poems that touch the heart. Their stories rank with Dickens and Jane Austen and Mark Twain. They gave the world new modalities of satire, muscular prose, marvelous characters that electrify the imagination, fresh and bounteous laughter.

The *shtetl* exists no more. Hundreds of thousands of Jews left those muddy, dreary clusters for cities and for England, France, Holland, Brazil and—America, America! Those who did not leave were rounded up, along with their brethren in Warsaw, Vilna, Kiev, Odessa—for the Nazis' "final solution."

It is not hard to write "six million were slaughtered." But it is impossible—simply *impossible*—to grasp the enormity of the horror. Even the survivors cannot do that. Read *Voices from the Holocaust*, edited by Sylvia Rothchild (New American Library). The simplicity and calmness of these recollections are a testimonial to human dignity and human endurance.

The consciousness of the spiritual richness that flourished amidst the squalor of the *shtetlekh* came surprisingly late in the West. The great 12-volume *Jewish Encyclopedia* (1901) has no entry for *shtetl;* nor does the *Encyclopedia of the Jewish Religion;* nor does the *New Standard Jewish Encyclopedia,* edited by Cecil Roth and Geoffrey Wigoder; and Chaim Potok's *Wanderings: A History of the Jews* contains one passing reference.

For a portrait of the physical attributes of a *shtetl* by one of its inhabitants, see Abraham Ains' "Swislocz," in *Voices from the Yiddish,* edited by Howe and Greenberg (University of Michigan). An informative, beautifully printed anthology of creative output is Joachim Neugroschel's *The Shtetl* (Richard Marek).*

---

* The best dramatizations of *shtetl* life are to be found in the writings of "Mendele" Mokher Seforim, Sholom Aleichem, I. L. Peretz, Sholem Asch, the plays of Peretz Hirschbein, the work of I. J. Singer (Isaac Bashevis' older brother). Excellent recollections adorned the pages of the *Jewish Daily Forward.*

The first ethnological account is *Life Is with People,* by Zborowski and Herzog, study supervised by Margaret Mead. Valuable insights will be found in *The Golden Tradition,* edited by Lucy Dawidowicz (Holt, Rinehart). A memoir I found utterly beguiling is Jacob Marateck's *The Samurai of Vishogrod* (Jewish Publication Society).

shtunk

Rhyme the *u* with the *oo* of "look." German: *Stunk:* a squabble.

(Vulgar, but not obscene)
1. A stinker, male, female or otherwise.
2. An ungrateful person.
3. An unpleasant, nasty, offensive mortal.
4. A mess, a scandal, a stink.

A *shtunk* is not as despicable as a *paskudnyak,* but is more contemptible than a *shmegegge.* From there on, you may construct your own obloquies.

△ △ △

In front of a window at Tiffany's the girl snuggled up to Jerry Frimkin, murmuring, "Oh, darling, just look at that diamond necklace!"

"I see it, I see it."

"Jerry, I would *love* a necklace like that."

"Baby," he said, "permit me to elucidate that certain exigencies pertaining to my arbitrage enterprises militate against my acquisition of such a refulgent artifact."

"Jerry . . . I don't get it."

"Right," leered the *shtunk.*

shtup

Use the vowel sound of "foot," not of "stoop" or "pup." German: *stupsen:* to push.

As a verb:
1. To push; to press. ("Don't *shtup*" means "Don't push." "She *shtups* to the high windows" means "She's a social climber.")
2. (Obscene) To fornicate. ("Does she *shtup?*" has nothing to do with square dancing.)

Once more we must acknowledge the formidable phonetic power of the *sh,* which dominates the lusty, vulgar or obscene words of Yiddish-Yinglish. *Shtup* is vulgar and obscene. I caution finicky readers: *Read no further: worse is yet to come!*

As a noun:
1. A push, a shove. ("I received a *shtup* from the man behind me.")
2. A sexual episode. ("She loves a good *shtup.*")

3. A fornicator. ("He's a very active *shtupper*.") If female: ("She's a good *shtup*.")

See YENTS.

△ △ △

"Do you think a father of forty should get married again?"

"Never! That's more than enough children for *any* man!"

shtus

Rhyme this with "puss," not "cuss." From Hebrew.

1. A noisy commotion. ("Can't they pipe down? It's late for such a *shtus*.")
2. An embroglio, a "stink," the result of energetic protests or complaints. ("The newspapers made such a *shtus* over the zoning code, the law was repealed.")
3. A *contretemps*, a rhubarb (in sports lingo), a fracas. ("With all the *shtus*, I couldn't see what was going on!")
4. Carrying on disproportionately about something. ("From the *shtus* they're making, that tricycle will end up in the Supreme Court.")

See TSIMMES.

△ △ △

"Good morning," smiled Nurse Finkelhoff, lifting the patient's chart. "Well, I see you delivered a baby eight hours ago. A healthy seven-pound boy. Have you decided on his name?"

"Arafat."

"*Arafat?!*" The nurse's jaw dropped. "Are you joking?"

"No."

"But—I—why, I never heard of a Jewish mother calling her child by such a hateful name, Mrs. Kassbein! Are you absolutely *sure*—"

"I'm sure, I'm sure. Stop making a *shtus*. . . . My name isn't Mrs. It's Miss."

✡ shul

Rhymes with "full." From Greek *schola*, via German: *Schule*.

School—(therefore) synagogue.

The *shul* was the center of the life of religious Jews. All day, all night, men sat there, read, studied, discoursed, debated. They stood up to pray.

Philo, who was a rabbi and a Platonist, said the *schola* made all Jews philosophers.

shvartz (adj.)

shvartzeh (noun, f.)

shvartzer (noun, m.)

> Rhymes with "parts." German: black.
>
> 1. Black.
> 2. A black.
> 3. A gloomy prospect, a dark forecast. "May a black year befall him!" is a common Yiddish curse.

△ △ △

The great pianist Vladmir Ostrovsky was rehearsing the "Emperor" Concerto. The phone rang. The maid said, "Ostrovsky residence."

"I must talk to the Maestro," said a woman's voice.

"He ain't here."

"But—I can hear him playing!"

"Uh . . . that ain't him playin'," said the *shvartzeh*. "That's me—dustin' the keys."

sicknik

> 1. One who is (or maybe is) sick most of the time.
> 2. A hypochondriac.
> 3. One who enjoys the usufructs of illness.
> 4. One who enjoys the psychological experience of *fearing* he will be sick.

The connotational advantage of *sicknik* over "hypochondriac" is that the latter describes a propensity, the former, a hang-up. Hypochondriacs cannot help themselves; sickniks choose not to. A hypochondriac pays the price of apprehension: anxiety, depression; but a sicknik, being as much a malingerer as an invalid, enjoys the attention he gives himself.

△ △ △

DOCTOR: What are you taking for that terrible cold?

PATIENT: Make me an offer.

△ △ △

"She is such a sicknik they should bury her next to her doctor."

△ △ △

DOCTOR: Do you feel listless?

MRS. KORN: If I felt that good would I be here?

△ △ △

DOCTOR (removing stethoscope): Lady, has any doctor treated you for this condition?

WOMAN: Never! I always pay.

sidonder

Gorgeous Yinglish. Pronounce it si-DON-dair or si-don-DAIR— "sit down there."

1. A *shamus* (sexton).
2. An instruction about where to take a seat.

The *shamus* who supervises seating in a synagogue or temple during the high holidays is very busy telling worshippers where to sit ("Mister Fleisher, *sidon*DAIR"), or ordering those who are standing to be seated ("*Si*DON*dair!*"). It was inevitable that such a bustling beadle would be called "The *Sidonder.*"

See SHAMUS.

△ △ △

One holy day, a young man came running to the entrance of a synagogue. The *shamus* barred his way. "Show me your ticket."

"I don't have a ticket."

"On this day of days no one gets in without a ticket."

"It's an emergency!" cried the young man.

"We are already full!"

"There's been an accident! Yonah Knippel's house! It will only take me ten *seconds!*"

"Go in," the *shamus* muttered. "But don't let me catch you praying!"

singlemon

Rhymes with "tingle John."

1. An unmarried male, whether young or old, who is not a widower or divorced.
2. A bachelor.
3. A prospect eligible for dating or marriage.

I offer three variations of *singlemon* to draw attention to the subtle shifts in the man's status—real, assumed, or implied.

The unmarried male in Jewish circles was widely noticed and fervently propagandized. The first positive injunction in the Bible, after all, commands man to be fruitful and multiply (Genesis 1:28). Marriage was regarded as the only proper way for a young man to live—not because marriage necessarily offered, much less promised, connubial bliss, but because marriage is holy, mystic—and a partnership with the Lord. There was intense pressure by the Jewish community to strengthen itself and enhance its future. Forget not the startling reminder in the Talmud (*Kiddushin,* 29b): "When a man reaches twenty and is still unmarried, the Holy One Himself says, 'Let his bones rot!' "

The appearance of a *singlemon* in a neighborhood galvanized the matchmakers, male or female—especially those with an unmarried daughter, niece, cousin, or however distant a member of the *meshpoche.* "Jews have no nunneries."

△ △ △

When a young man marries, he divorces his mother.

Bachelor: A man who comes to work each morning from a different direction.

When a bachelor dies a bachelor, all girls are avenged.

Even a bad marriage can produce good children.

—FOLK SAYINGS

Paradoxically, the very Jews who extolled marriage and pushed bachelors down the road thereto, voiced the most devastating comments about marital bliss.

The man who marries for money, earns it.

After the ceremony it's too late to regret.

It is as hard to arrange a good marriage as it was to divide the Red Sea.

—TALMUD *Sotah,* 2a

△ △ △

When a girl is told about a *singlemon,* her responses change with her age:

TWENTY: "Is he handsome?"
THIRTY: "Is he well off?"
FORTY: "Where is he?!"

△ △ △

Said Uncle Nate to his nephew, "You're over forty and still a *singlemon.* Didn't you ever think about getting married?"

"Many times. That's why I didn't."

△ △ △

Mr. Bliberg waited in line to pay the fee for his naturalization certificate. A guard said, "The line at the next window is shorter. Don't you want to stand there?"

"I can't."

"Why not?"

"I'm married." Bliberg pointed to the sign:

SINGLE LINE ONLY

△ △ △

"Who ever heard of a man shouldn't want to get married?" the astounded rabbi asked.

"*I* don't want to get married," said the *singlemon*. "I'm having the time of my life!"

The rabbi sighed. "You just don't know what it means to have a wonderful, loving woman at your side. Every night when I come home, wearied by the day's labor, my darling Brindeleh takes off my coat, brings me my slippers, my robe, the paper. My dinner is fit for a king. And after dinner, my Brindel covers me nice and warm in our bed. And as we lie there, man and wife, well fed, contented, my angel tells me what she did all day. She talks, I listen, the house is cozy. . . . And my Brindeleh talks, and talks and talks until—so help me God!—that woman is going to drive me out of my *mind!*"

so

Yinglish for *tsi* or *nu.*

The use of "So" to begin a question is characteristically Jewish, from *tsi*, which often opens a question in Yiddish: "So have you called your father?" "So did he like the book?" "So when can you get here?"

1. So?
2. So . . .
3. So!
4. So–o.
5. S–so?
6. So what?

Each vocalization contains its own distinct message. Thus:

So? ("Well? What are you going to do about it?")
So . . . ("Following that"; "In any event.")
So! ("Let's get on with it!")
So–o . . . ("Meanwhile"; "I think"; "Perhaps.")
S–so? ("What's *next?*" "What will you (he, she) do?"; "I'm afraid to hear your next words!")

△ △ △

"Hymie, are you listening?"

"Mmh."

"Hymie! You're reading the paper! I have to tell you something. This afternoon I went to see the doctor. . . ."

"So how is he?"

So it shouldn't be (wasted, a total loss, etc.)

Yinglish. From Yiddish: *Zol nit zayn aroysgevarfene verter:* So my words should not be entirely thrown away . . . wasted.

Our house rang with such declamatory invocations:

"So your visit shouldn't be a disappointment, take home a piece of cake."

"So it shouldn't be a shock, I'm telling you now that I'm not talking to Hester!"

some

This Yinglish usage serves two separate functions:

1. Synonym for "very." ("She is some smart!")
2. Synonym for "truly . . . certainly." ("You are some lucky!")

Usage 1 drops the noun to which the adjective was usually attached: "She is some smart [student, person]!" Usage 2 both omits the final noun and substitutes "some" for any adverb of emphasis ("truly," "certainly") or singularity: "You are some [really] lucky!"

This Brooklyn-Bronx invention (no other word can do it justice) is a distinctive, deplorable characteristic of certain schools of Yinglish. I heard it first in Hollywood, used by screenwriters who cherish their childhood.

△ △ △

"Dora! Dora!" cried Mr. Efron. "I just won a thousand dollars! In the state lottery! One of my tickets won!"

"*Mazel tov!* You are some lucky." Mrs. Efron paused. "What did you mean, '*one* of my tickets'?"

"I bought four, and one of them won."

"Dummy! Why did you need the other three?"

something

From Yiddish: *eppes.*

1. Remarkable.
2. Noteworthy.

I am not suggesting that the English use of "something" is in most cases anything but English. The Yinglish usage to which I refer, and the reason for this entry, is "something" employed in nonconventional ways, such as:

"Man, that's something!" (Meaning, "That's something remarkable.")

"He's something!" ("He's someone of great consequence.")

"At a keyboard, he's really something!"

These usages have become familiar in the cant spoken by the young, the black, the aberrant and the addicted. I believe the Yinglish usage, by Jews, long preceded that.

△ △ △

Among the ranks of the ingenious, the name of Emanuel Greengold, of DuBarry Coats, must rank high. After extolling his wares, he would say, "Lady, even your best friends won't recognize you in this garment! So put the coat on, go out in the daylight . . ."

The customer would step out. And when she returned to the store, Manny Greengold would say, "Come in, stranger. What can I show you today?"

Greengold was something.

So sue me

Go sue me

1. "Try and do something about it."
2. "There's not a thing you can do about it."

These crisp, defiant exhortations are scornful responses to an inquiry, contemptuous retorts to a question, confident "toppers" to a challenge.

"Sue me" is proper English, of course, but the prefixed "So" or "Go" or even "So go and . . ." bristle with the taunting aspect of Yiddish.

The line "Sue me, sue me! (What can you do me?)" was immortalized in Nathan Detroit's protestations of ardor in the cantata "Sue Me," one of the many jewels in *Guys and Dolls*.

△ △ △

Mortimer Struzinsky, a fishing nut, was angling in a lovely lake in the Adirondacks. A local watched him for a spell, then called, "Hi, stranger. Are you fishin'?"

"Nope," said Morty, who was well known for laconic wit.

"Then why are y' standin' there with a fishin' pole?"
"So sue me: I like to drown worms."

So what?

So what else is new?

> From Yiddish: *Iz vus?* "Is what?"

1. "So what?"
   A. What's the point of telling me that?
      ("I never answered her letter." "So what?")
   B. What difference does that make?
      ("They're going to paint the hall." "So what?")
   C. Who cares?
      ("She doesn't like you." "So what?")
   D. I can't do anything about that.
      ("They're leaving New York?" "So what?")

Few idiomatic phrases are used as often and as pertly as the flippant, caustic "So what?" It is, indeed, a substitute for repartee in circles not noted for originality of language or inventiveness of rejoinder. "So what?" has become a popular improvement upon the defiant "Sez who?" which peppered the patois of the 1920s.

2. "So what else is new?"

This is a deceptive idiom. It has a slightly different function from "So what?" It is not only a comeback; it contains reproval—slightly mocking, somewhat crowing, meaning:

> A. Did you really think I didn't know that?
>   ("They're moving to Texas." "So what else is new?")
> B. Don't bore me with more of this.
>   ("People are buying bonds because of the interest rate." "So what else is new?")
> C. Do you know how many times I've heard that before?
>   ("She's going to buy a new car." "So what else is new?")
> D. But you've said that before—and didn't.
>   ("I'm going to contribute a thousand dollars!" "So what else is new?")
> E. That's hardly news to anyone.
>   ("She's been sleeping with that no-goodnik for years!" "So what else is new?")

Never place a comma after "so" ("So, what else is new?"); that converts "so" into "well," and separates "so" from "what"—which kills both the point and the pungency.

spynik

1. Someone who is hooked on spy stories, fictional or real.
2. An authority, with no official connections, on spies.
3. A writer/reporter who concentrates on stories about spies.

stood (for "stayed")

"You should of stood in bed."

The most celebrated instance of this usage was when Mike Jacobs, the fight promoter, observing the small line at his ticket windows, moaned, "I should of stood in bed!"

Stood is a calque for the Yiddish *geshtanen,* which can mean both "stood" and "remained." Mr. Jacobs' use of "of" simply followed the speech pattern of his childhood. He could have resorted to the barbarism had he been Irish, Italian, Polish. But H. L. Mencken and other language-watchers credit the American-Yiddish influence.

T

talis (standard)
taleysem (pl.)

> Rhymes with "solace." Hebrew: prayer shawl.

> 1. The long prayer shawl used by Jewish males at morning religious services, and at all services on Yom Kippur.
> 2. The prayer shawl used by the cantor at all services during Jewish holidays.

The *talis* reminds worshippers of their bond to the Almighty. In America, Jewish fathers give their sons a *talis* upon Bar Mitzve. A bride may give her groom a beautiful *talis*. Orthodox Jewish men are buried in their *posele* (invalidated *taleysem*).

. . . talk to the wall

> From Yiddish: *Red tsu der vand.*

> 1. It won't do a bit of good.
> 2. You can't get through to him (her).
> 3. Don't waste your time.

△ △ △

At the fifth floor nurses' desk, late one night, the phone rang. "Nurse, can you please tell me the condition of one of your patients—Myer Fleischman?"

"One moment . . ." The nurse got a chart out of the rack. "Yes. Mr. Fleischman is doing very well."

"His blood pressure is okay now?"

"Oh, yes. Mr. Fleischman is doing so well the doctor says he will be discharged tomorrow. . . . Who shall I tell him called?"

"No one. *I'm* Fleischman. That doctor—go talk to the wall!—won't tell me a damn thing!"

✡ Talmud

> Rhymes with "Dollwood." Hebrew: *lamod:* to teach; to study.

> The massive compendium of discussions, debates, commentaries, analyses and legal decisions of the Torah applied to the problems and obligations of life, religion, ethics, law, liturgy, truth, heaven, guilt, marriage, sex, children, the earth, the cosmos . . . The encyclopedia of "divine knowledge."

The Talmud is not the Bible, not the Old Testament, not the Torah (the five books of Moses). It is the assembled, centuries-long analysis, debate and legal findings of Jewish scholars, jurists, philosophers and sages—from the fifth century before the Christian era until the second century after. I know of no body of seminars with which to compare it. It is a stenographic report of a millennial discussion of the Torah. It is majestic, profound, bursting with insights. It is also maddening: hairsplitting, superstitious, pedantic. Sophistry jostles reason, mythology confounds logic. But the intellectual totality is staggering.

> . . . for generation after generation, the wits of the Jew were sharpened by continuous exercise from earliest youth upon the acute Talmudic dialectic. But the Talmud meant much more to him than this. It brought him another world, vivid, calm, and peaceful, after the continuous humiliation of ordinary existence. It provided him with a second life, so different from the sordid round of everyday. After each successive outbreak was stilled, and the shouting of the mob had died down, he crept back to the ruins of his home, and put away his Jewish badge of shame, and set himself to pore again over the yellowed pages. He was transported back into the Babylonian schools of a thousand years before, and there his troubled soul found rest.
>
> —Cecil Roth, *A History of*
> *the Jews* (Schocken)

tararam

tarrarom

> Onomatopoetic. Rhymes with "bar a bomb."

1. Big noise, hullabaloo, ruckus.
2. A big fuss, argument, *shtus.*

"What a *tararam* he made in the restaurant!"

"Calm down; don't make a *tararam* over it."

See SHTUS.

△ △ △

At the crowded chaise longue area around a pool in Miami Beach, a heated argument was heard above the lotioned bodies.

"Oh, God," moaned a sunbather. "What's all that *tararam* about?"

"It's a battle of wits."

"Wits? *Here?* Who?"

"Mirawitz, Branowitz, Golowitz and Shmulewitz."

△ △ △

Hollywoodniks love the following whopper:

When Moses reached the Red Sea he blew his ram's horn and shouted, "Sid! Sid! Where are you?"

Up ran his publicity man. "Yes, Chief?"

"Okay, Sid. Launch the boats."

"What?"

"The *boats*," said Moses. "Launch—"

"Oh, God," wailed Sid. "In all the excitement and *tararam*, I forgot!"

"You forgot to order the *boats?*" shouted Moses. "You fool—the Egyptians will be here in twenty minutes! What do you expect me to do, talk to God? Get Him to part the waters? Let us Jews across and drown all the Egyptians?"

"Boss," cried Sid, "pull that off and I'll get you two pages in the Old Testament!"

Tata

Tate (standard)

Tateleh (diminutive)

Tatenyu (affectionate)

> Rhyme respectively with "gotta" (*not* with "gate"), "stop at a," "Martin Yew."

> 1. Papa.
> 2. Father.

Tata is colloquial, used much more often than *foter* or *futer*.

Tata-Mama

Tate-Mame (standard)

Rhymes with "pot a . . . bomb a . . ."

Father and mother: parents.

✡ tefillen

tfiln (standard)

Rhymes with "a'willin'." Hebrew: *tefillin:* prayers. The English "phylacteries" comes from the Greek *phylakterim:* protection . . . amulet.

Phylacteries.

Thanks a lot

From Yiddish: *A sheynem dank aykh* (Pretty thanks to you . . .).

An ironic inversion of "Thank you" meaning "Thanks for nothing," or "*That* you call doing me a favor?"

This sarcastic response came into English in the late 1940s and 1950s from comedy sketches on radio and television. "Thanks a *lot*" became superdry repartee.

The gibe relates to the ironic Yiddish phrases *A groysn dank dir* ("Huge thanks to you") or *A sheyner, reyner dank* ("A pretty, pure thank you"). The latter gains force from its echo of the ago-old curse *A sheynem, reynem kapore of zey* ("May a beautiful, purified plague befall them (him, her, you)").

Yiddish maledictions are collected in James Matisoff's *Blessings, Curses, Hopes and Fears: Psycho-Ostensive Expressions in Yiddish.*

△ △ △

MOHAWK TRAILS CAMP
UPPER BEAR FALLS
NEW YORK

DEAR MR. AND MRS. KOSTER:

Your son Alfred is having a wonderful time here at Mohawk Trails! Every member of our staff likes him a lot, and he is popular with all the boys in his cabin.

You should be proud of your boy!

Yours truly,
RONALD FISHBACK
Director

WILLIAM KOSTER
309 WEST END AVENUE
NEW YORK, N.Y.

Dear Mr. Fishback:

My wife and I sure are happy to hear what a fine camper little Alfred is. Thanks a *lot.*

We happen to have a son at Mohawk Trails, too. His name is George. How is he doing?

Yours,
WILLIAM KOSTER
Father

That's all I need!

From Yiddish: *Dos felt mir nokh:* That's all I lack yet.

1. That's all I need (yet).
2. On top of everything else, do I need that?
3. (By inversion) That's one thing I certainly *don't* need!

This gem of irony has become Yinglish with celerity. And why not? It is a crisp, colorful variation of "From the frying pan into the fire," or "Are you kidding, Mac?"

"Another storm? That's all we need!"

"Her son is moving next door? That's all we need!"

"A broken filling? That's all I need yet."

See also NOKH.

△ △ △

WOMAN PATIENT (on couch): Oh, Doctor! If you would only— just once—kiss me!

PSYCHOANALYST: Kiss you? That's all I need! Why, I shouldn't even be lying next to you!

See WHO NEEDS IT?

That's for sure

From Yiddish: *Dos iz oyf zikher.*

"That's for sure" has become popular in colloquial English; it is quite serviceable for cheerful concurrence upon hearing such *aperçus* as these, say, from the folklore of the Jews:

"Out of snow, you can't make cheesecake."

"If you're doing something wrong, at least enjoy it."

"Never consult a coward about war, a salesman about a bargain, a woman about a rival."

△ △ △

Father Mulvaney, new to his parish, was walking down the street and saw a large sign over a store:

SPEIGELMAN AND MCCOY

HOME APPLIANCES

SINCE 1927

In went Father Mulvaney.

An old man with a beard and a *yarmulke* greeted him.

"I just came in to introduce myself," smiled Father Mulvaney, "and to say how wonderful it is to see Catholics and Jews joined in partnership. What a splendid surprise, Mr. Speigelman."

"A surprise it's for sure," said the old man. "A bigger surprise: I'm McCoy."

That should be . . .

Yiddish: *Zol dos zayn:* That should be . . .

1. May that be.
2. That should only be.

Notice the inversion so dear to Yiddish:

"Your hair is too thick? That should be your biggest problem!"

"Your son didn't graduate first in his class but third? That should be the biggest setback in his career!"

That's not chopped liver

Show-business lingo.

"That ain't hay!" "That's not peanuts!"

This declamatory judgment is favored by the natives of Broadway and Beverly Hills. It has often been uttered by Johnny Carson, doyen of television's "Tonight Show."

"Did you know she got fifty grand for one week in Las Vegas?"

"Man! That's not chopped liver."

That's what you say

Stress the pronoun. From Yiddish: *Azoy zugst du:* So say *you.*

The sarcastic rendition of an otherwise matter-of-fact observation conjures up contrasted meanings:

1. I don't believe you.
2. I take that with a grain of salt.
3. There is another and more plausible explanation.
4. What a story! What an invention! What a lie!

△ △ △

Arty and Mickey, approaching Honolulu on a Pan Am flight, on their first trip to the fabled island, began to argue about the right way to pronounce "Hawaii."

"You pronounce it just like it's spelled," said Arty. "Ha-why-ya."

"That's what *you* say," said Mickey. "You pronounce it with a *v*—like this: Ha-*vy*-ee!"

"Twenty bucks says you're wrong!"

"You're on."

Soon the two men hurried down the landing stairs. They spotted a group of native girls in hula skirts, dancing, and a group of native boys playing ukuleles for them. Arty went up to the leader of the ukulele combo. "Aloha!"

"Aloha."

Mickey said, "Mac, how do you pronounce the name of this here place?"

The native smiled, "Ha-*vy*-ee."

"There!" cried Mickey to Arty. And to the native: "Thanks a lot!"

The native beamed, "You're velcome."

There's no one here to talk to

Hyperbole from Yiddish: *Nito tsu vemen tsu reydn!*

1. It's useless for me to talk to you: you refuse to listen.
2. You are not *capable* of understanding!
3. You are too stubborn, too prejudiced to listen, so why waste my breath trying to reason with you?

The words are English and the syntax ordinary: What then makes the content Yinglish? The rhetorical murder of everyone except the aggrieved speaker.

toches

tokhes (standard)

> Rhyme this vulgar noun with "caucus." The *ch* is guttural, as in the German *Ach!* and not the English "Chickamauga." From Hebrew: *tahat:* bottom . . . under. The meaning "buttocks" is strictly Yiddish—although it has been adopted in Israeli Hebrew.

> *Vulgar, vulgar, and taboo.*
> The posterior, buttocks.

> "Get off your *toches* and work."
> "I gave the kid a slap on the *toches.*"

However common this usage, it still is common—and will remain so, in usage.

△ △ △

To describe someone who is a cold fish, street Yiddish goes *Er iz (hawt) a kalten toches:* He is (has) a cold ass.

. . . took a bath

> Yinglish. In Yiddish, "He led me to the bath" (*Er haut mikh gefirt in bod arayn*) means "He tricked (deceived) me," or "He led me up the garden path."

> Lost a great deal of money.

"I took a bath" does not (except when used in a report on hygiene) mean that the speaker bathed, or even showered. The Yinglish usage refers to monetary losses.

△ △ △

"How did that deal turn out?"
    "She took a bath."
    "What happened to the partners?"
    "They took a bath, too."
    There is, of course, a marked resemblance between "I took a bath" and the English "They cleaned me out," or "They took me to the cleaners."
    The etymology is fascinating: Guests in or from a poorhouse were urged, cajoled, pressured to take a bath (go to the *shvitsbod*), especially if

they seemed to have a communicable disease. When they were in the baths, their clothes were disinfected by steam. Since not all guests relished the prospect of being deloused or having their hair closely clipped, they were tricked, one way or another, into the baths. Hence: *M' firt im in bod arayn* ("They are tricking him into the bath").

△ △ △

APPLICATION FOR A PUBLIC LIBRARY CARD
Name: Joel Sonnenschein.
Born: Absolutely.
Address: 18 Avenue B.
Business: Terrible.

Torah

The Hebrew pronunciation is TOE-rah, the Yiddish TOY-rah. Hebrew: teaching; doctrine.

1. The first five books of the Bible, called the Five Books of Moses; the Pentateuch (Greek).
2. The scroll, used in readings in the synagogue, that contains the fine parchment roll on which the Five Books of Moses have been lettered.
3. One of the three cardinal aspects of Judaism, contained in the saying: "God, Torah, Israel."
4. The entire body of Jewish faith, morality, ethics, values, jurisprudence, social thought, culture.

The crowning ideal of religious Jews is the unending study of Torah. As Maimonides said:

> How long is one required to study Torah? Till the day of his death. . . . Some of the greatest of the wise men of Israel were woodchoppers, others drawers of water, some even blind—who, nevertheless, studied Torah day and night.

To bring Torah to even the least educated, the slow to learn or the backward, part of the Pentateuch is read aloud, *seriatim*, in the synagogue or temple every Monday and Thursday, every Sabbath, and on every holiday. (Why Monday and Thursday? Because in ancient Palestine, those were market days—when Jews congregated.)

By the end of the year, the congregation has gone from the first word in Genesis to the last word in Deuteronomy. And as soon as the long cycle has been completed, to the sounds of rejoicing and song (and dancing, among Hasidim), the holy scrolls are paraded around the synagogue seven times—when the reading anew, going back to Genesis, begins again. This dramatizes the conviction that the Torah has no end, and that its worship and study never end.

△ △ △

Torah . . . comprises every field and mark of culture—morality, justice, society, education, etc. The term aims to gather them all up as a unit because the Jewish view is that all the nobler manifestations of human conduct must be connected with religion.

—LOUIS GINZBERG, in *Students, Scholars and Saints* (The Jewish Publication Society of America)

T.O.T.

(Vulgarism)
1. The genteel acronym for *toches oyfn tish:* backside on the table. But wait. T.O.T. does not mean "Place your buttocks on the table." T.O.T. means:
2. Put all your cards on the table.
3. Stop beating around the bush.
4. Put up or shut up.
5. Let's get down to brass tacks (or *tachlis*, which is in no way related to *toches*).

T.O.T. is an effective challenge in circumstances where *toches oyfn tish* would be taboo.

tough toches

Gargle the *ch* as *kh.*

(Taboo)
1. (Literally) Tough ass.
2. Tough luck.
3. Too bad.
4. Nothing can be done about it.
5. (Ironically) You better learn to like it.

△ △ △

"The judge knocked my case out. I'll lose a mint."
"Tough *toches.*"

"If I have to pay you, I won't be able to go to Vegas!"
"Tough *toches.*"

Travel in good health

Go in good health

> From Yiddish: *for gezunterhayt;* or, in Polish/Galician pronunciation: *für gezinterhayt.* Pronounce the former FAWR ge-ZOON-ter-hate; the latter FOOR ge-ZIN-ter-hite. For the plural, add a *t* to *for/fur.*
>
> Travel (happily and) healthily.

Anglo-Saxons are taken aback upon hearing such a *Bon voyage!* The English is undoubtedly awkward and alien, but the sentiment is amiable. I would not myself use the salutation, but I hear the natives use it right and left.

△ △ △

Ari Zitlow was disappointed when the newly elected Prime Minister of Israel offered him the cabinet post of Minister of Health and Transportation. Said Zitlow: "Have you forgotten how I, once an American citizen, came to work for you in Israel? Have you forgotten how much I personally donated to your election campaign? Have you forgotten you promised me an important post in your cabinet? What kind of joke is Health and Transportation?!"

"I am giving you a *prize* position! You will get a fine apartment in Haifa with a balcony overlooking the harbor. And you will sit on that balcony where everyone can see you. And whenever a ship leaves the harbor, you will get up and wave and call out, in a strong, official voice, through a bullhorn, '*Fort gezunterhayt!*' "

treppverter

> From German: *Treppe:* steps, and *Verter:* words.
>
> Those brilliant rejoinders you wish you had uttered, but think of only when you are going down the steps—on the way home.

It always surprises me to find words for which there are no words in English. The same is true, of course, for any language: German had no word for "bully" and no phrase for "fair play" until the 1920s. French appropriated a German phrase, during the occupation of Paris in 1870, for a fanlight or transom: *Vas ist das?* (What is that?); you will find *vasistas* in any French dictionary. So I nominate *treppverter* as an addition to our tongue.

treyf (standard)

trayf

> Rhymes with "safe." Hebrew: *treyfa:* originally, "cattle killed by predators," later, "torn to pieces."
>
> 1. An animal not slain according to the ritual laws, and by an authorized *shochet.*
> 2. Any food that is not kosher.

treyfener (male)

treyfeneh (female)

> One who eats *treyfes.*

treyfnyak (male)

treyfenyitse (female)

> 1. Someone not to be trusted.
> 2. Someone who flouts Jewish ways.
> 3. A Jew who has embraced non-Jewish cuisine/mores.

△ △ △

Into the fanciest deli in Manhattan marched a white-bearded patriarch, with fine *peyes,* wearing a broad black hat and a long black coat. Surveying the meats so beautifully arrayed behind the glass, he pointed to a slab. "I'll take a half-pond nice corn biff."

"Mister," said the clerk, "that's not corned beef. It's ham!"

The old man murmured, "Did I esk you?"

trombenik

trombenyik (standard)

> Rhymes with "fond o'Nick." Polish: a blower of a horn or trumpet.
>
> 1. A boastful loudmouth.
> 2. A fourflusher.
> 3. A lazy faker.
> 4. A *fonfer—plosher—bluffer—shtarker—hoo-ha-nik.*

If definition 4 does not give you the picture, nothing will. The word is unique.

△ △ △

The owner of a movie house emblazed his marquee with this historic boo-boo.

NOW PLAYING
ADAM and EVE
with a cast of thousands!

The showman was a *trombenik.*

△ △ △

"Jenny," said Bernie, a *trombenik,* "open the little case."

Inside the case was a thin gold ring, in the center of which was a tiny, tiny diamond.

"Jenny, it may look small, but there isn't a single flaw in it."

"Bernie, inside such a ring there's no *room* for a flaw."

✡ tsadik (standard)

tzaddik

> Pronounced TSAH-d'k. Hebrew: a righteous man.
>
> 1. A man of surpassing virtue.
> 2. A saint.
> 3. One who possesses mystical, arcane powers; a wonder or miracle worker.

An old legend holds that there are on earth thirty-six saints *(Lamed-vov Tsadikim),* anonymous and unidentifiable, on whose goodness the world itself exists: that is to say, the thirty-six are God's agents—but they do not know they are saints. Nor does anyone else. This means that your grocer, barber, a mendicant or a derelict may be one of the fateful thirty-six.

During a great crisis, a *Lamed-vov* may reveal his mission by performing some miraculous feat (rescuing a child, bringing a stricken scholar back from the dead). Then the *tsadik* vanishes. At once.

The idea of doing good secretly is, of course, the crowning act of *tsedaka* (righteousness, sacred obligation). But the secret is no secret to the Lord, and He never forgets.

The place of the vanished *tsadik* is instantly taken by another unaware soul; earth is never left by the Almighty without thirty-six truly just mortals. (You ought to read the novel by André Schwarz-Bart, *The Last of the Just.*)

△ △ △

For a week, the beloved *tsadik* of Tarnapolchev had lain in a fever. The end was near: A disciple leaned over the old saint's form and in the gentlest tone asked, "*Rebbe* . . . have you made your peace with—*baruch ha-Shem*—the Lord?"

Wheezed the old man, "Who told you we ever quarreled?"

△ △ △

One of my favorite tales concerns the venerable *tsadik* who was being introduced to a congregation. The rabbi declaimed: "How fortunate are we to hear from a *tsadik* who is so learned that the deepest scholars come to him for interpretations of Torah. A man so compassionate that little children confide their hopes to him. A man so truthful that judges swear by him. A man so saturated with virtue—"

The old man tugged at the eulogist's sleeve and whispered, "Don't forget my modesty."

tsatske (standard)

tshatshke

> Yinglish with éclat. Pronounced TSATS-ka or CHOTSH-ka. From Slavic: jewel, trinket, toy.

1. A toy.
2. An inexpensive thing. ("Don't make a fuss: it's only a *tsatske*.")
3. A precious person. ("That baby is her *tshatshke*.")
4. A fop.
5. (Sarcastic) Anything superelegant or ornate.
6. A girl who fools around or lets males take liberties.
7. A sexy but brainless female.
8. A mistress; a kept woman. (A certain avenue on New York's West Side was once called "Tsatske Row.")

You may judge for yourself how resourceful, how versatile, how delightful this word is. Its very sound signals amusement.

△ △ △

> FIRST TSHATSHKE: I dated Myron Paletsky last night. What a classy dresser!
> SECOND TSHATSHKE: I know. And so *fast.*

△ △ △

The wrinkled, white-haired man with big pouches under his eyes was the talk of the Fountainbloom Hotel—every day with a different *tshatshke,* every night on the dance floor until dawn.

After a week of observing this, Mr. Frakish went up to the nonpareil: "Mister, it's positively *amazing* the way you live! Excuse me—but how *old* are you?"

The roué yawned. "Twenty-seven."

△ △ △

Two Jews were seated on a bench at the edge of Lake Michigan, watching a motorboat with a beautiful girl water-skiing behind. Said one man: "What a *tsatske!*"

"Yeah." The other rose. "But we may as well go. She'll never catch it."

△ △ △

"Who said money is everything?" asked the *tshatshke.*

"You don't believe it?"

"Of course not. Remember diamonds."

tsedreyt

tsedreyteh (f.)

tsedreyter (m.)

> Rhyme *tsedreyt* with "berate." Yiddish: confused . . . twisted.
>
> 1. A scatterbrain, one who is mixed up, a screwball.
> 2. An impractical innocent.
> 3. A lunatic.

"That woman? No one believes her. She's a *tsedreyteh*" (or: "She's *tsedreyt*").

"All day he's been acting like a *tsedreyter.*"

> See FARMISHT, TSEDUDLT, TSETUMLT.

△ △ △

"What do you mean, what would I do if I found a million dollars in the street? I would try to find out who lost it. And if it was a poor man, I *swear* to you I would return it!"

tsedudlt (adj.)

tsedudlteh (noun, f.)

tsedudlter (noun, m.)

> Yinglish, now and then, because colorful and echoic. Pronounce it tse-DO-d'lt. Possibly from *tsedrudelt,* a variant of *tsedreyt;* or from the English "doodle."

As an adjective:
1. Confused, bewildered, mixed up.
2. Wacky, scatterbrained.
3. Crazy.
As a noun:
"That *tsedudlteh* can't make a decision."
"Don't ask that *tsedudlter* professor for advice."

See also TSEDREYT, TSETUMLT, FARMISHT, FARFUFKET.

tsetumlt

tsetumlter (m.)

tsetumlteh (f.)

> Pronounced with the *u* of "put," not "cut." tse-TOOM-elt. From German.

> A vivid synonym for *farmisht, tsedudlt,* with this difference: *tsetumlt* suggests a momentary, not a permanent, state of discombobulation.

"Every time the rent's due, she gets *tsetumlt.*"

"He may act like a *tsetumlter,* but he doesn't miss a trick."

"That *tsetumlteh* can't make a decision."

△ △ △

Dr. Isenberg, a conscientious healer, was absentminded. In fact, he was once so *tsetumlt* while presiding at a meeting of the Brownsville Medical Society that he said, "Gentlemen, you have heard the resolution. All in favor say 'Ah.' "

tsimmes

tsimes (standard)

> Rhymes with "Guinness." Yiddish. From old German: *Zumus:* food, porridge.

> Stew of fruit/vegetables, served as a side dish or dessert.

Tsimmes has become an English word. The *American Heritage Dictionary* defines it as:

> 1. A stew (vegetable or fruit) that is cooked slowly, over very low heat.

2. The overcomplication of a relatively simple situation: a state of confusion. ("She made a whole *tsimmes* out of planning the birthday party.")

The A.H.D. is right, but by no means complete. Since making *tsimmes* takes a long time, the word has come to mean:

3. An involved or prolonged procedure. ("Keep it simple; don't make a *tsimmes* out of it!")
4. Troubles, irksome details, contretemps. ("Within a week, their marriage was nothing but *tsimmes*.")

△ △ △

A television commercial for interstate bus travel contained the inspired jingle:

> Why not skip the fuss?
> Leave the *tsimmes* to us!

See MEGILLA, MISH-MASH, SHTUS.

△ △ △

When Mr. Marx opened an account in a Beverly Hills bank, a vice-president of the bank wrote him, "If I can ever be of assistance to you, please let me know."

Marx replied, without *tsimmes:*

> The best assistance you can give me is to steal some money from the account of one of your richer clients and credit it to mine.
>
> Yours,
> GROUCHO MARX

tsitser

Rhymes with "fits 'er." Echoic.

1. One given to uttering *ts–ts!* in friendly commiseration.
2. A bystander who offers interjections of sympathy, but does nothing useful for a victim.

The *tsitser,* who makes our misfortunes easier to endure through his dentalized sympathy, is a psychological type dear to Jewish hearts. (Almost any psychological type except the psychopath is dear to Jewish hearts.)

The utterance of sounds of solace is a staple of decorum in Mediterranean and Middle Eastern cultures: *Tsk-tsk! Tchk-tchk!* or *Ay-yay-yay!* may be heard puncturing the air from Lisbon and Rome to Baghdad and Tel Aviv.

"You broke your elbow? *Ts-ts!*"

"She married an eighty-year-old? *Ts-ts!*"

The do-nothing *tsitser* is also called (with scorn) a *doppess*, which I urge you to look up. It will enrich your life as much as your vocabulary.

△ △ △

An old Jew was looking over the shoulder of an artist who was painting a scene in Crotona Park. After a while, the old man said, "It's beautiful! How long you had to study painting?"

"I never studied."

"*Tchk! Tchk!*" marveled the old gent. "Then it must be inherited. From your mother or father—"

"N–not necessarily. Take Vermeer. Did you ever hear of Vermeer's father?"

"No."

"Or Vermeer's mother?"

"No."

"So," smiled the artist, "you see what I mean."

The old man screwed up one eye. "I never hoid of Vermeer eider."

tsores (standard)
tsuris

> Yiddish. Rhymes with "Horace." Hebrew: *tsarah:* trouble.

> 1. Troubles, worries, problems.
> 2. Afflictions.

> The singular is *tsore,* but it is less frequently used than *tsores,* for who ever heard of only one trouble?

> "Is he *uf tsores!*" (Does *he* have problems!)
> "She's really *uf tsores.*" (She really is depressed.)

Tsores and *tsuris* appear in many an English dictionary.

△ △ △

> What a pleasure it is to talk about *tsores* that have passed.

> Why worry about tomorrow? Who knows what will hit you today?

> Troubles prefer wetness: tears—or whiskey.

> —FOLK SAYINGS

△ △ △

Isadore Boris Poliakoff was packing. The Commissariat of Electrical Planning in Moscow had ordered him to a post in Outer Mongolia. "Papa, I'll write, but the censorship is very strict. We'll have to use a code."

"My boy, codes are dangerous. If your letter is written in blue ink, I'll know everything is true. But if your letter is in red ink, I'll know it's all baloney!"

A month passed. Then a letter arrived, in blue ink:

> DEAR PAPA,
>   I live in a gorgeous new apartment. The butcher has meat every day. There are many cultural facilities. I have no *tsores* at all.
>   Your son,
>   YITZCHOK BORIS.
> P.S. There's only one thing I couldn't find here: red ink.

✡ **tumler** (standard)
tummler

> Well ensconced in the argot of show business. Rhymes with "Broomler." From Yiddish: *tuml:* noise; racket; disorder.
>
> 1. A noisy, lively creator of commotions; the "life of the party."
> 2. A busybody who makes a lot of *tuml* (noise, confusion) but does not accomplish much.
> 3. The social director or M.C. of a resort in the Catskills.

△ △ △

An astonishing array of gifted writers, actors, comedians first learned their trade as (or with) *tumlers* in the "Borsht Belt" of Catskill summer resorts where the patrons were emphatically Jewish: among them, Jerry Lewis, Phil Silvers, Moss Hart, Milton Berle, Danny Kaye, Clifford Odets, John Garfield, Shelley Winters, Sid Caesar, Joey Bishop, Red Buttons, Henny Youngman, Garson Kanin, Dore Schary and countless others.

tush

tushy

> Rhyme with "push" and "bushy." From Yiddish: *toches*, via Galician *tukhes*, which became a euphemism by softening the *kh* into a *sh* and sometimes adding the *y*, as in baby talk.
>
> Buttocks (euphemism).

This genteel diminutive is often used by American mothers in talking to a child about its posterior, or when referring to anyone's buttocks. *Tushy* is popular in metropolitan and suburban zones where nice-Nellyisms thrive.

"He fell down so hard he almost broke his *tush*."

"You know what, dolling? I think you have a rash on your *tushy*."

△ △ △

BOY: Mama, Mama! Can I go out and watch? There's going to be an eclipse!

MOTHER: Go, go. But don't stand too close—or I'll give you a slap on the *tushy*.

type ("of" omitted)

From Yiddish: *tip*, and German: *typ*.

Type (of).

The blithe banishment of the preposition, creating such solecisms as "type book," "type friend," or even "type type," fills me with dismay. Yet this direct transfer of Yiddish to English usage has taken a firm foothold in the American vernacular.

"That's the type English I find awful."

"She's the type author who doesn't talk much."

"They're the type neighbors you dream of having."

Ugh!

△ △ △

"Your application," said the *balebos*, "says you left your last job because of—a disease."

"That's right."

"Miss Gottlieb, would you mind telling me what type sickness was it?"

"The boss got sick of me."

U

utz

> Bronxese. Rhymes with "foots." German: *uzen:* to tease. Recommended without reservation for Yinglish.
>
> *Verb:*
> 1. To needle.
> 2. To nag.
> *Noun:*
> 1. A verbal goading.
> 2. A piece of barbed criticism.

Here are some classic examples of the use of *utz:*

Old Mr. Tenzer took a chair in Korschik's barbershop.
Korschik whipped on the cover and asked, "So—a haircut?"
"No," *utzed* Mr. Tenzer, "I just dropped by for an estimate."

"Excuse me, lady. Are you going to have a baby?"
"No. I'm just carrying it for a friend."

△ △ △

A New Yorker in Israel was boasting to his Israeli cousin, "Why, at Columbia University there's a professor who speaks thirteen languages!"
"My!" sighed the cousin, "I don't think we have a hundred men in Tel Aviv who can do that."

△ △ △

As Mr. Kovitz entered the gilded elevator of the posh department store, the *soigné* operator closed the door with insolent force. "What floor do *you* want?"
"Four," said Mr. Kovitz, "if it isn't out of your way."

V

vaiduh

A fricative gloss on "waiter."

Waiter.

Rare is the visitor to Manhattan who is not flabbergasted by the Jewish waiter. He is thin-skinned, cynical, temperamental and deadly in ripostes. He acts like a philosopher condemned by fate to serve peasants. "When you go to a restaurant, get a table near a waiter."

After prolonged research, I have come to the following conclusions:

1. A New York waiter hates to tell anyone the time. Once, I asked a passing menial, "What time is it?" He answered, "You're not my table."

2. He hands you the menu upside down. This is done in order to exercise the customer's wrist.

3. He asks you how you like your meat done, so he can tell the cook how long to overcook it.

4. He writes your order in a secret code. In this way, he can give you the wrong check.

△ △ △

"*Vaiduh!* I can't eat this meat. Get the owner!"

"Don't waste your time; he won't touch it either."

△ △ △

CUSTOMER: Are you sure you're the *vaiduh* I gave my order to?
WAITER: What makes you ask?
CUSTOMER: By now I expected a much older man.

△ △ △

WAITER: *Nu,* I'm ready to take your order.
CUSTOMER: But I gave my order to a waiter an hour ago!
WAITER: That *vaiduh* . . . can't serve you.
CUSTOMER: Did he leave any family?

Vuden?

Voden? (standard)

> Pronounced vu-DEN or vaw-DEN. Yiddish: What (where) then?

1. What then?
2. Naturally; of course.
3. So what can you expect?
4. So?
5. What else?
6. You mean to say you're *surprised?*

This juicy, many-layered expletive is a shaft of scorn, a dollop of disdain. It is a question that answers—and annihilates:

1. "You mean to say he ran away with the proceeds?" (With arched eyebrows) *"Vuden?"*

2. "If you go to Washington you'll meet the President?" (With aplomb) *"Vuden?"*

3. "If you take that treatment, your hair will fall out?" (With a shrug) *"Vuden?"*

4. "You think he's *sleeping* with her?" (With a knowing smile) *"Vuden?"*

5. "You're too busy, of course, but if they offer to make you chairman, will you accept?" (With a modest sigh) *"Vuden?"*

6. "Two minutes after he took office, he broke all his campaign promises!" (With a superior sneer) *"Vuden?"*

△ △ △

Second Avenue was deserted, so fierce was the downpour. The deli was about to close when an apparition appeared: a bedraggled man, his umbrella blown inside-out, his hair streaming water. "An onion roll," he gasped.

The owner nodded. "What else?"

"That's all."

"That's *all?* No cream cheese?"

"No cream cheese."

"Coffee, I suppose?"

"No coffee."

The *balebos* said, "On a terrible night like this you come out just for one . . . onion . . . roll—"

"That's what she wants."

"Aha! I suppose 'she' is your wife?"

"Vuden? . . . You think my *mother* would send me out on a night like this?"

W

Wear it in good health

Wear in the best of health

> Often introduced by the interjection *nu* or the conjunction "so."
> Thus: "So wear it in good health," or "*Nu,* wear it in the best of health."

> A conditioned reflex among Jews when giving presents, or upon noticing a new article of clothing.
>
> △ △ △

BORKIN: My God, Shulman, what happened to you?

SHULMAN: I broke my arm in three places. I have to wear this cast for six weeks.

BORKIN: Wear it in good health.

What gives?

> From Yiddish: *Vi geyt's?* ("How goes it?")

> 1. What's going on?
> 2. What's new?
> 3. What's the matter? What's wrong?
> 4. Tell me the whole story.
>
> △ △ △

The psychiatrist was giving a pilot his annual checkup. "And when was the last time you slept with a woman, Captain?"

"1959."

"That long ago?"

"What gives?" the pilot frowned. "It's only 23:10 right now."

△ △ △

Onto the used-car lot drove a magnificent new Lincoln Continental, out of which stepped Mrs. Lustig, dressed all in black. "I want to sell this car."

"What's wrong with it?" asked Mr. Gutfleish, owner of Motor Mavens.

"Absolutely nothing."

Mr. Gutfleish glanced at the speedometer (only 2,100 miles!), got in the driver's seat, turned on the ignition, listened to the perfect motor . . . "Uh—how much do you expect to get?"

"Twenty-five dollars."

Gutfleish's jaw dropped. "Is this a joke?"

"No. Just give me twenty-five dollars—"

"Lady, is this a stolen car?"

"No."

"Is there a lien on it?"

"Absolutely not."

"Lady, what *gives?*"

"What gives," iced Mrs. Lustig, "is that my husband, who just died, was having an affair with the bookkeeper, and his will says she should get the money from the sale of his new Continental."

What is, is

What was, was

Yinglish, and philosophically definitive.

△ △ △

Mrs. Korngold greeted a newcomer to the canasta tables: "So welcome to our group . . . We *never* tell a lady how she *should* have played a hand. We don't discuss our husbands. We don't boast about our grandchildren. Finally, we never discuss S–E–X. The way we all feel is: What was, was."

What's to . . . ?

From Yiddish: *Vos iz tsu . . .*

This elimination of "there" ("What is there—") is indubitable Yinglish, and thrives in such popular phrasings as:

What's to lose?
What's to forgive?
What's to regret?

The only comment I care to make about such diction is: "What's to comment?"

What's with . . . ?

From Yiddish: *Vos iz mit . . . ?*

1. What's wrong with . . . ?
2. Please explain that.
3. Why are you (he, she) acting this way?

The proper English phrasing would be "What's the matter with . . . ?" or "What's wrong with . . . ?" or "What's bothering . . . ?" The syntax of "What's with . . . ?" is distinctly Yiddish; its popularity in American and British slang has made it Yinglish.

△ △ △

One night when the air-raid sirens began to shriek all over Haifa, Mr. and Mrs. Gruenfeld leaped toward the corridor and the air-raid shelter, when suddenly Mrs. Gruenfeld cried, "Wait! My false teeth!"

"What's with the teeth?" cried Mr. Gruenfeld. "What do you think they're going to drop: sandwiches?"

Who knows?

From Yiddish: *Ver veyst?*

1. I don't know.
2. Maybe someone, somewhere, knows the answer, but I doubt it.
3. You may search the whole world for an answer to that question but—believe me!—there is none.

Any language contains the neutral interrogation "Who knows?" But as rendered in Yinglish ("*Who* knows?" or, with umbrage, "Who *knows?*"), the phrase is not interrogatory; it is declarative. It is also accusatory ("Why do you ask me for an answer to a question that is clearly unanswerable?"), or sarcastic ("What a dope you are to think I can answer something like that!"), or philosophical ("Beware the surface innocence of the question; to answer is to risk entrapment in epistemology").

The ironic ploy of "Who knows?" may be transferred to any number of pseudo-interrogative asseverations: "Who *cares?*" "Who could?" "Who should?"

4. It's Greek to me.

Digression: What does a Greek say in order to confess total noncomprehension? A Greek says, "Stop talking Chinese!" Bravo—but what does a Chinese say? What a Chinese says is staggering: "Your words are like a Buddha twelve feet tall, whose head and feet I cannot recognize!" Eloquent though this is, it cannot begin to match the way Malayans voice their ignorance: "I do not perceive the dried ginger of it!"

When Poles, on the other hand, are unable to understand something, they blurt, "I am hearing a sermon in Turkish!" Frenchmen, who are especially irritated by incomprehensibility, murmur, "Pray stop talking Hebrew!" And Jews dismiss ensnarled (or foolish) statements with a crisp "Stop knocking a teapot!" (See DON'T KNOCK A TEAPOT.)

△ △ △

> DR. METSER: God, I'm so *tired!* All day long, day in and day out, all I hear are stories of such pain, suffering, conflict. Hermie, how do you manage to look so *serene* after listening all day—?
>
> DR. PFLAUM: Who listens?!

Who needs it?

> From Yiddish: *Ver darf es?* Who needs it?

> Who *needs* it?

The phrase comes directly from Yiddish—and, apart from being widely used, has given birth to an amusing covey of children:

> Who *wants* it?

> With friends like I have, who needs enemies?

> That's something I *need?*

△ △ △

Advertising and headline writers have seized upon the locution as a "grabber":

> *Advertisement for a co-op on the Palisades, facing Manhattan:*
> With this view, who needs Palm Beach?

> *Insurance company ad, showing a smug smart guy:*
> Medical insurance? Who *needs* it?

> *Magazine ad for carpets:*
> This is Acrylan, so who needs wool?

Y

Yahveh

Yahweh

> Pronounced YAH-vay. Probably the way the "sacred letters" YHVH or YHWH (Hebrew has no *W* sound; in German the letter *W* is pronounced *V*) were pronounced in ancient times.

> Jehovah.

This name/pronunciation is unmistakably wrong.

> See ADONAI, JEHOVAH, YHVH.

△ △ △

In his seventieth year, the old Jew, alone in the synagogue, addressed the Lord: "Oh, God, Blessed by Thy Name, have I not every day celebrated Your Glory? Is there a more devout, observing soul in all Your fold? . . . And now I'm old, I'm sick, I'm poor. . . . But my partner, Velvel! That no-good! That *apikoros!* Not *once* has he made a prayer! Not a penny has he given to the synagogue! He drinks, he gambles, he runs around with loose women—and he's worth a *fortune!* Dear God, I am not asking You to punish him, but please tell me: Why, *why* have You treated *me* this way?"

The synagogue rumbled as the Voice boomed: "Because all you do, day after day, is *nag* me!"

△ △ △

Emperor Hadrian once asked Rabbi Joshua ben Hananiah, "I desire to see your God, Yahveh."

Rabbi Joshua said, "Face the sun, sire, and gaze into it."

"I cannot! It is too bright. It blinds my eyes."

Said Rabbi Joshua, "If you are not able to look upon the sun, which is only a servant of God, how much less can you gaze upon the Divine Presence?"

yak
yak-yak

yakkety-yak

> Onomatopoeia. Not to be confused with *yok*.
>
> 1. To chatter away.
> 2. To gossip.

Unlike *shmoos, yak* entirely lacks the idea of a warm, heart-to-heart exchange. *Yak* is derogatory, said about talk that is of irritating length and trivial substance. *Yakkety-yak* is more so.

> 3. To laugh.

What makes *yok* or *yak* Yinglish? Its persistent use in show business by Jewish comedians, writers, ad-libbers. I welcome correction.

✡ yarmulke
yarmilke (standard)

> Pronounced YAR-m'l-keh. From Turkish via Polish: skullcap.
>
> The small caplet perched on the top of the head by a religious Jew.

Reform Jews do not as a matter of course wear a *yarmulke*, although they often (as do nonobserving Jews) don one for a religious ceremony: a wedding, a *bris*, a funeral.

△ △ △

The most charming comment ever about the skullcap appeared in 1964 in a cartoon in a Tel Aviv newspaper. The cartoon showed the Pope and the President of Israel, side by side, during the Holy Pontiff's history-making trip. The caption:

"The Pope is the one wearing a *yarmulke*."

yente (standard)
yenta

> Pronounced YEN-ta. From Spanish or French.

1. A gossipy woman; a blabbermouth.
2. Someone who can't keep a secret.
3. A vulgar, ill-mannered woman.
4. A shrew.
5. A man who acts as the above do.

A *yente* and a *yachne* are difficult to tell apart: these types are universal.

Marcel Proust was a genius—and a *yente.* The television character "Maude," played to the rasp by Bea Arthur, was a liberal *yente.*

△ △ △

Yentes separate friends.

The tongue has no bones, so it's loose.

Your friend has a friend, so shut up.

△ △ △

Our fingers are shaped like nails, so that we can put them in our ears when ugly gossip reaches us.

—TALMUD: *Kethuboth,* 109b

△ △ △

PLACE: *Miami*

NETTIE: Belle, have you been through the menopause yet?

BELLE: I haven't even gone to the Fontaineblue.

△ △ △

Into Mrs. Peltsner's home hurried her friend Alice, blurting, "Ranna, listen! I'm so excited." A blush turned her cheeks rosy. "I—have to tell someone!"

"Me you can tell, Alice."

"Ranna—I'm having an affair!"

"Oh, super, Alice! Who's catering?"

yents

Infra dig but widely used in slang. Rhymes with "tents." Yiddish: *yents:* that thing. *Cf.* German: *jenes.*

(Obscene, vulgar, taboo)
1. To copulate; to *shtup.*
2. To seduce.
3. To cheat, deceive, swindle. "He'll *yents* you out of your last dollar."

This vulgar word, a synonym for the slang "screw" (the sexual act, not the threaded fastener), is solidly established in American speech after a long apprenticeship in the lingo of the underworld.

Modern Hebrew has no explicit words for sex organs or parts thereof: there once were straightforward names, of course, but they perished from disuse. So the penis, in Hebrew/Yiddish, became "that organ"; the vagina, "that place"; testicles, "eggs."

I hope you will be as surprised as I was when I learned that *yents* is a proper Yiddish word meaning "that thing" or "the other." It also serves as the euphemism in rabbinical literature for a dozen "unmentionables": genitalia, urine, dung, a devil, a demon. It is the ironic fate of euphemisms to replace the unacceptable and themselves become taboo.

German servants, maids, governesses used the German *jenes* (YEN-es), which means "that (thing)," as a genteelism for the sexual or excretory organs of the children they attended.

See SHMUCK.

△ △ △

The attitude of Jews to sex is at once relaxed and repressive. The sexes were carefully segregated. In the old country, men never danced with women. The marriage canopy was a sacrosanct symbol. All marriages were arranged. Illegitimacy was virtually unknown.

On the other hand, sex was no shameful thing, surely no sin. Indeed, the sexual aspect of marriage is celebrated in the Talmud and in rabbinical writings. Rare among religions, Judaism recognized women's right to, and need for, sexual satisfaction. Rabbi Akiba called the Song of Songs the "holiest of holies."

△ △ △

A friend tells me that in the old country his mother protested to her father that she did not want to marry the man chosen to be her husband. "Why not?" asked her father.

"B—because I don't *love* him!"

To which the old man bellowed, "You want to love him *before* you marry him?!"

✡ yeshiva

yeshive (standard)

> Pronounced y'-SHEE-vah. From Hebrew: *yeshov:* to sit. (The places where students sat whilst studying were *yeshivot.*)
>
> 1. A rabbinical seminary.
> 2. (In the U.S.) A secondary Hebrew school.

It should be emphasized to American readers that only a small proportion of the students at a yeshiva intended to become rabbis. Jewish boys attended a yeshiva to fulfill God's commandment: to study Torah; to become well versed in the Talmud; to prepare themselves for lifelong discussions of the holy texts. No secular courses (science, philosophy, mathematics) were offered. The intellectual regimen was extremely demanding. The first yeshiva in America was founded in 1886 in New York.

yeshiva bokher

> Pronounced y'SHEE-vah BOO-kher (or BAW-khar), using the throat-clearing *kh,* not the voiced aspirate *ch* of "China."
>
> 1. A boy *(bokher)* or young man enrolled at a yeshiva.
> 2. A shy, unsophisticated young man. ("He never dated a girl; he might just as well be a *yeshiva bokher.*")
> 3. A gullible, inexperienced fellow. ("He can't handle an assignment like that; he's a *yeshiva bokher.*")

"The scholar takes precedence over the king," says the Talmud. So the Jewish communities of Eastern Europe lovingly supported the *yeshiva bokher.* It was considered a *mitzve* to lodge and feed him. The students were ascetic. Many lived on the edge of starvation. They studied from early morning until late at night. They walked about with eyes cast downward, to avoid worldly temptations. For a classic rendition, see I. J. Singer's *Yoshe Kalb.*

The *yeshiva bokher* was much sought after by the parents of a nubile girl. Large dowries often rewarded the students. The Talmud tells the pious to "sell everything, if you must, [to] marry your daughter off to a scholar."

△ △ △

> Student life began for the Jewish youth when, at the age of seventeen or eighteen, he left home and fared forth, defying hunger and cold, only to drink in the words of a far-famed master. He would wander about for half a year across ditches and mountains for the sake of a Talmudic explanation to be had from an Italian scholar. There were no entrance examinations, no graduating exercises. The schools made demands upon the students without conferring privileges.
>
> —LOUIS GINZBERG, "The Rabbinical Student," in
> *A Treasury of Judaism,* edited by Philip Birnbaum

△ △ △

Postcard from nine-year-old at camp for the first time:

DEAR MAMA:

Having good time, I think. We take long hikes. Send my other sneaker.

Your son
MOISHE

I think Moishe grew up to become a true *yeshiva bokher*.

yet

From Yiddish: *nokh*.

Don't jump to conclusions: this common English adverb as used in Yinglish does not mean what it does in English. In Yinglish, "yet" is umbrageous, indignant, or a cry against the unjust.

1. On top of everything else.
2. Even after all that.
3. Can you imagine such bad luck?

Thus:

"—and for doing me such a crummy favor, he wants to be *paid,* yet."

"It wasn't enough he borrowed my car for a day and kept it a week: he burned a hole in the seat, yet."

YHVH

The four sacred letters for the name of God.

Often rendered (in translations from the Hebrew) as *Yahweh, Yahveh, Yehova, Jehovah*. All of these are arbitrary—for no one is certain how YHVH was pronounced.

See ADONAI, JEHOVAH.

Yid

Yinglish, and undesirable.

A Jew (pejorative).

If pronounced "Yid" in American, the word is as unwelcome as "kike." (Yes, I know that Litvaks use the short *i* and give no offense thereby.) If pronounced "Yeed," the word is fine, dandy, sweet.*

△ △ △

Mrs. James Hale Rillington III telephoned the headquarters of the Infantry base several miles from Forty Elms, her ancestral home. "This is Mrs. James Hale Rillington the Third. With Thanksgiving coming up," she said, "I would like to invite ten of your enlisted men to share our family feast at Forty Elms."

"That's wonderful, Mrs. Rillington."

"Only one thing. We—prefer not to have any Yids. I'm sure you understand."

"Madam, I *quite* understand."

When her bell rang on Thanksgiving Day, Mrs. Rillington hurried to the door herself. "Welcome to Forty—" She stopped. Under the great portico stood ten black soldiers. "My God!" she gasped. "There has been a terrible mistake!"

The black sergeant said, "Oh, no, ma'am. Captain Kaminsky *never* makes a mistake."

△ △ △

During the Nazi occupation of Paris an old, well-dressed French Jew entered the offices of Thomas Cook. "I want to buy a ticket on the next ship out of Cherbourg."

"Certainly, monsieur. Where do you want to go?"

"Where? . . . May I see that globe?"

"Of course." The clerk placed the globe before the old man, who put on reading glasses and turned the globe very slowly. In a few minutes the old man removed his glasses. "Tell me, do you have anything else?"

△ △ △

One Friday night in Peking, George Simkess of Staten Island, wandering around, came upon—a synagogue! He hurried in. The worshippers were Chinese, as was the rabbi, and so was the cantor. The service had begun. Simkess happily joined in.

Afterward he went to the rabbi and said, "I'm from America, Rabbi. You can't imagine how happy I am to be with you tonight."

---

* In Hebrew, *Yehudi* means an inhabitant of *Yehuda* (romanized: Judea). Jews called themselves "Yehudi" in every language they were obliged to speak; but the word suffered syncopation, so to speak: *e.g.*, in the Talmud, Rabbi "Yuda" replaced "Yehuda," and "Yuda" became "Yudi." By the thirteenth century, says Dr. Nathan Susskind, every accented *u* that is followed by an *i* of the next syllable became an umlauted *ü* in German. In Yiddish, the umlauted *ü* was unrounded into an *i*. Hence the progression: Yehudi, Yudi, Yüde, Yid.

The rabbi beamed. "Ah . . . for us is honor. . . . But excuse. . . . You a Yid?"

"Certainly."

"That's funny. You don't look Jewish."

✡ Yiddish

From German: *judisch.*

The language of the Jews of Eastern Europe: the Ashkenazim. (The comparable vernacular for the Sephardim is Ladino, also called Dzhudesmo or Judesmo.)

Do not say, "He talked Jewish," for "Jewish" refers to a people, "Yiddish" to a language.

A "Jewish journal" may be printed in English or Swahili, if it focuses on Jewish topics; a Yiddish text, even if it deals with the rise of Hitler or the fall of Idi Amin, is in Yiddish.

Nor is Yiddish, by any stretch of the imagination, Hebrew. Yiddish and Hebrew are entirely separate and emphatically different languages. What confuses people is that Yiddish uses the alphabet of Hebrew, and a good many Hebrew words, and, like Hebrew, is written and printed from right to left, in this fashion:

.aciremA sselb doG

Hebrew is an ancient tongue; Yiddish was born a mere thousand years ago (give or take a hundred), which, nevertheless, makes it older than English or German.

yingatsh

yungatsh

Pronounced YIN-gotch. Yiddish: *ying:* a young fellow.

1. A large young man.
2. A bold, brave boy.
3. A clever, resourceful male.
4. A rough young man; a hoodlum.
5. A rascal.

Yingatsh is usually a term of admiration, similar to *shtarker,* with this difference: *shtarker* is often used sarcastically to denote one who is not *shtark* (strong), or who only pretends to be so; but *yingatsh* is not used in derogation.

△ △ △

The *shadchen* shook his head. "But how is it that an intelligent, handsome *yingatsh* like you isn't married?"

The *yingatsh* replied: "Every time I meet a nice girl, a girl who would make a good wife, take care of a home, even cook like my mother . . . she looks like my father."

✡ Yizkor

Pronounced YISS-koar. Hebrew: May (God) remember.

The memorial service, held in a synagogue, for the dead.

△ △ △

Part of the *Yizkor* service is a memorial to the martyrs of all generations. Many synagogues recite a special prayer for the six million victims of the Nazis. In Israel, *Yizkor* is said for the men and women who fell in the various wars of survival.

yok

yak (standard)

Do not confuse with the entry *yak*.

1. To laugh loudly.
2. A belly laugh.

This slang neologism is theatrical argot, born in vaudeville, used by stage comedians, then by radio comics.

I first encountered *yok* in the 1930s in *Variety* and the *Hollywood Reporter,* and as used by newspaper columnists who were Jewish: Walter Winchell, Leonard Lyons, Louis Sobol, Irving Hoffman. . . . S. J. Perelman, meticulous chronicler of Yiddishisms, loved *yok.*

△ △ △

Jack Benny drew many a *yok* when, accepting an award, he would say, "I really don't deserve this beautiful award. But I have arthritis, and I don't deserve that either."

yold

Yinglish. Rhymes with "bald" or "told."

1. A dolt.
2. A naive, gullible sort.
3. A fool.

A *yold* is a clone of a *shlemiel,* or a hybrid of a *shlemiel* and a *nebech,* or a brother to a *lemish,* or a blood cousin to a *nayfish.* One has a certain protective sympathy for these. A *putz* and a *shmuck* lack a *yold*'s tenderness of character.

See KUNYE LEML, ZHLUB.

✡ Yom Kippur

Yom Kiper (standard)

> In Yiddish, this is pronounced yum KIP-per; in Hebrew, it is pronounced yom ki-POOR. (This confused many listeners during broadcasts of the war so named.) Hebrew: Day of Atonement.
>
> The last of the annual Ten Days of Penitence (Rosh Hashanah), *Yom Kippur* has the strongest hold on the Jewish conscience.

△ △ △

Even the most God-fearing Jew may offer his orisons in a freewheeling manner that is garnished with complaints and irony. On the eve of Yom Kippur, an old Jew prayed: "Dear God, listen: The butcher in our village is a good man who never cheats anyone and never turns away the needy; yet he is so poor that he sometimes goes without meat. Or take our shoemaker, a model of piety, yet his beloved wife is dying in great pain. And our *melamed* [teacher], loved by all who know him, lives hand to mouth and has an eye disease that may leave him blind. I ask you bluntly: God, are such things *fair* of You? I repeat: *Are such things fair?* . . . So I'll tell you something: tomorrow, O Adonai, on Yom Kippur, Your most solemn and sacred day—if You will forgive us, we will forgive You."

△ △ △

"Cronin, Floyd and Lipstein," crooned the operator.
    "May I talk to Mr. Lipstein?"
    "Mr. Lipstein is out, sir; this is Yom Kippur."
    "Oh. Well, Mr. Kippur, please tell him his car is fixed."

yontif

yontef (standard)

> Yinglish no less than Yiddish. Pronounced YUN-tiff. From Hebrew: *yom:* day; *tov:* good.

1. Holiday. ("The post office is closed; it's *yontif*." Third-generation Jews would say: "a *yontif*.")
2. A celebration, a festivity.
   "I felt *yontifdik* [in a holiday mood] that day."
3. (Sarcastically) Oh, my! Thanks a *lot*.
   ("There will be a penalty for back taxes."
   "Good *yontif*.")

△ △ △

Who suggested that on Christmas we should send the Pope this greeting card?

"Good *yontif*, Pontiff."

Yortsayt (standard)

Yortzeit

Yahrzeit

> Pronounced either YAWR-tzite or YAR-tzite. German: year's time; anniversary.

> The anniversary of someone's death.

Many Jews fast all day on *Yortsayt*.

A memorial candle or lamp is lighted in the home and/or in the synagogue. The light burns from sunset to sunset, perhaps to symbolize immortality. (Proverbs 10:17: "The spirit of man is the candle of the Lord. . . .")

Yortsayt is the one Jewish religious ritual that has no Hebrew name! (*Yom hashana* means "day of the year" in Hebrew.)

△ △ △

I know no jokes about *Yortsayt;* and if I did, I would not put them here, for two candles burn in my mind until I die too.

You don't have to put a finger in his mouth

> More exactly, "Him, no one need put a finger in his mouth": *Im (aym) darf men keyn finger in moyl nit araynleygen.*

1. To him you don't have to explain.
2. He can take a hint.

This picturesque phrase provides an image that has haunted me ever since I heard it: a finger inserted into a mouth to arrange the letters into comprehensibility.

△ △ △

My favorite Marxism, of the hundreds I cherish, involves the time Groucho was driving back from Mexico. He pulled up to the U.S. Immigration Post on the California border, where the government officer asked him the usual questions:

> "Are you an American citizen?"
> "Sure," replied Marx.
> "Where were you born?"
> "New York."
> "Occupation?"
> "Smuggler."

. . . you should excuse (the expression; me; my frankness)

> From Yiddish: *Zolst mir antshuldigen:* You should excuse me.
>
> Please excuse . . .

"You should excuse" is synonymous with "*if* you'll excuse" or "if you'll pardon [the expression, my candor] . . ." Yes, it's deplorable, substandard English, but Yinglish to the core.

This genteelism, long a feature of New Yorkese and of vaudeville/ radio comedy, takes on a satirical note in conversation among the sophisticated:

> "He is a Good Humor (you should excuse the expression) salesman."

Intramural aspersions are more easily expressed in this barbarism than in naked disdain:

> "Professor Montzer is a (excuse the expression) Keynesian."
>
> "Professor Tunkel is a (pardon the expression) monetarist."
>
> "He wants to play rock-and-roll (excuse the expression) music."

You want to hear something?

> Yinglish for *Ir vilt eppes her'n?*

Do not mistake this for, say, "Do you want to hear what happened?" or "Do you want to hear how we got home?" These convey precise information: ". . . what happened" and ". . . how we got home."

"You want to hear something?" is an invitation to the revelation of unspecified information. The question is a tease, an offer, open-ended bait.

One may answer the question "Do you want to hear what we ate?" with a polite "Not really." But I cannot imagine anyone asked "Do you want to hear something?" replying, "No."

The most revealing use of this interrogative prod was told to me by Professor Joshua Fishman. "In the middle of the night, my wife and I were awakened by our son, standing at our bedside in his pajamas. 'You wanna hear somep'n?' "

Z

zaftik (standard)

zaftig

> Pronounced ZOFF-tig. From German: juicy.
>
> 1. Juicy. ("What a *zaftik* plum.")
> 2. Plump, buxom, well-rounded (to describe a female). This is the most frequent American usage.

Zaftik describes in one word what it takes two hands to do.

△ △ △

SCENE: *A bus, Los Angeles*

Two *zaftik* girls are deep in discussion, seated in front of Mrs. Lederer.

ROSALYND: You actually auditioned for the part?

CHERYLL: Did I ever!

ROSALYND: So did you get it?

CHERYLL: Get it? I was *made* for that part!

MRS. LEDERER: Excuse me, dollink, but do you have to tell *strangers?*

zeyde (standard)

zayde

zaydie

> Pronounced ZAY-deh or, as some American grandchildren prefer for greater affection, ZAY-dee. Slavic origin.
>
> 1. Grandfather.
> 2. An old man.

You may address any elderly Jew as *Zeyde*.

△ △ △

A *zeyde* is best defined, I think, as "the press agent for his grandchildren."

△ △ △

Letter from a ten-year-old at summer camp:

> Dear Zaydie:
>   Remember I told you if my parents made me go to camp, *something terrible would happen??* Well, it did.
>
> Love,
Amy

△ △ △

There is a story about the legendary Zeyde of Shpolle, who became so heartsick about the injustices and horrors of life that—he put God on trial!

He appointed nine friends as judges, himself being the tenth (to make a *minyen*) and summoned the Almighty to the witness stand. (Since God is everywhere, the Zeyde simply opened his door.)

For six days and nights this remarkable jury tried the Lord: They presented charges, defenses, prayed, fasted, consulted Torah and Talmud.

Finally, in solemn consensus, they issued their verdict: *God was guilty!* In fact, they found Him guilty on two counts: (1) He had Himself created the spirit of Evil, which He let loose among innocent and temptable people; (2) He failed to provide widows and orphans with decent food and shelter.

△ △ △

For weeks Mrs. Kotskin had been nagging her husband to join her in the séances at the home of Madame du Brillof. "She calls up spirits from the dead. We *talk* to them! Lenny, you keep saying how much you miss your old *zeyde*. Isn't it worth twenty dollars to talk to him?"

At the next séance, Kotskin sat at the table. Madame du Brillof peered into a ghostly crystal ball. "And what dear departed one do you seek?"

"My grandfather."

The medium closed her eyes, moaned, hummed—and soon a voice quavered, "I . . . am here . . . Who . . . calls me?"

"*Zeyde!* It's Lenny. Are you happy in *Yenner velt* [the other world]?"

"Happy? . . . Very . . . I am . . . in eternal bliss. . . ."

"And do you ever see the others in our family?"

"I am with them. . . . We dine on milk and manna together . . . we laugh . . . we sing. . . . Oh, it's wonderful!"

A dozen questions did Lenny Kotskin ask of his *zeyde*, and each